THE
PUSHCART
BOOK OF POETRY

The Pushcart Book of Poetry:

The best poems from three decades of The Pushcart Prize

Edited by Joan Murray
with the Pushcart Prize poetry editors

PUSHCART PRESS

811,508
Pus

Poems are reprinted with permission of
poets, or their agents or publishers. We have made
every reasonable effort to contact all poets.
If we have not found you, please write to Pushcart
for more information and your copy of this book.
Rights revert to poets on publication.

"Power" © 2002 Adrienne Rich, © 1978 W. W. Norton & Co.

For information address:
Pushcart Press
PO Box 380
Wainscott, NY 11975

Distributed by W. W. Norton Co.
500 Fifth Ave.
New York, NY 10110

PUBLISHER'S NOTE

I am enormously grateful to Joan Murray for assembling this monumental volume. When I approached Joan about editing an anthology of the Pushcart's best poetry, she had the inspired notion to contact the nearly 50 poets, who, like herself, had taken their turns as Pushcart's guest poetry editors over its 30-volume history. Though she was unable to reach a few (and a few are no longer with us), the response was enthusiastic, almost joyous. The editors revisited the volumes they had edited and picked the poems that seemed to have held up best over the passage of years. The names of all the original guest editors of the series follow.

ABOUT JOAN MURRAY: Joan is a poet whose five volumes include *Dancing on the Edge* and the verse-novel *Queen of the Mist* (Beacon) and *Looking for the Parade* (W. W. Norton). She is also editor of two Beacon anthologies, *Poems to Live By in Uncertain Times* (2001) and *Poems to Live By in Troubling Times* (2006). Winner of the National Poetry Series and the Wesleyan New Poets Series competitions, she has also won awards from Poetry Society of America and fellowships from the National Endowment for the Arts and the New York Foundation for the Arts. Former Poet in Residence at the New York State Writers Institute, she has been a repeat guest on NPR's *Morning Edition*.

To Joan, and her many guest co-editors, I am profoundly grateful.

Bill Henderson

THE PUSHCART PRIZE POETRY EDITORS AND EDITORS OF THE PUSHCART BOOK OF POETRY

(in chronological order)

Lloyd Van Brunt
Naomi Lazard
Lynn Spaulding
Herb Leibowitz
Jonathan Galassi
Grace Schulman
Carolyn Forché
Gerald Stern
Stanley Plumly
William Stafford
Philip Levine
David Wojahn
Jorie Graham
Robert Hass
Philip Booth
Jay Meek
Sandra McPherson
Laura Jensen
William Heyen
Elizabeth Spires
Marvin Bell
Carolyn Kizer
Christopher Buckley
Chase Twichell

Richard Jackson
Susan Mitchell
Lynn Emanuel
David St. John
Carol Muske
Dennis Schmitz
William Matthews
Patricia Strachan
Heather McHugh
Molly Bendall
Marilyn Chin
Michael Dennis Browne
Kimiko Hahn
Billy Collins
Joan Murray
Judith Kitchen
Sherod Santos
Pattiann Rogers
Carl Phillips
Martha Collins
Carol Frost
Jane Hirshfield
Dorianne Laux
David Baker
Linda Gregerson

INTRODUCTION
by JOAN MURRAY

THE PUSHCART PRIZE has been rolling along for thirty years—longer than than the Concorde, which was launched the same year but is now a cumbersome museum piece. That the cart is still in motion owes to its simple, intelligent design: it was created by a man determined to lift the thing up and move it forward himself. I'm referring, of course, to Bill Henderson, founder, publisher, editor, and sometime ringmaster of the Pushcart Prize.

Henderson (as almost everyone in the literary community affectionately calls him) launched the Pushcart in a defiant spirit of Promethean empowerment. If the commercial publishing industry (for which he worked) and the mainstream media took scant notice of the brilliant and varied writing being published by hundreds of American literary journals and alternative presses, Henderson was going to carry those publications and their writers to the public himself. And so in 1976, he created the glitteringly self-deprecating "Pushcart Prize"—which has become a proud credential on the dust jackets of leading writers.

Though he still edits the Pushcart in a no-tech garage behind his house, Henderson never meant it to be merely a one-man show. From the start, he invited the literary community to join him in his mission. Their overwhelming response has helped make the Pushcart a cultural icon and communal phenomenon. Now, every year, some 8000 poems and works of fiction and non-fiction are nominated for "the prize" by independent publishers, along with Pushcart's Contributing Editors (an ever-expanding "peer group" of writers who've appeared in the Pushcart themselves). Because of this, the Pushcart is widely acknowledged as the vehicle by which America's literary editors and writers celebrate one another's work.

Now when the cart rolls into town, loaded with the best offerings from America's small presses, it gets heaped with high praise from readers and reviewers alike. Famous names flash from its pages, yet part of the annual excitement comes from discovering new names—both of writers and publications. By being open and innovative while keeping focused on quality, the Pushcart has become (as the commercial guys might put it), a "trusted brand." Despite its often empty money coffers, The Pushcart has to be counted—along with Apple, Google, Microsoft and Amazon—as one of the great garage-enterprises of our era. It's also the only one still in a garage.

❧

That the Pushcart emerged in 1976 isn't especially surprising. It was a fertile year for changing the old order of things. Besides being, aptly, a leap year, it was also America's dizzyingly exuberant bicentennial year—and the election-year when Jimmy Carter defeated Gerald Ford. It was a year of multi-cultural literature (before "multi-cultural" was on everyone's lips). On the bestseller list were Alex Halley's *Roots*, Maxine Hong Kingston's *The Woman Warrior*, and Gabriel Garcia Marquez's *Autumn of the Patriarch*. 1976's Album of the Year was Paul Simon's *Still Crazy After All These Years*—whose title seemed a sobriquet for a ripened generation.

During the decade that preceded it, many of us had directed our poetry and larger energies to the urgent concerns of the day: the war in Vietnam, the criminal scandals in the White House, the civil rights and women's liberation movements, and the redress of social inequality and ethnic invisibility. By 1976 our culture had expanded beyond the confines of a predominant middle-class, white, male perspective, and our poetry had shrugged off the decorum of academic models and intellectualized alienation in favor of a poetry of engagement. We'd learned the power of collective initiatives and grass-roots activism: we'd brought down a corrupt president and ended a bloody, protracted, and immoral war.

In that expansive mood, small presses and literary journals were springing up all across the nation—many of them with the mission of bringing aesthetically exciting and socially relevant poetry to a broad new readership. This was no easy task. Macs and PCs hadn't arrived

8

on the scene yet—even Kinkos was a thing of the future. Yet more daunting than the difficulties faced in production, were the formidable challenges of publicizing, marketing, and distributing small press poetry—when the mainstream media snubbed it and most bookstores refused to carry it.

Into that thorny yet fertile field, rolled the Pushcart Prize—gathering the best independently published poems into a handsome, hefty literary digest that couldn't be ignored. The Pushcart won national distribution, national media attention, and a national readership. Now, thirty years later, the Pushcart is still in the business of introducing readers to poets and writers as well as to the journals and presses that publish their work. A little bit like speed-dating, those brief introductions can lead to reader relationships for life.

❧

It shouldn't be hard to imagine how a fledgling writer must feel on learning that a poem of hers will appear in the Pushcart Prize. (In my own case, the peer nominator wasn't exactly a peer—it was Joyce Carol Oates.) Such moments in the lives of even fully-fledged poets account for some of the enthusiasm poets have for the Pushcart. But our greater enthusiasm—the one we share with readers—is for what's in its pages. Each year I've found myself on the phone (more recently on the computer) telling some friend or fellow writer or former student about a terrific poem or publication I've just seen in the new volume. And every year, I've nodded in gratitude to Henderson and the hundreds of others who've helped him bring it into being.

Still, I had no idea what that task meant for the volume's Poetry Editors—these are usually two poets whom Henderson invites to join him (plus a couple of other Fiction Editors) for the annual task. Along with the rest of the literary community, I was aware that the Poetry Editors were always outstanding poets—poets like Philip Levine, William Stafford, Jorie Graham, Gerald Stern, William Matthews, and Carolyn Kizer. So naturally I was honored when Henderson invited me and Billy Collins to be the Poetry Editors for the 25th Anniversary Volume.

Henderson explained that the Poetry Editors were changed each year since they were usually left shattered and exhausted by the task. I thought he was joking. More than once he warned me of what was ahead, but since I'd worked for a poetry press, edited a poetry journal, and served on the National Endowment's Literature panel, I thought no mere mountain of poems could daunt me. Not until 3000 enthusiastically nominated, proudly published poems were heaped on my desk waiting to be judged. (Billy had the other 3000.)

The sheer variety of the poems was fascinating. Had I a lifetime to peruse them, it might have been a satisfying pastime. But I had an obligation—and a two-and-a-half month deadline. I read, I winnowed, I worried down the mountain to a sizable foothill of 200 poems. But I had only 15 slots. I read and winnowed and worried some more till I'd found "The Best." Just as I'd been asked to do. Now when Billy and I meet, we mention our Pushcart experience in whispers—the way POWs do.

Not long after Henderson issued that 25th Anniversary Volume, he sat back for a few minutes, surveyed all the remarkable things the Pushcart had published in its twenty-five-year history, and issued two outstanding "Best of the Best" volumes: *The Pushcart Book of Short Stories*, edited by Henderson, and *The Pushcart Book of Essays*, edited by Anthony Brandt. I waited for the third one.

Henderson's explanations for its absence went like this: "Timing's bad" (in the aftermath of September 11th many cultural ventures had to be postponed). "Money's scarce" (Pushcart suffers the same affliction as the rest of the independent publishing field). And (mistakenly) "I don't really know much about poetry." True, Henderson the writer is known for his books of prose, but Henderson the reader is known to have a keen and substantial interest in poetry. And his eclectic tastes in it pretty much match my own. Which is probably why he asked me to edit the volume—"when time and money allow." I said I'd think about it.

What finally won my assent was the idea that I could *share* the task. Instead of choosing the poems myself (though that might have yielded a fine book too), I would ask the almost fifty poets who had been Pushcart Poetry Editors to choose the poems from *their* volumes. Not only would that spare me a lot of winnowing and worrying, it would also relieve me from the inevitable second-guessing I'd do when my own tastes veered from the known tastes of those Editors. But what I liked most about the idea was a gut-feeling that the book should be done communally—or, as Henderson likes to say," in the Pushcart spirit."

I wasn't at all surprised that Henderson liked my idea. Yet both of us wondered whether the Poetry Editors would respond to it. After all, they might still be recovering from their first Pushcart galley-ship experience. And most probably they were as busy as hell. Nonetheless, every poetry editor I contacted agreed to participate—many with considerable enthusiasm.

While I waited for them to send me their choices (three selections and three other outstanding poems each), I occupied myself with looking over all the poetry in Pushcart's thirty volumes. There were nearly a thousand poems, but since *all* were Pushcart-Prize winners, reading them was a pleasure rather than a task. Going first volume through last, I observed some rather general shifts in content and style over the years—from the socially conscious early volumes, through the casually ironic middle ones, to the eclectically postmodern and technically ambitious later ones. I observed the penchants of individual editors for such things as narrative, humor, experiment or diversity. And I couldn't help picking some favorites.

Months before, at the moment I decided to open the editing of this book to many poets (all with different styles, passions, and aesthetic loyalties), I knew—and also *intended*—that the resulting book wouldn't reflect my own tastes and interests, but would represent the field. That it does so—so well—pleases me immensely. Yet at that same moment, I knew I'd also have regrets over some extraordinary poems and poets who wouldn't be here. Still, I was glad to see that, more often than not, the poems selected for this book are the ones I'd have chosen myself.

And what a stunning book this is! It includes the work of 19 Pulitzer Prize Winners, 17 National Book Award Winners, 11 National Book Critics Circle Award Winners, 10 US Poets Laureate, and 4 Nobel Prize Laureates. It offers a dazzling selection by Pushcart's editors of the voices, styles, and subjects that have defined American poetry for the past 30 years. Here are the poems of such celebrated poets as Seamus Heaney, Billy Collins, Mary Oliver, John Ashbery, Gerald Stern, Amy Clampitt, Derek Walcott, and Adrienne Rich (to name only a few)—along with remarkable poems by poets only few have heard of *yet*.

Here are poems of nearly every definable subgenre: lyrical poems, surreal poems, meditative poems, experimental poems, narrative poems, formal poems, humorous poems, elegiac poems, political poems, nature poems, identity poems, love poems—and many others. Anyone with a curiosity about what American poetry has been doing for the past thirty years is bound to be as hooked by this book as I am.

∽❧

In writing his annual introductions for Pushcart's thirty volumes, Henderson's made it a principle never to single out individual work. (Perhaps the Pushcart Spirit raises a brow at that sort of thing.) Yet it struck me that the very nature of this book might permit me to point out a few things as a way to orient readers to the whole.

Let me begin by calling attention to some of the poems that touch on the issues and concerns of the past thirty years—like Galway Kinnell's "The Fundamental Project of Technology" (a chilling poem about nuclear annihilation) and Mark Doty's "Turtle, Swan" (a gripping love poem in the era of AIDS), and Sharon Olds' "May 1968" (a harrowing vision of police violence), and Lucille Clifton's "Jasper, Texas, 1998" (a heart-rending look at a lynching). Along with those, you'll want to read Michael Hogan's quietly affecting prison poem "Spring," and William Stafford's poignant salute to the elderly, "Waiting in Line," and Larry Levis's "To a Wren on Calvary," an exquisite exploration of indifference.

Take a look too at some of the remarkable poems that focus on origins, family, or roots—among them, Philip Levine's "A Poem with No Ending" (a brilliant long-poem that circles through the bleakness of urban-industrial America) and Linda Gregerson's "Salt" (an unrelenting glimpse of rural despondency). Also not to be missed are David Mura's "Listening" (a flourishing welcome for an unborn child); Jack Marshall's "Sesame" (a beautifully leavened remembrance of a mother); and two stunning quests for still elusive fathers: Li-Young Lee's "Furious Versions" and Kwame Dawes' "Inheritance." You'll also want to see Etheridge Knight's "We Free Singers Be," (a wistful, jubilant, in-your-face celebration), Agha Shahid Ali's "The History of Paisley" (a tapestry of creation myth and history) and Eavan Boland's "Anna Liffey" (an immersion of the self into a river and a nation).

Let me alert you also to some stunning and seemingly unrelated poems that celebrate life and the sexual passion that infuses it: Pattiann Rogers' pulsing nature hymn, "The Power of Toads," Thom Gunn's small elegant treatise, "In a Woods Near Athens," Czeslaw Milosz's lambent art-exploration, "The Garden of Earthly Delights" and Gerald Stern's Edenic domestic portrait, "I Would Call it Derangement." And, yes, the book is full of astonishing "love poems"—like Jane Cooper's "Conversations by the Body's Light," Seamus Heaney's "The Otter," Stephen Dunn's "Tenderness," Cathy Hong's "All the Aphrodisiacs," and Eamon Grennan's "To Grasp the Nettle"—which exquisitely and explicitly demonstrate why "love" is still called "the poet's subject."

Yet that other great "poet's subject," death, is richly present too—in such superb poems as Allen Grossman's "By the Pool" and Miranda Field's "Cock Robin." Take a look at death's varied guises in such poems as Karen Volkman's "Sonnet," (a gem in the manner of Hopkins), Reginald Shepherd's "Also Love You," (a serenade from a surprising point of view), Robert Wrigley's "Horseflies," (a dizzying provocation of the senses), and Betty Adcock's "Penumbra" (a small formal masterpiece on childhood bereavement). Yet I was especially moved by three haunting poems of mature loss: Stanley Kunitz's "Quinnapoxet," Rosanna Warren's "Mediterranean," and Robert Creeley's "Mitch."

You'll also want to see some of the highly appealing poems that look at literary lives and cultural icons—among them David Baker's "Primer of Words," which glances over the shoulder of an aging Whitman, and Hilda Morley's "That Bright Grey Eye," which gazes at a hazy river with an aging Turner, and William Matthews' "Note I Left for Gerald Stern," which listens in on the musings of an office-bound poet. Especially entertaining is Edward Hirsch's series "The Lectures on Love," which stages dramatic appearances by the Marquis de Sade and Ralph Waldo Emerson (among others); and Kenneth Koch's "Vous Êtes Plus Beaux que Vous ne Pensiez" which burbles inspiredly about Sappho and Wittgenstein (to name just two)—and might be the funniest poem in the book.

Though all the poems I've mentioned won me with the completeness of their craft, I have to single out a few that swept me away with their language—like Charles Wright's luminous meditation, "The Southern Cross" and John Ashbery's shimmering pillow-talk, "All Kinds of Caresses," and Brenda Hillman's earth-shaking eruption, "Mighty Forms." You'll also want to see the linguistic virtuosity of

13

Katrina Robert's "The Cup" in all its glistening shards, and Brigit Pegeen Kelly's "Black Legs" with its splendid shape-shifting ambiguities. Also savor the sparkling word-horde in Grace Schulman's "The Button Box," and the forbidden mouthful in Heather McHugh's "I knew I'd Sing," and the unorthodox litany of Charles Harper Webb's "Biblical Also-Rans." Need I say more?

❧

I think I've said plenty to whet anyone's appetite for all the riches this book contains. But allow me to explain that in order to highlight poems from every volume (which is what I've just done) and draw attention to some relationships and differences among them, I've grouped them rather arbitrarily according to a few broad themes—which may be of no significance to the poets who wrote them—or to the readers who will read them. Let me also remind those readers that there are *many other poems* in this book—180 in all—and they're all "the best of the best."

Let me also point out that the Poetry Editors who chose those 180 poems, also chose *another 180* (they're noted at the end of this book as "more outstanding poems"). You can find them in Volumes I through XXX of *The Pushcart Prize*. And while you're looking for them, why not have a look at *all the other outstanding poems* in those thirty volumes—they're *all* Pushcart Prize winners!

I'm sure you'll also want to check out the journals and independent presses who first published the poems in this volume (and in all those other Pushcart volumes). Maybe you'll decide to subscribe to a few. And, after that, you might pick up some books by the poets who most appeal to you—and then you'll be a part of "the Pushcart spirit."

❧

And now (in that spirit) I want to thank the people who made this book possible:

First, to those 49 outstanding American poets—the Pushcart Poetry Editors (who are noted at the beginning of this book—my tremendous thanks for so generously and carefully selecting the poems for this volume (as well as for the thirty earlier Pushcart volumes). As you told me, it wasn't an easy task, but it's made this the fascinating, first-rate, comprehensive, representative book it is.

Great thanks too to the hundreds of independent publishers and journal editors and Pushcart's loyal Contributing Editors, who first nominated the poems in this book (along with thousands and thousands of other poems) over the past thirty years.

To the literary journals and independent presses who first published these poems, many thanks for the sharpness of your vision and the importance of your mission.

To the poets whose work is included here—my deep gratitude. Your poems *are* this book—it's you who have made it superb.

To my husband Jim—for technical feats involving mildewed volumes, exacto knives, proof pages and photocopiers—and other, more enduring acts of kindness, my always inadequate thanks.

My deepest gratitude and admiration go, of course, to Henderson—not only for making this landmark book a reality—but for so generously dedicating his past thirty years to creating and sustaining a major American cultural phenomenon—the Pushcart Prize! May it roll along for another thirty years—defiantly generous, dynamically stalwart, collectively brilliant and unpretentiously important! As for you, Henderson, this volume and all the rest are the true, sufficient and eloquent testimony to your achievement. You've become a hero in your own time—so poke your head out of the garage and listen to the thundering applause.

CONTENTS

I

II

III

16

IV

V

VI

VII

VIII

IX

X

XI

XII

XIII

XIV

XV

XVI

XVII

XVIII

XIX

XX

XXI

XXII

XXIII

XXIV

XXV

XXVI

XXVII

XXVIII

XXIX

XXX

I

POWER

by Adrienne Rich

from THE LITTLE MAGAZINE

Living   in the earth-deposits   of our history

Today a backhoe divulged   out of a crumbling flank of earth
one bottle   amber   perfect   a hundred-year-old
cure for fever   or melancholy   a tonic
for living on this earth   in the winters of this climate

Today I was reading about Marie Curie:
she must have known she suffered   from radiation sickness
her body bombarded for years   by the element
she had purified
It seems she denied to the end
the source of the cataracts on her eyes
the cracked and suppurating skin   of her finger-ends
till she could no longer hold   a test-tube or a pencil

She died   a famous woman   denying
her wounds
denying
her wounds   came   from the same source as her power

PEACE IN THE NEAR EAST

by **GERALD STERN**

from AMERICAN POETRY REVIEW

While I have been flooding myself with black coffee
and moving slowly from pajamas to underwear to blue corduroys
my birds have been carrying twigs and paper and leaves and straw
back and forth between the box elders and the maples.
—They are building the Aswan Dam out there;
they are pulling heavy wheelbarrows up the hillsides;
they are dragging away old temples stone by stone;
they are wiping the sweat from their black bodies.

Ah, soon, soon they will be sitting down
like rich Mamelukes in their summer palaces on the Nile,
greeting the Arabian ambassador on the right,
greeting the Russian ambassador on the left,
and finally even the Jew himself, a guest
in his own garden, a holder of strange credentials,
one who is permitted to go through the carrots
only with special consent, one who is scolded
if he gets too close to the raspberry bushes,
one who looks with loving eyes at the water
and the light canoes that float down to the locks
for the meeting of princes in their little rubber tents—
by the picnic tables and the pump and the neat pile of gravel and
    the naked sycamores;
by the cement spillway that carries a ton of water a minute
under the old generating plant;
by the sandy beach down below where the fishermen sit
on their canvas stools feeding worms to the river—
worm after worm to the starving river,
in exchange for the silver life in their tin buckets,
in exchange for silence.

THE GRIOTS WHO KNEW BRER FOX

by COLLEEN J. MCELROY

from YARDBIRD READER

There are old drunks among the tenements,
old men who have been

lost

forever from families, shopping centers
starched shirts and

birthdays.

They are the griots, the story tellers
whose faces are knotted and swollen

> into a black patchwork
> of open sores and
> old scabs; disease
> transforms the nose
> into cabbage; the eyes
> are dried egg yolks.

They grind old tobacco between scabby gums
like ancient scarabs rolling dung from tombs

in their

mother country.

In this country, they are scenic, part of the

view from Route 1, Old Town.

Don't miss them; they sit in doorways
of boarded houses in the part of town
that's nested between wide roads, roads
named for English kings and tourists.

> These old men sit like moldy stumps
> among the broken bricks of narrow
> carriage streets, streets paved with
> the Spirit of '76, the Westward Movement
> and Oz.

The old men never travel the wide roads;

they sit in the dusk, dark skinned as Aesop,

remember their youth. They chant stories

to keep themselves awake another day,

> tales of young girls bathing in kitchens
>
> before wood stoves, smells of
>
> > the old South,
>
> or Northern tales of babies bitten by rats,
>
> women who have left them or how they
>
> were once rich.

They'll spin a new Brer Rabbit story for a nickel;

tell you how he slipped past the whistle-slick fox

to become

> the Abomey king.

But you must listen closely,
it moves fast, their story;
skipping and jumping childlike,
the moral hidden in an enchanted forest

                                        of word games.

            These stories are priceless,
            prized by movie moguls
            who dream of Saturday matinees
            and full houses.

You have to look beyond the old men's faces,

beyond the rat that waits to nibble the hand

when they sleep. The face is anonymous,

                              you can find it anywhere.

but the words are as prized

as the curved tusks of the bull elephant.

SPRING

by MICHAEL HOGAN

from LETTERS FOR MY SON (Unicorn Press); Cold Mountain
Press Post Card Series; THE AMERICAN PEN

Ice has been cracking all day
and some boys on the shore
pretending it is the booming of artillery
lay prone clutching imaginary carbines.
Inside the compound returning birds ·
peck at bread scraps from the mess hall.
Old cons shiver in cloth jackets
as they cross the naked quadrangle.
They know the inside perimeter is exactly
two thousand and eighty-four steps
and they can walk it five more times
before the steam whistle blows for count.
Above them a tower guard dips his rifle
then raises it again dreamily.
He imagines a speckled trout
coming up shining and raging with life.

VARIATIONS ON THE MOUND OF CORPSES IN THE SNOW

by STEPHEN BERG

from CHICAGO REVIEW

For Bill Arrowsmith

Sleet blows through the city,
gray. An old Jew's black skull-cap's
flecked with snow. He looks
into the sky. Nothing. Flakes
spin into his mouth and eyes.
For two years

I've been reading
an Israeli poem about God's silence in evil,
about a child
watching Nazis murder his father in the snow
then fling him on a mound of corpses.
First they made him undress

but he left his underpants and socks on.
When the officer saw this
he walked up behind him and rammed
the butt of his rifle between the shoulders
of the boy's father, who coughed and fell down.

The officer smoked.
"The snow on both sides of my father's face
was melting, reddening,
because of the blood
that came out of his mouth, from his burst lungs."
Like prayers spilled into the earth.

I keep trying to find out why we do these things
and hear my mother scream "Your father
used to pinch me at parties whenever I spoke
or he'd disappear and shack-up with his secretary.
After he died I found eight hundred-dollar
checks he wrote to a woman nobody knew!"

At Arrowsmith's the goats, the boulders
strewn over the hillside across from the studio,
his wife's chickens in the barn and the vegetables
she grew, sheep cropping grass, melted into
the son, the father, all of us.
The rocks lay down, the Jew

was a rock, the rock was his back,
his face was in the grass so deep I couldn't
even see his ears. When Bill and I talked this week
he said the first snow had blinded
everything except the crests of the rocks,
which the wind blew clean.

One morning last summer when I drove to see him
we stood very close to each other, watching the air clear.
It was like being with my father again.
A mist like fine snow hung over the valley, then thinned off.
The rocks appeared, scarred humps
clawed out of the ground by retreating ice. Oh

that shy man who had stood naked only in front of his wife! And
    God? Listen—
"When the night fell the stars
glittered, the pile of corpses
lay in the field,
and snow came down out of the night
with soft, cruel abundance."

MUSICAL SHUTTLE

by HARVEY SHAPIRO

from LAUDS (Sun Press) and UNDINE

Night, expositor of love.
Seeing the sky for the first time
That year, I watched the summer constellations
Hang in air: Scorpio with
Half of heaven in his tail.
Breath, tissue of air, cat's cradle.
I walked the shore
Where cold rocks mourned in water
Like the planets lost in air.
Ocean was a low sound.
The gate-keeper suddenly gone,
Whatever the heart cried
Voice tied to dark sound.
The shuttle went way back then,
Hooking me up to the first song
That ever chimed in my head.
Under a sky gone slick with stars,
The aria tumbling forth:
Bird and star.
However those cadences
Rocked me in the learning years,
However that soft death sang—
Of star become a bird's pulse,
Of the spanned distances
Where the bird's breath eddied forth—
I recovered the lost ground.
The bird's throat
Bare as the sand on which I walked.
Love in his season
Had moved me with that song.

II

THE END OF SCIENCE FICTION

by LISEL MUELLER

from THE OHIO REVIEW

This is not fantasy, this is our life.
We are the characters
who have invaded the moon,
who cannot stop their computers.
We are the gods who can unmake
the world in seven days.

Both hands are stopped at noon.
We are beginning to live forever,
in lightweight, aluminum bodies
with numbers stamped on our backs.
We dial our words like muzak.
We hear each other through water.

The genre is dead. Invent something new.
Invent a man and a woman
naked in a garden;
invent a child that will save the world,
a man who carries his father
out of a burning city.
Invent a spool of thread
that leads a hero to safety;
invent an island on which he abandons
the woman who saved his life,
with no loss of sleep over the betrayal.

Invent us as we were
before our bodies glittered
and we stopped bleeding:
invent a shepherd who kills a giant,
a girl who grows into a tree,
a woman who refuses to turn
her back on the past and is changed to salt,
a boy who steals his brother's birthright
and becomes the head of a nation.

Invent real tears, hard love,
slow-spoken, ancient words,
difficult as a child's
first steps across a room.

RABBIT TRANCE

by JAROLD RAMSEY

from ONTARIO REVIEW

Once on a clear November morning
I saw a rabbit pad out of cover
and into the silent frost and stubble of my field
the old battleground, where a thousand roaring
regiments still fall down some days like wheat.
I saw the rabbit creep into the bright
open, targeted beyond the hope
of safety, then crouch and stare
so long the seasons seemed to roll around
and it was Fall again another year.
The huge horizons shrank and kept their distance,
the rabbit's trance and gaze redeemed the air
and all unquiet life quickened in silence
except my voice chirping in my ear
little totem carry me through

THE SAGE OF APPLE VALLEY ON LOVE

by EDWARD FIELD

from THE TEXAS SLOUGH

Seeker, whatever you love
that is your path
for truly, love is the path.

Do not believe them when they say
what you love is wrong—
it is part of the great love.

Nobody's road is better than yours.
Nobody else's road is yours.
The important thing is to follow it.

Romantics love their loved ones
the way religious people love God:
It opens you up
either way.

Both kinds of people
get from their love
the same thing:

they stay open
and adore.

To love is the path.

Thank whoever
opened that place in you
we call falling in love.

It is the beloved
and woke in you the sacred feeling.

That is what love is about,
feeling, not possession.
It doesn't matter how far it goes
but thank him, whoever he is,
whether or not he responds.

Through him you worship:
He is the path.

WE FREE SINGERS BE

by ETHERIDGE KNIGHT

from NEW LETTERS

> *If we didn't have the music, dancers*
> *would/be soldiers too, holding guns*
> *in their arms, instead of each/other.*
> *—Fr. Boniface Hardin*

We free singers be
sometimes swimming in the music,
like porpoises playing in the sea.
We free singers be
come agitators at times, be
come eagles circling the sun,
hurling stones at hunters, be
come scavengers cracking eggs
in the palm of our hands.
(Remember, oh, do you remember
the days of the raging fires
when I clenched my teeth
in my sleep and refused to speak
in the daylight hours?)
We free singers be, baby,
tall walkers, high steppers,
hip shakers, we free singers be
still waters sometimes too.
(Remember, oh, do you remember
the days when children held our hands

and danced
around us in circles, and we laughed
in the sun, remember
how we slept in the shade of the trees
and woke, trembling in the darkness?)
We free singers be
voyagers
and sing of cities
with straight streets
and mountains piercing the moon—
and rivers that never run dry.
(Remember, oh, do you remember
the snow
falling
on broadway
and the soldiers marching
thru the icy streets
with blood on their coat sleeves.
remember how we left the warm movie house
turned up our collars
and rode the subway home?)
We free singers be, baby,
We free singers be.

ALL KINDS OF CARESSES

by JOHN ASHBERY

from CHICAGO REVIEW

The code-name losses and compensations
Float in and around us through the window.
It helps to know what direction the body comes from.
It isn't absolutely clear. In words
Bitter as a field of mustard we
Copy certain parts, then decline them.
These are not only gestures: they imply
Complex relations with one another. Sometimes one
Stays on for awhile, a trace of lamp black
In a room full of gray furniture.

I now know all there is to know
About my body. I know too the direction
My feet are pointed in. For the time being
It is enough to suspend judgment, by which I don't mean
Forever, since judgment is also a storm, i.e., from
Somewhere else, sinking pleasure craft at moorings,
Looking, kicking in the sky.

Try to move with these hard blues,
These harsh yellows, these hands and feet.
Our gestures have taken us farther into the day
Than tomorrow will understand.

They live us. And we understand them when they sing,
Long after the perfume has worn off.
In the night the eye chisels a new phantom.

THE SLEEP

by PHILIP DACEY

from PRAIRIE SCHOONER

In memory of Anne Sexton, 1928–1974

It is an answer, a going-into.
The soft helmet slowly eases over the head.
The limbs begin to believe in their gravity,
The dark age of faith begins, a god below
Draws down the body, he wants it
And we are flattered.
We are going to the level of water.
(Don't hold on. Drop fair, drop fair.)
This is fine seepage, we think,
Seepage ravelling to a river
To set ourselves upon. So
What is the price of dark water?
Where is the weight going?
The body powers the vaguest of shapes,
Pilot-boat, the falls collapse
And collapse upon themselves. We hear them
In time and imitate them.
We would turn to water that has lost
Its floor, water surprisingly
In space and beading,
A glittering disintegration.

　　　　　Now, what was a bed
Rocks just perceptibly, this is a cradle
In search of a captain, the bone-cargo
Settles, the medium

Washes up over and across and fills
The spaces we have been keeping empty just for this,
The palpable black herein
Barbarian, riding us down.

                    There will be a level
We come to, will we know it?
A flat place with, look, a light.
It is a guess as our loins give way.
Already we are forgetting
Where we were
And left from, the human
Faces like sunglare hurting our eyes.
Did we even wave goodbye? Yet could there
Possibly be someone here now,
That this going down
Not be so sole, and sore,
A cup, a cupped hand, a basket,
These forms of containment
Forms of Person
Where, when we're water, we're caught?
Listen. It is the sound of ourselves,
This passage: a breath.
We are almost not here.
If we break up this softly,
We must be incomparably lovely.

III

THE BREAKER

by NAOMI CLARK

from BURGLARIES AND CELEBRATIONS (Oyez Press) and
SOUTHWEST: A CONTEMPORARY ANTHOLOGY (Red Earth Press)

Maria we called you:
a Spanish mare, they said, up from Mexico—
born to the saddle, but skittish, liable to panic.
We were not, anymore, the kind of family to keep saddle horses.
Straddled bareback, past dry holes and dry grey slush pits, past the
mound where
we buried the cows, I'd stolen time from field and chickens
to ride low, nag transformed, under the scrub oak branches,
through darkening johnson grass where puma screamed, out onto
the Great Staked Plains.
You sold cheaper than a nag,
kicked out the end of the trailer, the gate off the horselot.
All night I heard you circling the barbed wire, stamping.
All night I rode through the sky.
You were a small, dark mare, Spanish, bought for a plowhorse.

I remember you in chains, Maria, the day he broke you to
plow-harness.
Tied to a post, you drag the heavy iron beam, the heavy log
chains,
twist and kick, whipped, driven round
and round. Foam flies, and blood, with the broken har-
ness,
with the tangled harness, the slipped chains. Your eyes
turn white.
Only when you both fall does it end. Next day
you plow ten rows before it starts.

51

You come to me now, Maria,
in so many dreams: your mad eyes,
your flinches, your broken stance, the slouch in the heavy harness,
your bowed head blindered, the break into frenzy.
My hands burn to heal you, to gentle you, to gentle your eyes.
Maria, you lift strong black wings,
rise free over the mesquites and the prickly pear, over the Caprock,
over the untrampled high grass of the Llano into the age of
    Comanche, Apache.

    And the man who broke you?

How shall I heal him, how stretch out my hand
in healing, my cold hands in healing
and warmth, how gentle?
O father, how shall I heal you?
What wings from the fire where you burn, and I the breaker?

WEST VIRGINIA
SLEEP SONG

by RUTHELLEN QUILLEN

from MAGDALEN (Sibyl-Child Press)

(for Jim Redmond and Doris Mozer)

You must teach him that when the deer comes into
the corn you shoot without question, and the runts
must be drowned in the kitchen well. Those who pray
they'll die asleep, hands on heart, are choked backwards
into pillow slips and tatted counterpanes.
When the heart is stillborn there is no answer.
An ectoplasm masks the face that will not cry.
This child, you teach him good and more. The nighttime's

made of horses who run on shattered legs.
The blinded pheasant is in its trap to judas
sing. Geraniums in coffee cans and tires
of marigolds spindle when there is no sun.
Those who come from churches never dream there're some
whose fathers lock closet doors on fists that pray
they haven't sinned. A great moon rises on all
the tar-papered shacks and cinderblocks; some

fire blindly at Orion unable to touch
a moment of their lives. I will or can't or
must: there's no necessity. You rhyme or scan
this song which settles where the roofs are tin and
the houses bluer than violets or pink as glazes

on supper rolls, where children take worms
into their feet and mouths, and dulcimers hang from
gouty hands. I give you penny whistles,

washboards, cups, and pans to bang the spooks away.
Jefferson County, home of pole beans, black lung,
twists in the road, and chevvies of sudden death,
some lullaby on bone pipes ought to be played
cross the fields of sorghum and civil war; it
staggers. I am afraid of music. I
buck and clog over this sag of porch and think:
my babies, this dirt will catch you when you fall from me.

Your cowls are going to be buried where the roads
cross, soon the rags of curtains will flap like crows
above your cradles. God help you. Here's grief pushed
into a corner of broken looking-glass
and comb, with patched-up screens and the husks of moths.
Those who think of other things, they can bind
the cut cord or let you bleed. I bleed. I ache
because I'm out of joint. The sons and daughters

damned to hell, the country stores, the glider swings,
the breasts tucked-in at underskirts, the river gnats,
the cataracts that half-cloud these eyes, the knives
too dull to cut even this simple pain, this fear
away. You keep this wrapped in eiderdown
for him who comes, half-dreamed of now on attic
stairs, in hunting roots, when cooling cider down.
You keep these patches and fits of love; they're all

I have to wrap him with against that night of
no sleep when I am plastered to this bed
of tied-up springs and corn and feather matresses
and bite down to crown his head or thrust his feet
into a world where lullabies slide out through broken teeth.

EVERYONE KNOWS
WHOM THE SAVED ENVY

by JAMES GALVIN

from ANTAEUS

It isn't such a bad thing
To live in one world forever.
You could do a lot worse:
The sexual smell of fresh-cut alfalfa
Could well be missing somewhere.
Somewhere you'd give in to some impetuous unknown,
And then stand guilty, as accused, of self-love.
It's better not to take such risks.

It's not as if we had no angels:
A handful remained when the rest moved on.
Now they work for a living
As windmills on the open range.
They spin and stare like catatonics,
Nod toward the bedridden peaks.
They've learned their own angelic disbelief.

The mountains still breathe, I suppose,
Though barely
The prairie still swells under a few small churches.
They are like rowboats after the ship's gone down.
Everyone knows whom the saved envy.
Runoff mirrors the sky in alpine pastures;
Imagine how quickly one's tracks unbloom there.
This world isn't such a bad world.

At least the angels are gainfully employed:
They know where the water is,
What to do with wind.
I try not to think of those others,
Like so many brides,
So many owls made of pollen
Wintering in a stand of imaginary timber.

THERE IS A DREAM DREAMING US

by NORMAN DUBIE

from PORCH

for Thomas James

Every little chamber was one reed long
from the gate to the roof of a chamber
to the roof of another, and door against
door. —found in a jar outside Cairo

We are seven virgins. Seven lamps.
Each with a different animal skin on our shoulders.
We had crowns made of black mulberry with the pyracantha,
Its white flowers in corymbs spotted with yellow fruit.
On my forehead, in charcoal, is the striking digit
Of an asp, and with all of this we were nearly nude.

The procession to the pyramid began at the pavilion
At the very edge of the thirteen acres that were sacred.
We walked ahead of everyone with our priest,
But we are the last to leave this world for the portico
And the first gallery which is dark and cold.

We stood on the terraced face of the pyramid witnessing
The long entrance of the king's family.
The queen carrieb a lamb made of papyrus: its eyes
Were rubies. The Queen's brother was dressed

In little rattles made of clay.
Even the King's nursery followed him with two slaves
To the Chamber where we would all stay.

The sun no longer touched us on the plateau. It was lost
Making the sand dunes beyond the cataract rise and fall
Like water rushing toward us.
The glass doll was smashed above the portico,
And the doors began to close! We were inside the galleries
Of sun and flour and our seven lamps guided us
To the underground chamber. We could no longer hear
The drums leaving the inner acre.
I am the initial lamp and so I broke the last bottles

And from the bottles sand poured:
This last gate had two flanking chambers full with sand
And on the sand was the weight of marble columns,
Columns that joined the limestone slab that was
The last seal lowering now as the sand spills
Into two fern boxes on the floor.

The children had all been smothered and washed in oils,
All of the family is poisoned.
They sprawl around the sarcophagus which is open.
The priest has stabbed my six companions—it is
A noise like a farmer testing river soil.
I'm to drain the cup of wine that the King's mother
Handed me before dying. I was the *first lamp*, but

This is my story. I spilled the wine down my leg
And pretended to faint away. The priest thinking everyone
Had crossed from his world stopped his prayer. He walked
To the girl with the third lamp.
He kissed my dead sister on the lips. He ripped the silk
From her breasts. And then he fell on her.
Her arms were limp, I imagine even as they would be
If she were alive doing this with him.

The heat must have been leaving her body. He finished
And turned to me: what I saw was the longest

Of the three members of an ankh, all red, and from it
Came a kind of clotted milk.
But his strength was leaving him visibly; he put his
Dagger in his neck and bled down his sleeve.
I don't understand. But now

I am alone as I had planned.
I'm a girl who was favored in the market by the King.
I've eaten the grapes that the slaves carried in for him:
If someone breaks into this tomb in a future time how
Will they explain the dead having spit grape seeds
Onto a carpet that was scented with jasmine?
The arrogance of the living never had a better monument

Than in me. I am going to sleep
In a bed that was hammered out of gold for a boy
Who was Pharoah and King of Egypt. My father died free.
My mother died a slave, here, at this site after being
Whipped twice in a morning. In the name of Abraham

I have displaced a King. I picked him up
And put him in the corner, facing in and kneeling.
He would seem to be a punished child.
What he did? I will tell you; you will be told many times again:

He killed four thousand of my people
While they suffered the mystery of this mountain appearing
Where there was nothing but moving sands and wind!

SWEENEY ASTRAY

by SEAMUS HEANEY

from ARMADILLO

*This run of verses occurs about half-way through a Middle-Irish work known as
BUILE SHUIBHNE, or SWEENEY ASTRAY, as I have rendered it, astray in his
mind and in his own country. It is the story, in prose and verse, of a king from the
north of Ireland called Sweeney who is cursed by one St. Ronan and turned into a
bird at the Battle of Moira. Sweeney had gone there to fight on behalf of another
king called Congal. The main body of the work is an account of his subsequent woes
and wanderings, such as his residence in a madman's glen called Glen Bolcain; his
pursuit by a posse of kinsmen headed by Lynchseachan; his hunger and exposure to
the elements; his various guilts; and his foreknowledge of his own death by the spear
at St. Mullin's church in Carlow.*

*Readers of Flann O'Brien's AT-SWIM-TWO-BIRDS will be familiar with
Sweeney as part of the comic apparatus of that novel. My sense of him is more
elegiac. His experiences are purgatorial. He physics his pomp, takes protective
colouring from the landscape itself, becomes its tongue. He is Lear and Poor Tom at
once, a type of the poet as inspired madman, paranoiac, schizophrenic, totally
sympathetic.*

*Some of the verse reworks older traditional material, such as the "tree alphabet" at
the beginning of this extract. It is composed in strict bardic forms, whose metronome
I do not try to follow. Instead, I have let the stanzas wear out a metrical or free shape
for themselves in response to the feel and sense of the original material.*

Seamus Heaney

Suddenly a clamour
and belling in the glen!
The little timorous stag
like a wild musician

saws across the heartstrings
a high homesick refrain
of deer on my lost hillsides,
flocks on my native plain.

Here bushy, leafy oak trees
climb up to the daylight,
the forking shoots of hazel
divulge their musky nut.

The alder is my darling,
all thornless in the gap,
some milk of human kindness
coursing in its sap.

The blackthorn is a jaggy creel
stippled with dark sloes;
green watercress is thatch on wells
where the drinking blackbird goes.

Sweetest of the leafy cliques,
the vetches strew the pathway;
the oyster-grass is my delight
and the wild strawberry.

Ever-generous apple-trees
rain big showers when shaken;
scarlet berries clot like blood
on mountain rowan.

Briars insinuate themselves,
arch a stickle back,
draw blood and curl up innocent
to sneak the next attack.

The yew tree in each churchyard
wraps night in its dark hood.
Ivy is a shadowy
genius of the wood.

Holly rears its windbreak,
a door in winter's face;
life-blood on a spear-shaft
darkens the grain of ash.

Birch-tree, smooth and blessed,
delicious to the breeze,
high twigs plait and crown it
queen of trees.

The aspen pales
and whispers, hesitates:
a thousand frightened scuts
race in the leaves.

But what disturbs me
more than anything
is an oak rod, always
swinging its thong.

                    *

Ronan was dishonoured,
he rang his little bell;
he clapped me in a labyrinth
of curse and miracle;

and noble Congal's armour,
that tunic edged with gold,
swathed me in doomed glory
with omens in each fold.

His lovely tunic marked me
in the middle of the rout,
the host pursuing, yelling,
—That's him in the gold coat.

—Get him, take him live or dead,
every man fall to.
Draw and quarter, pike
and spit him, none will blame you.

The horsemen still were after me
into the north of Down,
my back escaping nimbly
from every javelin thrown.

I fled, I must confess,
like a spear's trajectory,
my course a whisper in the air,
a breeze flicking through ivy.

I overtook the startled fawn,
outstripped his dainty toe,
I caught, ‘I rode him lightly—
from peak to peak we go;

from Inishowen's hilltops
I scorched along so free,
mountain after mountain
until I'm at Galtee

and from Galtee up to Liffey
I'm skipping terrified
and reach, towards evening,
Ben Bulben, where I hide.

Who on the even of battle thought
with me so puffed in pride
that I would spin off fortune's wheel
to scour that mountainside?

*

And then Glen Bolcain was my lair,
my earth and den;
I've roamed those slopes contented
by star and moon.

I wouldn't swap a hermit's hut
in that dear glen
for a world of mountain acres
or spreading plain.

Its waters' flashing emerald,
its wind so keen,
its tall brooklime, its watercress's
luscious green.

I love the ancient ivy-tree,
the merry sallow,
the birch's sibilant melody,
the solemn yew.

And you, Lynchseachan, can try
disguise, deceit,
the liar's mask, the shawl of night:
I won't be caught

again. You managed it the first time
with your litany of the dead:
father, mother, daughter, son,
brother, wife—you lied

but when you come the next time
Clear the Way!
Or face the heights of Mourne
and follow me.

                    *

I would lodge happily
in an ivy bush
high in some twisted tree
and never come out.

The skylarks'
unexpected treble
sends me pitching and tripping
over stumps on the moor

and my hurry
flushes the turtle dove.
I overtake it,
my plumage rushing,

am startled
by the startled woodcock
or a blackbird's sudden
volubility.

Think of my wild career,
my coming to earth
where the fox still
gnaws at the bones—

then away I go again
eluding the wolf in the wood,
athlete of air,
lifting off towards the mountain,

the bark of foxes
echoing below me,
the wolves howling
my send off,

their vapouring tongues,
their low-slung speed
shaken off like nightmare
at the foot of the slope.

Hobbled to the past,
I show my heels
and breast into guilt,
a sheep without a fold.

In the old tree at Killoo
I sleep soundly
dreaming back prosperous days
with Congal in Antrim.

A starry frost will come
dropping on the pools
and I'll be astray here
on the unsheltered heights:

herons calling
in cold Glenelly,
flocks of birds quickly
coming and going.

I prefer the elusive
rhapsody of blackbirds
to the garrulous company
of humans.

I prefer the squeal of badgers
in their sett
to the tally-ho
of the morning hunt.

I prefer the re-
echoing bellow of a stag
among the peaks
to that arrogant horn.

Those unharnessed runners
from glen to glen!
Nobody tames
that royal blood,

each one aloof
on a summit,
antlered, watchful.
Imagine them,

The stag of high Slieve Felim,
the stag of the steep Fews,
the stag of Duhallow, the stag of Orrery,
the fierce stag of Killarney.

The stag of Islandmagee, Larne's stag,
the stag of Moylinny,
the stag of Cooley, the stag of Cunghill,
the stag of the two-peaked Burren.

The mother of this herd
is old and grey,
the stags that follow her
are branchy, many tined.

I would creep beneath the grey
hut of her head,
would roost among
her mazy antlers,

would be dissembled
in this thicket of horns
that come sloping at me
over the belling glen.

I am Sweeney, the whinger,
the scuttler in the valley.
But call me, instead,
Peak Pate, Stag Head.

*

The springs I always liked
were the fountain at Dunmall
and the spring-well on Knocklayde
that tasted pure and cool.

Forever mendicant,
my rags all frayed and scanty,
high up in the mountains
like a crazed, frost-bitten sentry

I find no bed nor quarter,
no easy place in the sun:
not even in this reddening
covert of tall fern.

My only rest: eternal
sleep in holy ground
when St. Moling's earth lets fall
its dark balm on my wound.

But now that sudden clamour
and belling in the glen!
I am a timorous stag
feathered by Ronan Finn.

CONVERSATION BY
THE BODY'S LIGHT

by JANE COOPER

from WESTIGAN REVIEW OF POETRY

Out of my poverty
Out of your poverty
Out of your nakedness
Out of my nakedness
Between the swimmer in the water
And the watcher of the skies
Something is altered

Something is offered
Something is breathed
The body's radiance
Like the points of a constellation
Beckons to insight
Here is my poverty:
A body hoarded
Ridiculous in middle age
Unvoiced, unpracticed

And here is your poverty:
A prodigality
That guts its source
The self picked clean
In its shinning houses

Out of my nakedness
Out of your nakedness
Between the swimmer in the skies
And the watcher from the water
Something is braided
For a moment unbalanced
Caught—the barest shelter
Lost but reoccurring:
The still not-believed-in
Heartbeat of the glacier

IV

SNOW OWL

by DAVE SMITH

from ANTAEUS

In snow veined with his blood and the white bruise
of a broken wing, the hiss in the mouth
salutes my hand and will have still
its pink plug of flesh.
Big as I am he would nail me
if only the legs lasted, those numbs
never made for this crawling, for the wings,
all night, beat nowhere. He is himself. *Here*,

here, I say, on my knees edging toward him,
my own mastery the deceit of words.
His eye cocks, the hinged horn
of beak-bone cracks and rasps,
comes cold again, and shrill,
again, the shragged edge of wind
speaking the language of his world,

his kind, giving a blunt answer to all pain.
My words fall on his white attention
like a rain he can't escape.
At each angle his bad wing
sends a screen of snow
between us, a blind conceit,
until I leave him, beaten,
who I never leave in this life . . .

and go home, blood-specks and snow's feathering
for new clothes. In the spit of weather

I go without tracks, lips drawn
back for the least gusts
of harsh breath, and know
the moon that leads me is
an eye closed long ago
to the world's dark, large secrets.

RUNNING AWAY FROM HOME

by CAROLYN KIZER

from KAYAK

Most people from Idaho are crazed rednecks
Grown stunted in ugly shadows of brick spires,
Corrupted by fat priests in puberty,
High from the dry altitudes of Catholic towns.

Spooked by paster madonnas, switched by sadistic nuns,
Given sex instruction by dirty old men in skirts,
Recoiling from flesh-colored calendars, bloody gods,
Still we run off at the mouth, we keep on running.

Like those rattling roadsters with vomit-stained back seats.
Used condoms tucked beneath floor-mats.
That careened down hairpin turns through the blinding rain
Just in time to hit early mass in Coeur d'Alene!

Dear Phil, Dear Jack, Dear Tom, Dear Jim.
Whose car had a detachable steering-wheel:
He'd hand it to his scared, protesting girl
Saying, "Okay, *you* drive"—steering with his knees;

Jim drove Daddy's Buick over the railroad tracks,
Piss-drunk, just ahead of the Great Northern freight
Barrelling its way thru the dawn, straight for Spokane.
O the great times in Wallace & Kellogg, the good clean fun!

Dear Sally, Dear Beth, Dear Patsy, Dear Eileen,
Pale, faceless girls, my best friends at thirteen,
Knelt on cold stone, with chilblained knees, to pray.
"Dear God, Dear Christ! Don't let him go All the Way."

O the black Cadillacs skidding around corners
With their freight of drunken Jesuit businessmen!
Beautiful daughters of lumber-kings avoided the giant
Nuptial Mass at St. Joseph's, and fled into nunneries.

The rest live at home: bad girls who survived abortions,
Used Protestant diaphragms, or refused the sacred obligation
Of the marriage bed, scolded by beat-off priests,
After five in five years, by Bill, or Dick, or Ted.

I know your secrets: you turn up drunk by 10 a.m.
At the Beauty Shoppe, kids sent breakfastless to school.
You knew that you were doomed by seventeen.
Why should your innocent daughters fare better than you?

Young, you live on in me: even the blessed dead:
Tom, slammed into a fire hydrant on his Indian Chief
And died castrated; Jim, fool, fell 4 stories from the roof
Of his jock fraternity at Ag. & Tech.;

And the pure losers, cracked up in training planes
In Utah; or shot by a nervous rookie at Fort Lewis;
At least they cheated the white-coiffed ambulance chasers
And death-bed bedevillers, and died in war in peace.

Some people from Oregon are mad orphans
who claim to hail from Stratford-upon-Sodom.
They speak fake B.B.C.; they are Unitarian fairies,
In the Yang group or the Yin group, no Middle Way.

Some stay Catholic junkies, incense sniffers who
Scrawl JESUS SAVES on urinal walls, between engagements;
Or white disciples of Black Muslims; balding blonds
Who shave their public hair, or heads, for Buddha.

I find you in second-hand bookstores or dirty movies,
Bent halos like fedoras, pulled well down,
Bogarts of buggery. We can't resist the furtive questions:
Are you a writer too? How did you get out?

We still carry those Rosary scars, more like a *herpes
Simplex* than a stigmata: give us a nice long fit
Of depression; give us a good bout of self-hate;
Give us enough Pope, we pun, and we'll hang.

Hung, well hung, or hungover, in the world's most durable
Morning after, we'd sooner keep the mote and lose the eye.
Move over Tonio Kroger; you never attended
Our Lady of Sorrows, or Northwestern High!

Some people from Washington State are great poetasters,
Inbibers of anything, so long as it makes us sick
Enough to forget our sickness, and carry on
From the Carry Out: Hostess Winkies and Wild Duck.

We "relate", as they say, to Indians, bravest of cowards
Furtively cadging drinks with a shit-faced grin:
Outcasts who carry our past like a 90 lb. calcified foetus
We park in the bus-station locker, and run like sin.

Boozers and bounders, cracked-up crackerbarrel jockeys,
We frequent greasy bistros: Piraeus and Marseilles,
As we wait for our rip-off pimps, we scribble on napkins
Deathful verse we trust our executors to descry.

Wills. We are willess. As we have breath, we are wilful
And wishful, trusting that Great Archangel who Still Cares,
Who presides at the table set up for celestial Bingo.
We try to focus our eyes, and fill in the squares.

Some people from Spokane are insane salesmen
Peddling encyclopedias from door to door,
Trying to earn enough to flee to the happy farm
Before they jump from the Bridge, or murder Mom;

Or cut up their children with sanctified bread-knives
Screaming, "You are Isaac, and I am Abraham!"
But it's too late. They are the salutary failures
Who keep God from getting a swelled head.

Some shoot themselves in hotel rooms, after gazing
At chromos of the Scenic Route through the Cascades
Via Northern Pacific, or the old Milwaukee & St. Paul:
Those trains that won't stop rattling in our skulls!

First they construct crude crosses out of Band-Aids
And stick them to the mirror; then rip pages
From the Gideon Bible, roll that giant final joint,
A roach from *Revelations*, as they lie dying.

Bang! It's all over, Race through Purgatory
At last unencumbered by desperate manuscripts
In the salesman's sample-case, along with the dirty shirts.
After Spokane, what horrors lurk in Hell?

I think continually of those who are truly crazy:
Some people from Montana are put away;
They shake their manacles in a broken dance
With eyes blue-rimmed as a Picasso clown's.

Still chaste, but nude, hands shield their organs
Like the original Mom & Dad, after the Fall;
Or they dabble brown frescoes on the walls
Of solitary: their Ajanta and Lascaux.

While the ones that got away display giant kidneys
At the spiral skating-rink of Frank Lloyd Wright,
Or framed vermin in the flammable Museum
Of Modern Mart. But they're still Missoula

In their craft and sullen ebbing, Great Falls & Butte.
Meanwhile, Mondrian O'Leary squints at the light
Staining the white radiance of his well-barred cell,
Till ferocious blurs bump each other in Dodgem cars.

O that broken-down fun-house in Natatorium Park
Held the only fun the boy Mondrian ever knew!
Now seven-humped, mutated radioactive Chinook salmon
Taint the white radiance of O'Leary's brain.

O mad Medical Lake, I hear you have reformed:
No longer, Sunday afternoon, the tripper's joy.
Watch the nuts weep! or endlessly nibble fingers.
Funny, huh? The white ruin of muscular men.

Twisting bars like Gargantua; lewd Carusos,
Maimed Chanticleers, running off at the scars.
They hoot their arias through the rhythmic clashing
Of garbage-can lids that serve as dinner trays;

Inmates are slopped, while fascinated on-
Lookers watch Mrs. Hurley, somebody's grandma,
Eating gravy with her bare hands. Just animals, Rosetta.
She's not *your* mother. Don't let it get you.

Suddenly, Mr. Vincente, who with his eleven brothers
Built roads through the Spokane Valley
Where Italians moved like dreams of Martha Graham
As they laid asphalt over subterranean rivers,

Spots a distant cousin, Leonard, an architect
Until seventh grade, who seems to know him:
Leonard displays, by way of greeting.
His only piece of personal adornment:

How the tourists squeal! Watch them fumble at coat, and fly!
Girdled and ginghamed relatives disperse
Back to the touring car, the picnic basket
With its home-made grappa in giraffe-necked bottles.

As sun-scarred men urge olive children on,
Grandma Hurley, who thought the treat was for her,
Shyly waves her gravy-dappled fingers,
Couple-colored as her old brindled cat.

Enough of this madness! It's already in the past.
Now they are stabbed full of sopers, numbed & lobotomised
Is the privacy of their own heads. It's easier for the chaplain:
They're nodding. If you consent to be saved, just nod for God.

It's never over, old church of our claustrophobia!
Church of the barren towns, the vast unbearable sky,
Church of the Western plains, our first glimpse of brilliance.
Church of our innocent incense, there is no goodbye.

Church of the coloring-book, crude crayon of childhood,
Thank God at last you seem to be splitting apart.
But you live for at least as long as our maimed generation
Lives to curse your blessed plaster bleeding heart.

PIG 311

by MARGARET RYAN

from CEDAR ROCK

"In an experimental atomic explosion off the island
of Bikini. . . . among the animals exposed to
radiation was one pig, bearing the number 311. He
was placed in an old warship and was thrown into
the sea by the blast. He swam to an atoll, lived
for a long time and procreated in a perfectly
normal manner."

—One Hundred Thousand Years of Man's
Unknown History, by Robert Charroux

I was pickled in brine for a while,
all of me, not just the delicate feet;
the bristling body, the ugly snout,
even the much-maligned ears were blown
into the sea by a blast I knew nothing about.

The sleek-bodied goats, the intelligent monkies,
even the obese sheep in their expensive coats
disappeared into the unseen slaughter.
A great wind delivered me into the water.
I set my short legs churning the salt into foam.

I don't know who set this circle of coral
like a ring in the water, who gave me palmtrees,
coconuts, paradise—this other hard-nosed pig,
my bride. We have had daughters and sons
in a perfectly normal manner.

Our children cover the island now, a chosen,
cloven-footed race. They breed, repeople the land.
The children read about me, their father, how
I survived the great blast. Already the hooves
of the poets engrave my name in the sand.

From LAUGHING WITH ONE EYE

by GJERTRUD SCHNACKENBERG SMYTH

from POETRY

Walter Charles Schnackenberg
Professor of History (1917–1973)

NIGHTFISHING

The kitchen's old-fashioned planter's clock portrays
A smiling moon as it dips down below
Two hemispheres, stars numberless as days,
And peas, tomatoes, onions, as they grow
Under that happy sky; but, though the sands
Of time put on this vegetable disguise,
The clock covers its face with long, thin hands.
Another smiling moon begins to rise.

We drift in the small rowboat an hour before
Morning begins, the lake weeds grown so long
They touch the surface, tangling in an oar.
You've brought coffee, cigars, and me along.
You sit still as a monument in a hall,
Watching for trout. A bat slices the air
Near us, I shriek, you look at me, that's all,
One long sobering look, a smile everywhere

But on your mouth. The mighty hills shriek back.
You turn back to the lake, chuckle, and clamp
Your teeth on your cigar. We watch the black
Water together. Our tennis shoes are damp.
Something moves on your thoughtful face, recedes.
Here, for the first time ever, I see how,
Just as a fish lurks deep in water weeds,
A thought of death will lurk deep down, will show
One eye, then quietly disappear in you.
Its time to go. Above the hills I see
The faint moon slowly dipping out of view,
Sea of Tranquility, Sea of Serenity,
Ocean of Storms . . . You start to row, the boat
Skimming the lake where light begins to spread.
You stop the oars, mid-air. We twirl and float.

I'm in the kitchen. You are three days dead.
A smiling moon rises on fertile ground,
White stars and vegetables. The sky is blue.
Clock hands sweep by it all, they twirl around,
Pushing me, oarless, from the shore of you.

INTERMEZZO

Steinway in German script above the keys,
Letters like dragons curling stiff gold tails,
Gold letters, ivory keys, the black wood cracked
By years of sunlight, into dragon scales.
Your music breathed its fire into the room.
We'd hear jazz sprouting thistles of desire,
Or jazz like the cat's cry from beneath
The passing tire, when you played the piano
Afternoons; or "Au Clair de la Lune."
Scarlatti's passages fluttered like pages.
Sometimes you turned to Brahms, a depth, more true,
You studied him to find out how he turned
Your life into a memory for you.

* * *

In Number 6 of Opus 118,
Such brief directions, Andante, sotto voce:
The opening notes like single water drops
Each with an oceanic undertow
That pulled you deeper even as you surfaced
Hundreds of miles from where the first note drew
You in, and made your life a memory,
Something that happened long ago to you.

And through that Intermezzo you could see
As through a two-way mirror until it seemed
You looked back at your life as at a room,
And saw those images that would compose
Your fraction of eternity, the hallway
In its absolute repose, the half-lit room,
The drapes at evening holding the scent of heat,
The marble long-lost under the piano,
A planet secretive, cloud-wrapped and blue,
Silent and gorgeous by your foot, making
A god lost in reflection, a god of you.

WALKING HOME

Walking home from school one afternoon,
Slightly abstracted, what were you thinking of?
Turks in Vienna? Luther on Christian love?
Or were you with Van Gogh beneath the moon
With candles in his hatband, painting stars
Like singed hairs spinning in a candle flame?
Or giant maps where men take, lose, reclaim
Whole continents with pins? Or burning cars
And watchtowers and army-censored news
In Chile, in the Philippines, in Greece,
Colonels running the universities,
Assassinations, executions, coups—

You walked, and overhead some pipsqueak bird
Flew by and dropped a lot of something that
Splattered, right on the good professor, splat.

Now, on the ancient Rhine, so Herod heard,
The old Germanic chieftains always read
Such droppings as good luck: opening the door,
You bowed to improve my view of what you wore,
So luckily, there on the center of your head.

Man is not a god, that's what you said
After your heart gave out, to comfort me
Who came to comfort you but sobbed to see
Your heartbeat blipping on a TV overhead.

You knew the world was in a mess, and so,
By God, were you; and yet I never knew
A man who loved the world as much as you,
And that love was the last thing to let go.

"THERE ARE NO DEAD"

Outside a phoebe whistles for its mate,
The rhododendron rubs its leaves against
Your office window: so the Spring we sensed
You wouldn't live to see comes somewhat late.
Here, lying on the desk, your reading glasses,
And random bits of crimped tobacco leaves,
Your jacket dangling its empty sleeves—
These look as if you've just left for your classes.
The chess game is suspended on its board
In your mind's pattern, your wastebasket
Contains some crumpled papers, your filing cabinet
Heavy with years of writing working toward
A metaphysics of impersonal praise
Here students came and went, here years would draw
Intensities of lines until we saw
Your face beneath an etching of your face.
How many students really cared to solve
History's riddles?—in hundreds on the shelves,
Where men trying to think about themselves
Must come to grips with grief that won't resolve,
Blackness of headlines in the daily news,

And buildings blown away from flights of stairs
All over Europe, tanks in empty squares,
The flaming baby-carriages of Jews.

Behind its glass, a print hangs on the wall,
A detail from the Bayeux Tapestry.
As ignorant women gabbed incessantly,
Their red, sore hands stitched crudely to recall
Forests of ships, the star with streaming hair,
God at Westminster blessing the devout,
They jabbed their thousand needles in and out,
Sometimes too busy talking to repair
The small mistakes; now the centuries of grease
And smoke that stained it, and the blind white moth
And grinning worm that spiralled through the cloth,
Say death alone makes life a masterpiece.

The William of Normandy remounts his horse
A fourth time, four times desperate to drive
Off rumors of his death. His sword is drawn,
He swivels and lifts his visor up and roars,
Look at me well! For I am still alive!
Your glasses, lying on the desk, look on.

THE RITUAL OF MEMORIES

by TESS GALLAGHER

from UNDER STARS (Graywolf Press)

When your widow had left the graveside
and you were most alone
I went to you in that future
you can't remember yet. I brought
a basin of clear water where no tear
had fallen, water gathered like grapes
a drop at a time
from the leaves of the willow. I brought
oils, I brought a clean white gown.

"Come out," I said, and you came up
like a man pulling himself out of a river,
a river with so many names
there was no word left for it but "earth."

"Now," I said, "I'm ready. These eyes
that have not left your face
since the day we met, wash these eyes.
Remember, it was a country road
above the sea and I was passing
from the house of a friend. Look
into these eyes where we met."

I saw your mind go back through the years
searching for that day and finding it,
you washed my eyes
with the pure water
so that I vanished from that road
and you passed a lifetime
and I was not there.

So you washed every part of me
where any look or touch
had passed between us. "Remember,"
I said, when you came to the feet,
"it was the night before you would ask
the girl of your village to marry. I
was the strange one. I was the one
with the gypsy look.
Remember how you stroked these feet."

When the lips and the hands
had been treated likewise and the pit
of the throat where one thoughtless kiss
had fallen, you rubbed in the sweet oil
and I glistened like a new-made thing, not
merely human, but of the world gone past
being human.

"The hair," I said. "You've forgotten
the hair. Don't you know it remembers.
Don't you know it keeps everything. Listen,
there is your voice and in it the liar's charm
that caught me."

You listened. You heard your voice
and a look of such sadness
passed over your dead face that I wanted
to touch you. Who could have known
I would be so held? Not you
in your boyish cunning; not me
in my traveler's clothes.

It's finished.
Put the gown on my shoulders.
It's no life in the shadow of another's joys.
Let me go freely now.
One life I have lived for you. This one
is mine.

QUINNAPOXET

by STANLEY KUNITZ

from ANTAEUS

I was fishing in the abandoned reservoir
back in Quinnapoxet,
where the snapping turtles cruised
and the bullheads swayed
in their bower of tree-stumps,
sleek as eels and pigeon-fat.
One of them gashed my thumb
with a flick of his razor fin
when I yanked the barb
out of his gullet.
The sun hung its terrible coals
over Buteau's farm: I saw
the treetops seething.

They came suddenly into view
on the Indian road,
evenly stepping
past the apple orchard,
commingling with the dust
they raised, their cloud of being,
against the dripping light
looming larger and bolder.
She was wearing a mourning bonnet
and a wrap of shining taffeta.
"Why don't you write?" she cried
from the folds of her veil.
"We never hear from you."
I had nothing to say to her.

But for him who walked behind her
in his dark worsted suit,
with his face averted
as if to hide a scald,
deep in his other life,
I touched my forehead
with my swollen thumb
and splayed my fingers out—
in deaf-mute country
the sign for father.

V

THE OTTER

by SEAMUS HEANEY

from ANTAEUS

When you plunged
The light of Tuscany wavered
And swung through the pool
From top to bottom.

I loved your wet head and smashing crawl,
Your fine swimmer's back and shoulders
Surfacing and surfacing again
This year and every year since.

I sat dry-throated on the warm stones.
You were beyond me.
The mellowed clarities, the grape-deep air
Thinned and disappointed.

Thank God for the slow loadening.
When I hold you now
We are close and deep
As the atmosphere on water.

My two hands are plumbed water.
You are my palpable, lithe
Otter of memory
In the pool of the moment,

Turning to swim on your back,
Each silent, thigh-shaking kick
Re-tilting the light,
Heaving the cool at your neck.

And suddenly you're out,
Back again, intent as ever,
Heavy and frisky in your freshened pelt,
Printing the stones.

YOUNG WOMEN AT CHARTRES

by JAMES WRIGHT

from THE GEORGIA REVIEW

(in memory of Jean Garrigue)

> ". . . like a thief I followed her
> Though my heart was so alive
> I thought it equal to that beauty."
> ("The Stranger")

one

Halfway through morning
Lisa, herself blossoming, strolls
Lazily beneath the eastern roses
In the shadow of Chartres.
She does not know
She is visible.
As she lifts her face
Toward the northwest,
Mothwings fall down and rest on her hair.
She darkens
Without knowing it, as the wind blows on down toward the river
Where the cathedral, last night,
Sank among the reeds.

two

Fog
Rinses away for a little while the cold
Christs with their suffering faces.
Mist
Leaves to us solitary friends of the rain
The happy secret angel
On the north corner.

three

You lived so abounding with mist and wild strawberries,
So faithful with the angel in the rain,
You kept faith to a stranger.
Now, Jean, your musical name poises in the webs
Of wheatfield and mist,
And beneath the molded shadow of the local stones,
I hear you again, singing beneath the northwest
Angel who holds in her arms
Sunlight on sunlight.
She is equal
To you, to her own happy face, she is holding
A sundial in her arms. No wonder Christ was happy
Among women's faces.

I REMEMBER GALILEO

by GERALD STERN

from POETRY

I remember Galileo describing the mind
as a piece of paper blown around by the wind
and I loved the sight of it sticking to a tree
or jumping into the back seat of a car,
and for years I watched paper leap through my cities;
but yesterday I saw the mind was a squirrel caught
   crossing
route 80 between the wheels of a giant truck,
dancing back and forth like a thin leaf,
or a frightened string, for only two seconds living
on the white concrete before he got away,
his life shortened by all that terror, his head
jerking, his yellow teeth ground down to dust.

It was the speed of the squirrel and his lowness to the
   ground,
his great purpose and the alertness of his dancing,
that showed me the difference between him and paper.
Paper will do in theory, when there is time
to sit back in a metal chair and study shadows;
but for this life I need a squirrel,
his clawed feet spread, his whole soul quivering,
the hot wind rushing through his hair,
the loud noise shaking him from head to tail.
   O philosophical mind, O mind of paper, I need a squirrel
finishing his wild dash across the highway,
rushing up his green ungoverned hillside.

PORTRAIT OF

THE ARTIST WITH LI PO

by CHARLES WRIGHT

from DURAK: AN INTERNATIONAL MAGAZINE OF POETRY

The "high heavenly priest of the White Lake" is now
A small mound in an endless plain of grass,
His pendants clicking and pearls shading his eyes.
He never said anything about the life after death,
Whose body is clothed in a blue rust and the smoke of dew.

He liked flowers and water most.
Everyone knows the true story of how he would write his verses
    and float them,
Like paper boats, downstream
               just to watch them drift away.
Death never entered his poems, but rowed, with its hair down,
    far out on the lake,
Laughing and looking up at the sky.

Over a 1000 years later, I write out one of his lines in a notebook,
The peach blossom follows the moving water,
And watch the October darkness gather against the hills.
All night long the river of heaven will move westward while no
    one notices.
The distance between the dead and the living
          is more than a heart beat and a breath.

BREATH

by HEATHER McHUGH

from ASPEN ANTHOLOGY

What I want from God, feared to be
unlovable, is none
of the body's business, nasty
lunches of blood and host, and none

of the yes-man networks,
neural, capillary or electric.
No little histories recited
in the temple, in the neck and wrist.
I want the heavy air,
unhymned, uncyclical,
and a deep kiss: absence's.
I want to be rid of men

who seem friendly, but die,
and rid of my studies
wired for sound.
I want the space in which all names
for worship sink away,
and earth recedes
to silver vanishing, the point
at which we can forget
our history of longing, and become

his great blue breath,
his ghost and only song.

BY THE POOL

by ALLEN GROSSMAN

from THE PARIS REVIEW

Every dwelling is a desolate hill.
Every hill is a desolate dwelling.

The trees toss their branches in the dark air,
Each tree after its kind, and each kind after
Its own way. The wind tosses the branches
Of the trees in the dark air. The swimming
Pool is troubled by the wind, and the swimmers.

Even though this is not a tower, this is
Also a tower.

       Even though you are not
A watchman, you are also a watchman.

Even though the night has not yet come,
The night has come.

VI

CANTINA MUSIC

by DEREK WALCOTT

from ANTAEUS

A lilac sea between shacks,
and, at the Carenage overpass, the go-light
the exact hue of a firefly's faint emerald.
Coconuts, blasted with mildew,
rust between crusted roofs,
the pirogues seem soldered
to metal water, but, like paper lanterns,
rose, lilac, orange
the shacks shine through black hills like bullet holes.

Gauchos of the New World,
Rio, Buenos Aires,
the Wild West rumshops circling St. James,
your fantasies
thud to the rain's guitars
to the renegades whose names
darken on iron stallions,
directing traffic,
against a livid sunset whose palms droop,
morose moustaches of dead liberators,

as the foam's grey lather
shines like their horses.
Bandidos of the Old Republic,
your teeth flashed like daggers
your snarl like tom leather
you strode into the street
at the hour of the firefly
and, boots astride, facing the showdown,
you waltzed slowly to the dirt
to a flamenco from the tin cantinas.

Black hats of the double-feature,
Widmarks, Zapatistas, Djangos,
all revolution is rooted in crime.
Your dust is a cloud like a rose,
your hearts keep time
to the ruby beat of the jukebox
"adios muchachos,
compañeros de mi vida,"
from the grave of some boy shot by the police,
some wrong-sided leader
tenor-pan man from Renegades,
Gay Desperadoes.

When you fell there,
exactly as you had learnt to from the screen,
limp as a mountain lion
in whose glass amber eyes
there is no flickering question
about justice.

And the shot that flings
the bandit whirling
in perverse crucifixions
so that each frame, arrested,
repeats itself like a corrupt pietà
to the prodigal of The Mother of The World,
echoes as deep as any silver mine
from the rumshops,
from cantinas,

from the dark sky with a red flower in her hair,
from Rio, from Buenos Aires,
from Carenage,
from St. James,
and has more than they think to do with
the lilac sea between the shacks,
the highway overpass and the faint emerald
of the go-light
that unexpectedly
changes to red.

LAGOON

by JOSEPH BRODSKY

from THE PARIS REVIEW

I

Down in the lobby three elderly women, bored,
Take up, with their knitting, the Passion of Our Lord
    As the universe and the tiny realm
Of the *pension "Accademia,"* side by side,
with TV blaring, sail into Christmastide,
    A look-out desk-clerk at the helm.

II

And a nameless lodger, a nobody, boards the boat,
A bottle of grappa concealed in his raincoat
    As he gains his shadowy room, bereaved
Of memory, homeland, son, with only the noise
Of distant forests to grieve for his former joys,
    If anyone is grieved.

III

Venetian churchbells, tea cups, mantle clocks,
Chime and confound themselves in this stale box
    Of assorted lives. The brazen, coiled
Octopus-chandelier appears to be licking,
In a triptych mirror, bedsheet and mattress ticking,
    Sodden with tears and passion-soiled.

IV

Blown by nightwinds, an Adriatic tide
Floods the canals, boats rock from side to side,
    Moored cradles, and the humble bream,
Not ass and oxen, guards the rented bed
Where the windowblind above your sleeping head
    Moves to the sea-star's guiding beam.

V

So this is how we cope, putting out the heat
Of grappa with nightstand water, carving the meat
    Of flounder instead of Christmas roast,
So that Thy earliest back-boned ancestor
Might feed and nourish us, O Savior,
    This winter night on a damp coast.

VI

A Christmas without snow, tinsel or tree,
At the edge of a map-and-land corseted sea;
    Having scuttled and sunk its scallop shell,
Concealing its face while flaunting its backside,
Time rises from the goddess's frothy tide,
    Yet changes nothing but clock-hand and bell.

VII

A drowning city, where suddenly the dry
Light of reason dissolves in the moisture of the eye;
    Its winged lion, that can read and write,
Southern kin of northern Sphinxes* of renown,
Won't drop his book and holler, but calmly drown
    In splinters of mirror, splashing light.

VIII

The gondola knocks against its moorings. Sound
Cancels itself, hearing and words are drowned,
    As is that nation where among

*Sculptured figures placed along the enbankments of the Neva River in Leningrad

Forests of hands the tyrant of the State
Is voted in, its only candidate,
    And spit goes ice-cold on the tongue.

IX

So let us place the left paw, sheathing its claws,
In the crook of the arm of the other one, because
    This makes a hammer-and-sickle sign
With which to salute our era and bestow
A mute *Up Yours Even Unto The Elbow*
    Upon the nightmares of our time.

X

The raincoated figure is settling into place
Where Sophia, Constance, Prudence, Faith and Grace
    Lack futures, the only tense that is
Is present, where either a goyish or Yiddish kiss
Tastes bitter, like the city, where footsteps fade
    Invisibly along the colonnade,

XI

Trackless and blank as a gondola's passage through
A water surface, smoothing out of view
    The measured wrinkles of its path,
Unmarked as a broad "So long!" like the wide piazza's
        space,
Or as a cramped "I love," like the narrow alleyways,
    Erased and without aftermath.

XII

Moldings and carvings, palaces and flights
Of stairs. Look up: the lion smiles from heights
    Of a tower wrapped as in a coat
Of wind, unbudged, determined not to yield,
Like a rank weed at the edge of a plowed field,
    And girdled round by Time's deep moat.

XIII

Night in St. Mark's piazza. A face as creased
As a finger from its fettering ring released,
    Biting a nail, is gazing high
Into that *nowhere* of pure thought, where sight
Is baffled by the bandages of night,
    Serene, beyond the naked eye,

XIV

Where, past all boundaries and all predicates,
Black, white or colorless, vague, volatile states,
    Something, some object, comes to mind.
Perhaps a body. In our dim days and few,
The speed of light equals a fleeting view,
    Even when blackout robs us blind.

Translated by Anthony Hecht

WAITING IN LINE

by WILLIAM STAFFORD

from BARNWOOD PRESS

You the very old, I have come
to the edge of your country and looked across,
how your eyes warily look into mine
when we pass, how you hesitate when
we approach a door. Sometimes
I understand how steep your hills
are, and your way of seeing the madness
around you, the careless waste of the calendar,
the rush of people on buses. I have
studied how you carry packages,
balancing them better, giving them attention.

I have glimpsed from within the gray-eyed look
at those who push, and occasionally even I
can achieve your beautiful bleak perspective
on the loud, inattentive, shoving boors
jostling past you toward their doom.

With you, from the pavement I have watched
the nation of the young, like jungle birds
that scream as they pass, or gyrate on playgrounds,
their frenzied bodies jittering with the disease
of youth. Knowledge can cure them. But
not all at once. It will take time.

There have been evenings when the light
has turned everything silver, and like you
I have stopped at a corner and suddenly
staggered with the grace of it all: to have
inherited all this, or even the bereavement
of it and finally being cheated!—the chance
to stand on a corner and tell it goodby!
Every day, every evening, every
abject step or stumble, has become heroic:—

You others, we the very old have a country.
A passport costs everything there is.

FLOOR

by C. K. WILLIAMS

from THE AMERICAN POETRY REVIEW

A dirty picture, a photograph, possibly a tintype, from the turn of
    the century, even before that:
the woman is obese, gigantic; a broad, black corset cuts from
    under her breasts to the top of her hips,
her hair is crimped, wiry, fastened demurely back with a bow one
    incongruous wing of which shows.
Her eyebrows are straight and heavy, emphasizing her frank,
    unintrospective plainness
and she looks directly, easily into the camera, her expression
    somewhere between play and scorn,
as though the activities of the photographer were ridiculous or
    beneath her contempt, or,

rather, as though the unfamiliar camera were actually the much
    more interesting presence here
and how absurd it is that the lens be turned toward her and her
    partner and not back on itself.
One sees the same look—pride, for some reason, is in it, and a
    surprisingly sophisticated self-distancing—
in the snaps anthropologists took in backwaters during those first,
    politically pre-conscious,
golden days of culture-hopping, and, as Goffman notes, in certain
    advertisements, now.

The man is younger than the woman. Standing, he wears what
    looks like a bathing costume,
black and white tank-top, heavy trousers bunched in an ungainly
    heap over his shoes, which are still on.
He has an immigrant's mustache he's a year or two too callow for,
    but, thick and dark, it will fit him.
He doesn't, like the woman, watch the camera, but stares ahead,
    not at the woman but slightly over and past,
and there's a kind of withdrawn, almost vulnerable thoughtfulness
    or preoccupation about him
despite the gross thighs cast on his waist and the awkward, surely
    bothersome twist
his body has been forced to assume to more clearly exhibit the
    genital penetration.
He seems, in fact, deeply abstracted—oblivious wouldn't be too
    strong a word—as though, possibly,
as unlikely as it would seem, he had been a virgin until now and
    was trying amid all this unholy confusion—
the hooded figure, the black box with its eye—trying, and from
    the looks of it even succeeding
in obliterating everything from his consciousness but the thing
    itself, the act itself,
so as, one would hope, to redeem the doubtlessly endless nights
    of the long Victorian adolescence.

The background is a painted screen: ivy, columns, clouds, some
    muse or grace or other,
heavy-buttocked, whorey, flaunts her gauze and clodhops with a
    half-demented leer.

The whole thing's oddly poignant somehow; almost, like an
    antique wedding picture, comforting:
the past is sending out a tendril to us, poses, attitudes of stillness
    we've lost or given back.
Also there's no shame in watching them, in being in the tacit
    commerce of having, like it or not,
received the business in one's hand: there's no titillation either,
    not a tangle, not a throb,
probably because the woman offers none of the normal symptoms,
    even if minimal, even if contrived— ˎ
the tongue, say, wandering from the corner of the mouth, a glint
    of extra brilliance at the lash—
we associate to even the most innocuous, undramatic, parental
    sorts of passion, and the boy,
well, dragged in out of history, off of Broome or South Street, all
    he is is grandpa;
he'll go back into whatever hole he's found to camp in, those
    higher contrast tenements
with their rows of rank, forbidding beds, or not even beds, rags
    on a floor, or floor.
On the way there, there'll be policemen breaking strikers' heads,
    or Micks' or Sheenies',
there'll be war somewhere, in the sweatshops girls will turn to
    stone over their Singers.
Here, at least, peace. Here, one might imagine, after he
    withdraws, a kind of manly focus taking him,
the glance he shoots to her is hard and sure, and, to her, a
    tenderness might come,
she might reach a hand—Sweet Prince—to touch his cheek, or
    might—who can understand these things?—
avert her face and pull him to her for a time before she squats to
    flush him out.

FOR ELIZABETH BISHOP

by SANDRA MCPHERSON

from THE AMERICAN POETRY REVIEW

The child I left your class to have
Later had a habit of sleeping
With her arms around a globe
She'd unscrewed, dropped, and dented.
I always felt she *could* possess it,
The pink countries and the mauve
And the ocean which got to keep its blue.
Coming from the Southern Hemisphere to teach,
Which you had never had to do, you took
A bare-walled room, alone, its northern
Windowscapes as gray as walls.
To decorate, you'd only brought a black madonna.
I thought you must have skipped summer that year,
Southern winter, southern spring, then north
For winter over again. Still, it pleased you
To take credit for introducing us,
And later to bring our daughter a small flipbook
Of partners dancing, and a ring
With a secret whistle.—All are
Broken now like her globe, but she remembers
Them as I recall the black madonna
Facing you across the room so that
In a way you had the dark fertile life
You were always giving gifts to.
Your smaller admirer off to school,
I take the globe and roll it away: where
On it now is someone like you?

117

WORLD BREAKING APART

by LOUISE GLÜCK

from WATER TABLE

I look out over the sterile snow.
Under the white birch tree, a wheelbarrow.
The fence behind it mended. On the picnic table,
mounded snow, like the inverted contents of a bowl
whose dome the wind shapes. The wind,
with its impulse to build. And under my fingers,
the square white keys, each stamped
with its single character. I believed
a mind's shattering released
the objects of its scrutiny: trees, blue plums in a bowl,
a man reaching for his wife's hand
across a slatted table, and quietly covering it,
as though his will enclosed it in that gesture.
I saw them come apart, the glazed clay begin
dividing endlessly, dispersing incoherent particles
that went on shining forever. I dreamed of watching that
the way we watched the stars on summer evenings,
my hand on your chest, the wine
holding the chill of the river. There is no such light.
And pain, the free hand, changes almost nothing.
Like the winter wind, it leaves
settled forms in the snow. Known, identifiable—
except there are no uses for them.

VII

I SING THE BODY ELECTRIC

by PHILIP LEVINE

from ANTAEUS

People sit numbly at the counter
waiting for breakfast or service.
Today it's Hartford, Connecticut
more than twenty-five years after
the last death of Wallace Stevens.
I have come in out of the cold
and wind of a Sunday morning
of early March, and I seem to be
crying, but I'm only freezing
and unpeeled. The waitress brings
me hot tea in a cracked cup,
and soon it's all over my paper,
and so she refills it. I read
slowly in *The New York Times*
that poems are dying in Iowa,
Missoula, on the outskirts of Reno,
in the shopping galleries of Houston.
We should all go to the grave
of the unknown poet while the rain
streaks our notebooks or stand
for hours in the freezing winds
off the lost books of our fathers
or at least until we can no longer
hold our pencils. Men keep coming
in and going out, and two of them
recall the great dirty fights

between Willy Pep and Sandy Sadler,
between little white perfection
and death in red plaid trunks.
I want to tell them I saw
the last fight, I rode out
to Yankee Stadium with two deserters
from the French Army of Indochina
and back with a drunken priest
and both ways the whole train
smelled of piss and vomit, but no
one would believe me. Those are
the true legends better left to die.
In my black raincoat I go back
out into the gray morning and dare
the cars on North Indemnity Boulevard
to hit me, but no one wants trouble
at this hour. I have crossed
a continent to bring these citizens
the poems of the snowy mountains,
of the forges of hopelessness,
of the survivors of wars they
never heard of and won't believe.
Nothing is alive in this tunnel
of winds of the end of winter
except the last raging of winter,
the cats peering smugly from the homes
of strangers, and the great stunned sky
slowly settling like a dark cloud
lined only with smaller dark clouds.

FROM MY WINDOW

by C. K. WILLIAMS

from THE PARIS REVIEW

Spring: the first morning when that one true block of
    sweet, laminar, complex scent arrives
from somewhere west and I keep coming to lean on the
    sill, glorying in the end of the wretched winter.
The scabby-barked sycamores ringing the empty lot across
    the way are budded—I hadn't even noticed—
and the thick spikes of the unlikely urban crocuses have
    already broken the gritty soil.
Up the street, some surveyors with tripods are waving
    each other left and right the way they do.
A girl in a gymsuit jogged by awhile ago, some kids
    passed, playing hooky, I imagine,
and now the paraplegic Vietnam vet who lives in a half-
    converted warehouse down the block
and the friend who stays with him and seems to help him
    out come weaving towards me,
their battered wheelchair lurching uncertainly from one
    edge of the sidewalk to the other.
I know where they're going—to the "Legion"; once,
    when I was putting something out, they stopped,
both drunk that time, too, both reeking—it wasn't ten
    o'clock—and we chatted for a bit.
I don't know how they stay alive—on benefits most likely.
    I wonder if they're lovers.
They don't look it. Right now, in fact, they look a wreck,
    careening haphazardly along,
contriving as they reach beneath me to dip a wheel from
    the curb so that the chair skewers, teeters,
tips, and they both tumble, the one slowly, almost
    gracefully sliding in stages from his seat,
his expression hardly marking it, the other staggering
    over him, spinning heavily down,
to lie on the asphalt, his mouth working, his feet shoving
    weakly and fruitlessly against the curb.
In the store-front office on the corner, Reed and Son,
    Real Estate, have come to see the show:

123

gazing through the golden letters of their name, they're
    not, at least, thank god, laughing.
Now the buddy, grabbing at a hydrant, gets himself erect
    and stands there for a moment, panting.
Now he has to lift the other one, who lies utterly still, a
    forearm shielding his eyes from the sun.
He hauls him partly upright, then hefts him almost all
    the way into the chair but a dangling foot
catches a support-plate, jerking everything around so that
    he has to put him down,
set the chair to rights and hoist him again and as he does
    he jerks the grimy jeans right off him.
No drawers, shrunken, blotchy thighs; under the thick
    white coils of belly blubber
the poor, blunt pud, tiny, terrified, retracted, is almost
    invisible in the sparse genital hair,
then his friend pulls his pants up, he slumps wholly back
    as though he were, at last, to be let be,
and the friend leans against the cyclone fence, suddenly
    staring up at me as though he'd known
all along that I was watching and I can't help wondering
    if he knows that in the winter, too,
I watched, the night he went out to the lot and walked,
    paced rather, almost ran, for how many hours.
It was snowing, the city in that holy silence, the last we
    have, when the storm takes hold,
and he was making patterns that I thought at first were
    circles then realized made a figure eight,
what must have been to him a perfect symmetry but
    which, from where I was, shivered, bent,
and lay on its side: a warped, unclear infinity, slowly, as
    the snow came faster, going out.
Over and over again, his head lowered to the task, he
    slogged the path he'd blazed
but the race was lost, his prints were filling faster than
    he made them now and I looked away,
up across the skeletal trees to the tall center-city
    buildings, some, though it was midnight,
with all their offices still gleaming, their scarlet warning-
    beacons signaling erratically,
against the thickening flakes, their smoldering auras
    softening portions of the dim, milky sky.
In the morning, nothing; every trace of him effaced, all
    the field pure white,
its surface glittering, the dawn, glancing from its glaze,
    oblique, relentless, unadorned.

THE JOURNEY

by JAMES WRIGHT

from A REPLY TO MATTHEW ARNOLD (Logbridge-Rhodes, Inc.)

Anghiari is medieval, a sleeve sloping down
A steep hill, suddenly sweeping out
To the edge of a cliff, and dwindling.
But far up the mountain, behind the town,
We too were swept out, out by the wind,
Alone with the Tuscan grass.

Wind had been blowing across the hills
For days, and everything now was graying gold
With dust, everything we saw, even
Some small children scampering along a road,
Twittering Italian to a small caged bird.
We sat beside them to rest in some brushwood,
And I leaned down to rinse the dust from my face.

I found the spider web there, whose hinges
Reeled heavily and crazily with the dust,
Whole mounds and cemeteries of it, sagging
And scattering shadows among shells and wings.
And then she stepped into the center of air
Slender and fastidious, the golden hair
Of daylight along her shoulders, she poised there,
While ruins crumbled on every side of her.
Free of the dust, as though a moment before
She had stepped inside the earth, to bathe herself.

I gazed, close to her, till at last she stepped
Away in her own good time.

Many men
Have searched all over Tuscany and never found
What I found there, the heart of the light
Itself shelled and leaved, balancing
On filaments themselves falling. The secret
Of this journey is to let the wind
Blow its dust all over your body,
To let it go on blowing, to step lightly, lightly
All the way through your ruins, and not to lose
Any sleep over the dead, who surely
Will bury their own, don't worry.

THE SOUTHERN CROSS

by CHARLES WRIGHT

from THE PARIS REVIEW

Things that divine us we never touch:

The black sounds of the night music,
The Southern Cross, like a kite at the end of its string,

And now this sunrise, and empty sleeve of a day,
The rain just starting to fall, and then not fall,

No trace of a story line.

————

All day I've remembered a lake and a sudsy shoreline,
Gauze curtains blowing in and out of open windows all over
    the South.

It's 1936, in Tennessee. I'm one
And spraying the dead grass with a hose.
The curtains blow in and out.

And then it's not. And I'm not and they're not.

Or it's 1941 in a brown suit, or '53 in its white shoes,
Overlay after overlay tumbled and brought back,
As meaningless as the sea would be
                if the sea could remember its waves . . .

————

Nothing had told me my days were marked for a doom
                              under the cold stars of the Virgin.
Nothing had told me that woe would buzz at my side like a fly.

The morning is dark with spring.
The early blooms on the honeysuckle shine like maggots
     after the rain.
The purple mouths of the passion blossoms
                              open their white gums to the wind.

How sweet the past is, no matter how wrong, or how sad.
How sweet is yesterday's noise.

———

All day the ocean was like regret,
                    clearing its throat, brooding and self-absorbed.

Now the wisteria tendrils extend themselves like swan's necks
     under Orion.

Now the small stars in the orange trees.

———

At Garda, on Punto San Vigilio, the lake,
In springtime, is like the sea,
Wind fishtailing the olive leaves like slash minnows beneath
     the vineyards,
Ebb and flow of the sunset past Sirmio,
                              flat voice of the waters
Retelling their story, again and again, as though to unburden itself

Of an unforgotten guilt,
                    and not relieved
Under the soothing hand of the dark,

The clouds over Bardolino dragging the sky for the dead
Bodies of those who refuse to rise,
Their orange robes and flaming bodices trolling across the hills,

128

Nightwind by now in the olive trees,
No sound but the wind from anything
                                    under the tired, Italian stars . . .

 And the voice of the waters, starting its ghostly litany.

————————

River of sighs and forgetfulness
                        (and the secret light Campana saw),
River of bloom-bursts from the moon,
                            of slivers and broken blades from the moon
In an always-going-away of glints . . .

Dante and Can Grande once stood here,
Next to the cool breath of S. Anastasia,
                                watching the cypress candles
Flare in their deep green across the Adige
In the Giusti Gardens.
                            Before that, in his marble tier,
Catullus once sat through the afternoons.
Before that, God spoke in the rocks . . .

And now it's my turn to stand
Watching a different light do the same things on a different water,
The Adige bearing its gifts
                            through the April twilight of 1961.

————————

When my father went soldiering, apes dropped from the trees.
When my mother wrote home from bed, the stars asked for a
        pardon.

They're both ghosts now, haunting the chairs and the sugar chest.

From time to time I hear their voices drifting like smoke through
        the living room,
Touching the various things they owned once,
Now they own nothing
                        and drift like smoke through the living room.

———

Thinking of Dante, I start to feel
What I think are wings beginning to push out from my shoulder
    blades,
And the firm pull of water under my feet.

Thinking of Dante, I think of La Pia,
                           and Charles Martel
And Cacciaguida inside the great flower of Paradise,
And the thin stem of Purgatory
                       rooted in Hell.

Thinking of Dante is thinking about the other side,
And the other side of the other side.
It's thinking about the noon noise and the daily light.

———

Here is the truth. The wind rose, the sea
Shuffled its blue deck and dealt you a hand:
Blank, blank, blank, blank, blank.
Pelicans rode on the flat back of the waves through the green
    afternoon.
Gulls malingered along its breezes.
The huge cross of an airplane's shadow hurried across the sand,
                         but no one stayed on it
For long, and nobody said a word.
You could see the island out past the orange gauze of the smog.

———

The Big Dipper has followed me all the days of my life.
Under its tin stars my past has come and gone.
Tonight, in the April glaze
                   and scrimshaw of the sky,
It blesses me once again
With its black water, and sends me on.

———

After 12 years it's hard to recall
That defining sound the canal made at sundown, slap
Of tide swill on the church steps,
Little runnels of boat wash slipping back from the granite slabs
In front of Toio's, undulant ripples
Flattening out in small hisses, the oily rainbows regaining their
    loose shapes
Silently, mewling and quick yelps for the gulls
Wheeling from shadow into the pink and grey light over the
    Zattere,

Lapping and rocking of water endlessly,
At last like a low drone in the dark shell of the ear
As the night lifted like mist from the Ogni Santi
and San Sebastiano
                into the cold pearl of the sky . .

All that year it lullabied just outside my window
As Venice rode through my sleep like a great spider,
Flawless and Byzantine,
                webbed like glass in its clear zinc.
In winter the rain fell
              and the locust fell.
In summer the sun rose
Like a whetstone over the steel prows of the gondolas,
Their silver beak-blades rising and falling,
                    the water whiter than ston
In autumn the floods came, and oil as thick as leaves in the entry
    way.
In spring, at evening, under the still-warm umbrellas,
We watched the lights blaze and extend
                along the rio,
And watched the black boats approaching, almost without sound.
And still the waters sang lullaby.

I remember myself as a figure among the colonnades,
Leaning from left to right,
              one hand in my pocket,
The way the light fell,
           the other one holding me up.

I remember myself as a slick on the slick canals,
Going the way the tide went,
The city sunk to her knees in her own reflection.
I remember the way that Pound walked
                              across San Marco
At *passeggiata*, as though with no one,
                              his eyes on the long ago.
I remember the time that Tate came.
                    And Palazzo Guggenheim
When the floods rose
                    and the boat took us all the way
Through the front doors and down to the back half
Of *da Montin*, where everyone was, clapping their hands.

What's hard to remember is how the wind moved and the reeds
      clicked
Behind Torcello,
                    little bundles of wind in the marsh grass
Chasing their own tails, and skidding across the water.
What's hard to remember is how the electric lights
Were played back, and rose and fell on the black canal
Like swamp flowers,
                    shrinking and stretching,
Yellow and pale and iron-blue from the oil.
It's hard to remember the way the snow looked
                              on San Gregorio,
And melting inside the pitch tubs and the smoke of San Trovaso,
The gondolas beached and stripped,
The huge snowflakes planing down through the sea-heavy air
Like dead moths,
                    drifting and turning . . .

————————

As always, silence will have the last word,
And Venice will lie like silk
                    at the edge of the sea and the night sky,
Albescent under the moon.

Everyone's life is the same life
                    if you live long enough.

Orioles shuttle like gold thread
                        through the grey cloth of daylight.
The fog is so low and weighted down
Crows fall through like black notes from the sky.
The orioles stitch and weave.
Somewhere below, the ocean nervously grinds its teeth
As the morning begins to take hold
                        and the palm trees gleam.

There is an otherness inside us
We never touch,
                        no matter how far down our hands reach.
It is the past,
                        with its good looks and *Anytime, Anywhere* . . .
Our prayers go out to it, our arms go out to it
Year after year,
But who can ever remember enough?

Friday again, with its sack of bad dreams
And long-legged birds,
                        a handful of ashes for this and that
In the streets, and some for the squat piano.

Friday beneath the sky, its little postcards of melancholy
Outside each window,
                        the engines inside the roses at half speed,
The huge page of the sea with its one word *despair,*

Fuchsia blossoms littered across the deck,
Unblotted tide pools of darkness beneath the ferns . . .
And still I go on looking,
                        match after match in the black air.

The lime, electric green of the April sea
                              off Ischia
Is just a thumb-rub on the window glass between here and there:
And the cloud cap above the volcano
That didn't move when the sea wind moved;
And the morning the doves came, low from the mountain's shadow,
                              under the sunlight.
Over the damp tops of the vine rows,
Eye-high in a scythe slip that dipped and rose and cut down
        toward the sea;
And the houses like candy wrappers blown up against the hillside
Above Sant' Angelo,
                    fuchsia and mauve and cyclamen;
And the story Nicola told,
How the turtle doves come up from Africa
On the desert winds,
                    how the hunters take the fresh seeds
From their crops and plant them,
The town windows all summer streaked with the nameless blooms .

The landscape was always the best part.

————————

Places swim up and sink back, and days do,
The edges around what really happened
                        we'll never remember
No matter how hard we stare back at the past:

One April, in downtown Seville,
                    alone on an Easter morning
Wasted in emerald light from the lemon trees,
I watched a small frog go back and forth on the lily pads
For hours, and still don't know
                    just what I was staying away from . . .

(And who could forget Milano in '59
                        all winter under the rain?
Cathedrals for sure,
And dry stops in the Brera,
            all of her boulevards ending in vacant lots.

134

And Hydra and Mykonos,
Barely breaking the calm with their white backs
As they roll over
                    and flash back down to the dark . . .)

Places swim up and sink back, and days do,
Larger and less distinct each year,
As we are,
                    and lolling about in the same redress,
Leaves and insects drifting by on their windows.

———————

Rome was never like that,
                    and the Tiber was never like that,
Nosing down from the Apennines,
                    color of *cafe-au-lait* as it went through town . . .

Still, I can't remember the name of one street
                                        near Regina Coeli,
Or one block of the Lungotevere on either side,
Or one name of one shop on Campo dei Fiori.
Only Giordano Bruno,
                    with his razed look and black caul,
Rises unbidden out of the blank
Unruffled waters of memory,
                                his martyred bronze
Gleaming and still wet in the single electric light.

I can't remember the colors I said I'd never forget
On Via Giulia at sundown,
The ochres and glazes and bright hennas of each house,
Or a single day from November of 1964.
I can't remember the way the stairs smelled
                                        or the hallway smelled
At Piazza del Biscione.
                    Or just how the light fell
Through the east-facing window over the wicker chairs there.

I do remember the way the boar hung
                            in the butcher shop at Christmas

Two streets from the Trevi fountain, a crown of holly and
        mistletoe
Jauntily over his left ear.
I do remember the flower paintings
Nodding throughout the May afternoons
                        on the dining room walls
At Zajac's place.
                    And the reliquary mornings,
And Easter, and both Days of the Dead . . .

At noon in the English Cemetery no one's around.
Keats is off to the left, in an open view.
Shelley and Someone's son are straight up ahead.

With their marble breath and their marble names,
                        the sun in a quick squint through the trees,
They lie at the edge of everywhere,
            Rome like a stone cloud at the back of their eyes.

————————

Time is the villain in most tales,
                        and here, too,
Lowering its stiff body into the water.
Its landscape is the resurrection of the word,
No end of it,
            the petals of wreckage in everything.

————————

I've been sitting here tracking the floor plan
                        of a tiny, mottled log spider
Across the front porch of the cabin,
And now she's under my chair,
                        off to her own devices,
Leaving me mine, and I start watching the two creeks

Come down through the great meadow
Under the lodgepole pine and the willow run,
The end of June beginning to come clear in the clouds,

Shadows like drowned men where the creeks go under the hill.

Last night, in the flood run of the moon, the bullbats
Diving out of the yellow sky
                    with their lonesome and jungly whistling,
I watched, as I've watched before, the waters send up their smoke
      signals of blue mist,
And thought, for the 1st time,
                    I half-understood what they keep on trying to say.

But now I'm not sure.
                    Behind my back, the spider has got her instructions
And carries them out.
Flies drone, wind back-combs the marsh grass, swallows bank and
      climb.
Everything I can see knows just what to do,

Even the dragonfly, hanging like lapis lazuli in the sun . . .

——————

I can't remember enough.

How the hills, for instance, at dawn in Kingsport
In late December in 1962 were black
                              against a sky
The color of pale fish blood and water that ran to white
As I got ready to leave home for the 100th time,
My mother and father asleep,
                    my sister asleep,
Carter's Valley as dark as the inside of a bone
Below the ridge,
              the 1st knobs of the Great Smokies
Beginning to stick through the sunrise,
The hard pull of a semi making the grade up US 11 W,
The cold with its metal teeth ticking against the window,
The long sigh of the screen door stop,
My headlights starting to disappear
                    in the day's new turning . . .

I'll never be able to.

137

———————

Sunday, a brute bumblebee working the clover tops
Next to the step I'm sitting on,
                                    sticking his huge head
Into each tiny, white envelope.
The hot sun of July, in the high Montana air, bastes a sweet glaze
On the tamarack and meadow grass.
In the blue shadows
                        moist curls of the lupin glide
And the bog lilies extinguish their mellow lamps . . .

Sunday, a *Let us pray* from the wind, a glint
Of silver among the willows.
                                    The lilacs begin to bleed
In their new sleep, and the golden vestments of morning
Lift for a moment, then settle back into place.
The last of the dog roses offers itself by the woodpile.
Everything has its work,
                            everything written down
In a second-hand grace of solitude and tall trees . . .

———————

August licks at the pine trees.
Sun haze, and little fugues from the creek.
Fern-sleep beneath the green skirt of the marsh.

I always imagine a mouth
Starting to open its blue lips
Inside me, an arm
                    curving sorrowfully over an open window

At evening, and toads leaping out of the wet grass.

Again the silence of flowers.
Again the faint notes of piano music back in the woods.
How easily summer fills the room.

———————

The life of this world is wind.
Wind-blown we come, and wind-blown we go away.
All that we look on is windfall.
All we remember is wind.

Pickwick was never the wind . . .

It's what we forget that defines us, and stays in the same place,
And waits to be rediscovered.
Somewhere in all that network of rivers and roads and silt hills,
A city I'll never remember,
                    its walls the color of pure light,
Lies in the August heat of 1935,
In Tennessee, the bottom land slowly becoming a lake.
It likes in a landscape that keeps my imprint
Forever,
                    and stays unchanged, and waits to be filled back in.
Someday I'll find it out
And enter my old outline as though for the 1st time,

And lie down, and tell no one.

EUROPA

by DEREK WALCOTT

from ANTAEUS

The full moon is so fierce that I can count the
coconuts' cross-hatched shade on bungalows,
their white walls raging with insomnia.
The stars leak drop by drop on the tin plates
of the sea almonds, and the jeering clouds
are luminously rumpled as the sheets.
The surf, insatiably promiscuous,
groans through the walls; I feel my mind
whiten to moonlight, altering that form
which daylight unambiguously designed,
from a tree to a girl's body bent in foam;
then, treading close, the black hump of a hill,
its nostrils softly snorting, nearing the
naked girl splashing her breasts with silver.
Both would have kept their proper distance still,
if the chaste moon hadn't swiftly drawn the drapes
of a dark cloud, coupling their shapes.

She teases with those flashes, yes, but once
you yield to human horniness, you see
through all that moonshine what they really were,
those gods as seed-bulls, gods as rutting swans—
an overheated farmhand's literature.
Who ever saw her pale arms hook his horns,
her thighs clamped tight in their deep-plunging ride,
watched, in the hiss of the exhausted foam,
her white flesh constellate to phosphorous

as in salt darkness beast and woman come,
Nothing is there, just as it always was,
but the foam's wedge to the horizon-light,
then, wire-thin, the studded armature,
like drops still quivering on his matted hide,
the hooves and horn-points anagrammed in stars.

THE SNAKES OF SEPTEMBER

by STANLEY KUNITZ

from ANTAEUS

All summer I heard them
rustling in the shrubbery,
outracing me from tier
to tier in my garden,
a whisper among the viburnums,
a signal flashed from the hedgerow,
a shadow pulsing
in the barberry thicket.
Now that the nights are chill
and the annuals spent,
I should have thought them gone,
in a torpor of blood
slipped to the nether world
before the sickle frost.
Not so. In the deceptive balm
of noon, as if defiant of the curse
that spoiled another garden,
these two appear on show
through a narrow slit
in the dense green brocade
of a north-country spruce,
dangling head-down, entwined
in a brazen love-knot.
I put out my hand and stroke
the fine, dry grit of their skins.

After all,
we are partners in this land,
co-signers of a covenant.
At my touch the wild
braid of creation
trembles.

VIII

MOLES

by MARY OLIVER

from THE OHIO REVIEW

Under the leaves, under
the first loose
levels of earth
they're there—quick
as beetles, blind
as bats, shy
as hares but seen
less than these—
traveling
among the pale girders
of appleroot,
rockshelf, nests
of insects and black
pastures of bulbs
peppery and packed full
of the sweetest food:
spring flowers.
Field after field
you can see the traceries
of their long
lonely walks, then
the rains blur
even this frail
hint of them—
so excitable,

so plush,
so willing to continue
generation after generation
accomplishing nothing
but their brief physical lives,
pushing and shoving
with their stubborn muzzles against
the whole earth,
finding it
delicious.

I KNEW I'D SING

by HEATHER MCHUGH

from KAYAK

A few sashay, a few finagle.
Some make whoopee, some
make good. But most make
diddly-squat. I tell you this

is what I love about
America—the words it put
in my mouth, the mouth where once
my mother rubbed a word away

with soap. The word
was cunt. She stuck that great
big bar in there until there was
no hole to speak of, so

she hoped. But still I'm full
of it, the cunt, the prick,
short u, short i, the words
for her and him. I loved

the things they must have done,
the love they must have made
to make an example of me.
After my lunch of Ivory I said

vagina for a day or two, but knew
from that day forth which word it was
that struck with all the force of sex itself.
I knew when I was big I'd sing

a song in praise of cunt. I'd want
to keep my word, the one with teeth in it.
And even after I was raised, I swore,
nothing, but nothing, would be beneath me.

PROCESSION

by PHILIP BOOTH

from THE HUDSON REVIEW

A white-throat flicked into the sunset window.
How small a thing to bury: his short neck limp,
eye perfectly blank, the feathers warm in my hand.

Nothing left now to whistle *Old Sam Peabody,*
Peabody, Peabody . . . The rest in their thickets,
knowing to go. The winter stars coming. Out early

this morning I see Orion, the first time this fall,
Aldebaran brilliant in Taurus, the Dipper's
handle tipped down toward daybreak. As sun-up

dims Venus, I walk the first frost out into ground fog,
as it happens. Slowly, it comes to me: today
would be father's 85th birthday. I hear

today's birds in the cedars, woken, knowing to go.
I think of a boy years beyond me, back in Council Bluffs,
a boy with father's name, out on a third-floor porch

after midnight, without knowing why, watching (he must
have told me hundreds of times) against his own horizon
these same winter stars beginning to show.

THE MAN OF MANY L'S

by MAXINE KUMIN

from THE SEATTLE REVIEW

My whole childhood I feared cripples
and how they got that way: the one-
legged Lavender Man who sold
his sachets by St. Mary's steeple,
the blind who tapped past humming what they knew,
even the hunchback seamstress, a ragdoll
who further sagged to pin my mother's hems
had once been sturdy, had once been whole.
Something entered people, something chopped,
pressed, punctured, had its way with them
and if you looked, bad child, it entered you.

When we found out what the disease would do,
lying, like any council's stalwarts,
all of us swore to play our parts
in the final act at your command.

The first was easy. You gave up your left hand
and the right grew wiser, a juggler for its king.
When the poor dumb leg began to falter
you took up an alpenstock for walking
once flourished Sundays by our dead father.
Month by month the battleground grew thinner.
When you could no longer swallow meat
we steamed and mashed your dinner
and bent your straw to chocolate soda treats.

152

And when you could not talk, still you could write
questions and answers on a magic slate,
then lift the page, like laundry to the wind.
I plucked the memory splinter from your spine
as we played at being normal, who
had cradled each other in the cold zoo
of childhood. Three months before
you died I wheeled you through the streets
of placid Palo Alto to catch
spring in its flamboyant tracks.
You wrote the name of every idiot flower

I did not know. Yucca rained.
Mimosa shone. The bottlebrush took fire
as you fought to hold your great head on its stem.
Lillac, you wrote. *Magnollia. Lilly.*
And further, *olleander. Dellphinium.*

O man of many L's, brother, my wily
resident ghost, may I never spell
these crowfoot dogbane words again
these showy florid words again
except I name them under your spell.

THE REEDBEDS OF THE HACKENSACK

by AMY CLAMPITT

from THE KENYON REVIEW

Scummed maunderings that nothing loves but reeds,
Phragmites, neighbors of the greeny asphodel
that thrive among the windings of the Hackensack,
collaborating to subvert the altogether ugly
if too down-to-earth to be quite fraudulent:
what's landfill but the backside of civility?

Dreckpot, the Styx and Malebolge of civility,
brushed by the fingering plumes of beds of reeds:
Manhattan's moat of stinks, the rancid asphodel
aspiring from the gradually choking Hackensack,
ring-ditch inferior to the vulgar, the snugly ugly,
knows-no-better, fake but not quite fraudulent:

what's scandal but the candor of the fraudulent?
Miming the burnish of a manicured civility,
the fluent purplings of uncultivated reeds,
ex post cliché survivors like the asphodel,
drink as they did the Mincius, the Hackensack
in absent-minded benediction on the merely ugly.

154

Is there a poetry of the incorrigibly ugly,
free of all furbishings that mark it fraudulent?
When toxins of an up-against-the-wall civility
have leached away the last patina of these reeds,
and promised landfill, with its lethal asphodel
of fumes, blooms the slow dying of the Hackensack,

shall I compare thee, Mincius, to the Hackensack?
Now Italy knows how to make its rivers ugly,
must, ergo, all such linkages be fraudulent,
gilding the laureate hearse of a defunct civility?
Smooth-sliding Mincius, crowned with vocal reeds,
coevals of that greeny local weed the asphodel,

that actual, unlettered entity the asphodel,
may I, among the channels of the Hackensack—
those Edens-in-the-works of the irrevocably ugly,
where any mourning would of course be fraudulent—
invoke the scrannel ruth of a forsooth civility,
the rathe, the deathbed generations of these reeds?

THAT BRIGHT GREY EYE

by HILDA MORLEY

from IRONWOOD

The grey sky, lighter & darker
greys,
    lights between & delicate
    lavenders also
blue-greys in smaller strokes,
                    & swashes
of mauve-grey on the Hudson—
                      openings
of light to the blue oblong
off-center
        where the door to the warehouse
shows—
        the larger smearings darkening
                        deep
into blues
        So alight that sky,
        late August,
early evening,
           I had to
gasp at it,
        stand there hardly moving

to breathe it,   using
whatever my body gave me,
                                    at
that moment   attending to it,
thinking:
              Turner   he should have
seen it,
              he would have given it
back to us,
              not let it die away
                                    And that other
evening, walking down Bank Street from marketing,
the sky fiery over the river,
                              luminous but
hot in its flowering also,
                        rich in color
as Venice seen by Guardi—more aflame even,
the sky moving in a pulse,
                              its fire breathing in
a pulse verging on danger—mane of a lioness
affronted.
              That brilliance—the eye of the lion
filled to the lids with
flame
              And his eyes, Turner's, that bright grey eye
at seventy-six,
              "brilliant as
the eye of a child"
              who grew his thumbnail
in the shape of an eagle's claw,
                              the better
to use it in painting
              In Kirby Lonsdale, Yorkshire,
where Turner first drew mountain-landscapes,
              I found Blake's *Marriage
of Heaven and Hell*—sold for two guineas, 1821
& Turner aged 46 that year
                        & there I read:
"And when thou seest
an Eagle, thou seest a portion of genius.

                                            Lift up
thy head," says Blake.
                          These afternoons now,
                          late in September, '76,
the sky, the river are lit up
at the end of Bank Street, at Bethune.
                                       The pavement
trembles with light pouring
upon it.
                    We are held in it.
We smile.
              I hold my breath to see if
the cashier in the supermarket
will be gentle with the old lady who cannot
read the price-tag on
a loaf of bread.
                       Then I breathe freely,
for yes, she is helpful, yes, she is
kind.
            Outside on
the pavement, the light pouring itself away
is the light in the eagle's
eye   or the eye of a child
                         (I saw it in a man's eye once:
                         but he's dead now more than
                         four years)
Drawing heat out of
surfaces,
              the light is
without calculation,
                         is a munificence now,
is justified.

IX

CONSOLATION

by DANIEL BERRIGAN

from HOME PLANET NEWS

Listen
if now and then
you hear the dead
muttering like ashes
creaking like empty
rockers on porches

filling you in   filling you in

like winds in empty
branches   like stars
in wintry trees—
so far
so good

you've mastered finally
one foreign tongue

THE POWER OF TOADS

by PATTIANN ROGERS

from THE IOWA REVIEW

The oak toad and the red-spotted toad love their love
In a spring rain, calling and calling, breeding
Through a stormy evening clasped atop their mates.
Who wouldn't sing—anticipating the belly pressed hard
Against a female's spine in the steady rain
Below writhing skies, the safe moist jelly effluence
Of a final exaltation?

There might be some toads who actually believe
That the loin-shaking thunder of the banks, the evening
Filled with damp, the warm softening mud and rising
Riverlets are the facts of their own persistent
Performance. Maybe they think that when they sing
They sing more than songs, creating rain and mist
By their voices, initiating the union of water and dusk,
Females materializing on the banks shaped perfectly
By their calls.

And some toads may be convinced they have forced
The heavens to twist and moan by the continual expansion
Of their lung-sacs pushing against the dusk.
And some might believe the splitting light,
The soaring grey they see above them are nothing
But a vision of the longing in their groins,
A fertile spring heaven caught in its entirety
At the pit of the gut.

And they might be right.
Who knows whether these broken heavens
Could exist tonight separate from trills and toad ringings?
Maybe the particles of this rain descending on the pond
Are nothing but the visual manifestation of whistles
And cascading love clicks in the shore grasses.
Raindrops-finding-earth and coitus could very well
Be known here as one.

We could investigate the causal relationship
Between rainstrom and love-by-pondside if we wished.
We could lie down in the grasses by the water's edge
And watch to see exactly how the heavens were moved,
Thinking hard of thunder, imagining all the courses
That slow, clean waters might take across our bodies,
Believing completely in the rolling and pressing power
Of heavens and thighs. And in the end we might be glad,
Even if all we discovered for certain was the slick, sweet
Promise of good love beneath dark skies inside warm rains.

THE TRICKLE-DOWN THEORY OF HAPPINESS

by PHILIP APPLEMAN

from POETRY

It starts in the penthouses, drizzling
at first, then a pelting allegro
falling nowhere except the high places,
and Dick and Jane pull on bikinis
and go boogieing through the azaleas,
and Daddy, ecstatic, comes running
with pots and pans, glasses, and basins
and tries to keep all of it up there,
but no use, it's too much, it keeps coming,
and pours off the edges, down limestone
to the buckets and pails on the ground floor
where delirious citizens catch it,
and bucket brigades keep it moving
inside, until bathtubs are brimful,
but still it keeps coming, that shower
of silver in alleys and gutters,
all pouring downhill to the sleazy
red brick, and the barefoot people
who romp in it, squishing, but never
take thought for tomorrow, all spinning
in a pleasure they catch for a moment;
so when somebody turns off the spigot
and the sky goes as dry as a prairie,

164

then Daddy looks down from the penthouse,
down to the streets, to the gutters,
and his heart goes out to his neighbors,
to the little folk thirsty for laughter,
and he prays in his boundless compassion:
on behalf of the world and its people
he demands of the sky, give me more.

THE EXPLOSION

by SUSAN MITCHELL

from IRONWOOD

No one is crying.
In fact, there isn't a sound, as if on this street
it has been snowing for years, muffling
the noises of three men and one woman
staring out of the factory window.
That is why it is so hard to find the children.
With so much silence, how could you hear
a child exploding?
The fathers, though, are easy enough to locate.
Theirs are the arms reaching in
from another world.
The children, when they find them, are absolutely white.
In another world they might be made of snow.
You think if a father brushed away the ashes
from his child's face,
he would remember.
The father knows better.
He knows if you saw his child in a dream
you would run away.
The miracle is its almost human form,
the arms spread wide like a snow angel's,
the pencil-thin legs sharpened to points so fine
you cannot see what they are writing on the pavement.
The miracle is the child hasn't blown away yet.
The child does this for the father.
It wants him to find it.

That is why the father is fighting the other men
to get at it. He points to the single shoe as proof.
The others know he is lying.
They know his child has vanished into the pavement.
His child is only that outline drawn hastily
with white chalk.

GROUND ZERO

by WILLIAM STAFFORD

from FIELD

While we slept—
    rain found us last night, easing in
    from The Coast, a few leaves at first,
    then ponds. The quietest person in the state
    heard the mild invasion. Before it was over
    every field knew that benediction.

At breakfast—
    while we talked some birds passed, then slanted
    north, wings emphasizing earth's weight
    but overcoming it. "There's no hope,"
    you said. Our table had some flowers
    cascading color from their vase. Newspapers
    muttered repression and shouted revolution.
    A breeze lifted curtains, they waved
    easily. "Why can't someone do something!"
    My hand began its roving, like those curtains,
    and the flowers bending, and the far-off bird wings.

UKIYO-E

by SIV CEDERING

from CALLIOPEA PRESS

What explanation is given for the phosphorus light
That you, as boy, went out to catch
When summer dusk turned to night.
You caught the fire-flies, put them in a jar,
Careful to let in the air,
Then you fed them dandelions, unsure
Of what such small and fleeting things
Need, and when
Their light grew dim, you
    Let them go.

There is no explanation for the fire
That burns in our bodies
Or the desire that grows, again and again,
So that we must move toward each other
In the dark.
We have no wings.
We are ordinary people, doing ordinary things.
The story can be told on rice paper.
There is a lantern, a mountain, whatever
    We can remember.

Hiroshige's landscape is so soft.
What child, woman, would not want to go out
Into that dark, and be caught,
And caught again, by you?
Let these pictures of the floating world go on
Forever, but when
This light must flicker out, catch me,
Give me whatever a child imagines
To keep me aglow, then
　　Let me go.

X

THE FUNDAMENTAL PROJECT OF TECHNOLOGY

by GALWAY KINNELL

from AMERICAN POETRY REVIEW

"A flash! A white flash sparkled!"
Tatsuichiro Akizuki, Concentric Circles of Death

Under glass: glass dishes which changed
in color; pieces of transformed beer bottles;
a household iron; bundles of wire become solid
lumps of iron; a pair of pliers; a ring of skull-
bone fused to the inside of a helmet; a pair of eyeglasses
taken off the eyes of an eyewitness, without glass,
which vanished, when a white flash sparkled.

An old man, possibly a soldier back then,
now reduced down to one who soon will die,
sucks at the cigaret dangling from his lips, peers
at the uniform, scorched, of some tiniest schoolboy,
sighs out bluish mists of his own ashes over
a pressed tin lunch box well crushed back then when
the word *future* first learned, in a white flash, to jerk tears.

On the bridge outside, in navy black, a group
of schoolchildren line up, hold it, grin at a flash-pop,
scatter like pigeons across grass, see a stranger, cry,
hello! hello! hello! and soon *goodbye! goodbye!*
having pecked up the greetings that fell half unspoken

and the going-sayings that those who went the day
it happened a white flash sparkled did not get to say.

If all a city's faces were to shrink back all at once
from their skulls, would a new sound come into existence,
audible above moans eaves extract from wind that smoothes
the grass on graves or raspings heart's-blood greases still
or wails infants trill born already skillful at the grandpa's rattle
or infra-screams bitter-knowledge's speechlessness
memorized, at that white flash, inside closed-forever mouths?

To de-animalize human mentality, to purge it of obsolete
evolutionary characteristics, in particular of death,
which foreknowledge terrorizes the contents of skulls with,
is the fundamental project of technology; however,
pseudologica fantastica's mechanisms require:
to establish deathlessness you must first eliminate
those who die; a task attempted, when a white flash sparkled.

Unlike the trees of home, which continually evaporate
along the skyline, the trees here have been enticed down
toward world-eternity. No one knows which gods they enshrine.
Does it matter? Awareness of ignorance is as devout
as knowledge of knowledge. Or more so. Even though not
    knowing,
sometimes we weep, from surplus of gratitutde, even though
    knowing,
twice already on earth sparkled a flash, a white flash.

The children go away. By nature they do. And by memory,
in scorched uniforms, holding tiny crushed lunch tins.
All the ecstasy-groans of each night call them back, satori
their ghostliness back into the ashes, in the momentary shrines,
the thankfulness of arms, from which they will go
again and again, until the day flashes and no one lives
to look back and say, a flash, a white flash sparkled.

BIRTHDAY STAR ATLAS

by CHARLES SIMIC

from THE MISSOURI REVIEW

Wildest dream, Miss Emily,
Then the coldly dawning suspicion—
Always at the loss—come day
Large black birds overtaking men who sleep in ditches.

A whiff of winter in the air. Sovereign blue,
Blue that stands for intellectual clarity
Over a street deserted except for a far off dog,
A police car, a light at the vanishing point

For the children to solve on the blackboard today—
Blind children at the school you and I know about.
Their gray nightgowns creased by the north wind;
Their fingernails bitten from time immemorial.

We're in a long line outside a dead letter office.
We're dustmice under a conjugal bed carved with exotic fishes
    and monkeys.
We're in a slow drifting coalbarge huddled around the television
    set
Which has a wire coat-hanger for an antenna.

A quick view (by satellite) of the polar regions
Maternally tucked in for the long night.
Then some sort of interference—parallel lines

Like the ivory-boned needles of your grandmother knitting our
    fates together.

All things ambiguous and lovely in their ambiguity,
Like the nebulae in my new star atlas—
Pale ovals where the ancestral portraits have been taken down.
The gods with their goatees and their faint smiles

In company of their bombshell spouses,
Naked and statuesque as if entering a death camp.
They smile, too, stroke the Triton wrapped around the mantle
    clock
When they are not showing the whites of their eyes in theatrical
    ecstasy.

Nostalgias for the theological vaudeville.
A false springtime cleverly painted on cardboard
For the couple in the last row to sigh over
While holding hands which unknown to them

Flutter like bird-shaped scissors . . .
Emily, the birthday atlas!
I kept turning its pages awed
And delighted by the size of the unimaginable;

The great nowhere, the everlasting nothing—
Pure and serene doggedness
For the hell of it—and love,
Our nightly stroll the color of silence and time.

VESPER SPARROWS

by DEBORAH DIGGES

from ANTAEUS

I love to watch them sheathe themselves mid-air,
shut wings and ride the light's poor spine

to earth, to touch down in gutters, in the rainbowed
urine of suicides, just outside Bellevue's walls.

From in there the ransacked cadavers are carried
up the East River to Potter's Field

as if they were an inheritance,
gleaned of savable parts,

their diseases jarred and labeled, or incinerated,
the ashes of metastisized vision

professing the virus that lives beyond the flesh,
in air . . .

       The first time I saw the inside of anything
alive, a downed bird opened cleanly

under my heel. I knelt
to watch the spectral innards shine and quicken,

the heart-whir magnify.
And though I can't say now what kind of bird it was,

nor the season, spring or autumn, what
dangerous transition,

I have identified so many times that sudden
earnest spasm of the throat in children,

or in the jaundiced faces of the dying,
the lower eye-lids straining upward.

Fear needs its metaphors.
I've read small helplessnesses make us maternal.

Even the sparrows feel it
nesting this evening in traffic lights.

They must have remembered, long enough to mate,
woods they've never seen,

but woods inbred, somehow, up the long light of instinct,
the streaked siennas of a forest floor

born now into the city,
the oak umbers, and the white tuft

of tail feathers, like a milkweed meadow
in which their song, as Burroughs heard it,

could be distinguished:
come-come-where-where-all-together-

down-the-hill . . .
here, where every history is forfeited,

where the same names of the different dead greet
each other and commingle

above the hospital's heaps of garbage.
From the ward windows, fingerprinted,

from the iron-grated ledges,
hundreds flock down for the last feed of the day

and carry off into the charitable dusk what
cannot be digested.

RAIN COUNTRY .

by JOHN HAINES

from NEW ENGLAND REVIEW AND BREAD LOAF QUARTERLY

> *Earth. Nothing more.*
> *And let that be enough for you.*
>   *Pedro Salinas*

I

The woods are sodden,
and the last leaves
tarnish and fall.

Thirty-one years ago
this rainy autumn
we walked home from the lake,
Campbell and Peg and I,
over the shrouded Dome,
the Delta wind in our faces,
home through the drenched
and yellowing woodland.

Bone-chilled but with singing
hearts we struck our fire
from the stripped bark
and dry, shaved aspen;
and while the stove iron
murmured and cracked
and our wet wool steamed,
we crossed again
the fire-kill of timber
in the saddle of Deadwood.

Down the windfall slope,
by alder thicket, and now
by voice alone, to drink
from the lake at evening.

A mile and seven days
beyond the grayling pool
at Deep Creek, the promised
hunt told of a steepness
in the coming dusk.

II

Light in the aspen wood
on Campbell's hill,
a fog trail clearing below,
as evenly the fall distance
stretched the summer sun.

Our faces strayed together
in the cold north window—
night, and the late cup
steaming before us . . .
Campbell, his passion
tamed by the tumbling years,
an old voice retelling.

As if a wind had stopped us
listening on the trail,
we turned to a sound
the earth made that morning—
a heavy rumble in the grey
hills toward Fairbanks;
our mountain shivered
underfoot, and all
the birds were still.

III

Shadows blur in the rain—
they are whispering straw
and talking leaves.

I see what does not exist,
hear voices that cannot speak
through the packed
earth that fills them:

Loma, in the third year
of the war, firing at night
from his pillow
for someone to waken.

Campbell, drawing a noose
in the dust at his feet:
"Creation was seven days—
no more, no less . . ."
Noah and the flooded earth
were clouded in his mind.

And Knute, who turned
from his radio one August
afternoon, impassioned
and astonished:
                        "Is that
the government? I ask you—
is *that* the government?"

Bitter Melvin, who nailed
his warning above the doorway:

Pleese don't shoot
the beevers
They are my friends.

IV

And all the stammering folly
aimed toward us
from the rigged pavilions—
malign dictations, insane
pride of the fox-eyed men
who align the earth
to a tax-bitten dream
of metal and smoke—

2

all drank of the silence
to which we turned:

one more yoke at the spring,
another birch rick balanced,
chilled odor and touch
of the killed meat quartered
and racked in the shade.

It was thirty-one years ago
this rainy autumn.

Of the fire we built to warm us,
and the singing heart
driven to darkness
in the time-bitten earth—

only a forest rumor
whispers through broken straw
and trodden leaves
how late in a far summer
three friends came home,
walking the soaked ground
of an ancient love.

V

Much rain has fallen. Fog
drifts in the spruce boughs,
heavy with alder smoke,
denser than I remember.

Campbell is gone, in old age
struck down one early winter,
and Peg in her slim youth
long since become a stranger.
The high, round hill of Buckeye
stands whitened and cold.

I am not old, not yet, though
like a wind-turned birch
spared by the axe,

I claim this clearing
in the one country I know.

Remembering, fitting names
to a rain-soaked map:
Gold Run, Minton, Tenderfoot,
McCoy. Here Melvin killed
his grizzly, there Wilkins
built his forge. All
that we knew, and everything
but for me forgotten.

VI

I write this down
in the brown ink of leaves,
of the changed pastoral
deepening to mist on my page.

I see in the shadow-pool
beneath my hand a mile
and thirty years beyond
this rain-driven autumn.

All that we loved: a fire
long dampened, the quenched
whispering down of faded
straw and yellowing leaves.

The names, and the voices
within them, speak now for
the slow rust of things
that are muttered in sleep.

There is ice on the water
I look through, the steep
rain turning to snow.

A POEM WITH NO ENDING

by PHILIP LEVINE

from THE PARIS REVIEW

So many poems begin where they
should end, and never end.
Mine never end, they run on
book after book, complaining
to the moon that heaven is wrong
or dull, no place at all to be.
I believe all this. I believe
that ducks take wing only
in stories and then to return
the gift of flight to the winds.
If you knew how I came to be
seven years old and how thick
and blond my hair was, falling
about my shoulders like the leaves
of the slender eucalyptus
that now blesses my driveway
and shades my pale blue Falcon,
if you could see me pulling
wagon loads of stones across
the tufted fields and placing
them to build myself and my brother
a humped mound of earth where
flowers might rise as from a grave,

185

you might understand the last spring
before war turned toward our house
and entered before dawn, a pale
stranger that hovered over each bed
and touched the soft, unguarded faces
leaving bruises so faint
years would pass before they darkened
and finally burned. Now I can sit
calmly over coffee and recover
each season, how the rains swelled
the streets, how at night I mumbled
a prayer because the weight
of snow was too great to bear
as I heard it softly packing
down the roof, how I waited
for hours for some small breeze
to rise from the river dreaming
beside me, and none came, and morning
was so much mist rising
and the long moaning of ore boats
returning the way they'd come,
only now freighted with the earth
someone would carve and cook.
That is the poem I called "Boyhood"
and placed between the smeared pages
of your morning paper. White itself,
it fell on the white tablecloth
and meant so little you turned
it over and wrote a column
of figures you never added up.
You capped your gold fountain pen
and snapped your fingers to remind
yourself of some small, lost event.
My poem remained long after you'd
gone, face down, unread, not even
misunderstood, until it passed,
like its subject, into the literatures
of silence, though hardly first
among them, for there have always
been the tales the water told

the cup and the words the wind
sang to the windows in those houses
we abandoned after the roads
whispered all night in our ears.

I passed the old house and saw
even from the front that four trees
were gone, and beside the drive
a wire cage held nothing. Once
I stopped and rang the bell.
A woman said, No! before I asked,
and I heard a child say, Who
is he? and I turned away
from so many years and drove off.
Tomorrow my train will leave
the tunnel and rise above this town
and slowly clatter beside block
after block of buildings that fall
open like so many stunned faces
with nothing to hide. The cold odor
of smoke rises and the steeped smell
of wood that will not hold our words.
Once I saw the back of a closet
that burst unto sky, and I imagined
opening a familiar door and stepping
into a little room without limits.
I rose into a blue sky as undefined
as winter and as cold. I said, Oh my!
and held myself together with a wish!
No, that wasn't childhood, that
was something else, something
that ended in a single day and left
no residue of happiness I could
reach again if I took the first turn
to the left and eyes closed walked
a hundred and one steps and spoke
the right words.
                    I sit for days
staring at the dusty window
and no word comes to tell me what I

left behind. Still, I regret nothing,
not the little speeches I wrote
to the moon on the warm spring nights
I searched for someone other
than myself and came home empty
at sun-up among bird calls
and the faint prattle of rain.
I do not regret my hands
changing before me, mottling
like the first eggs I found
in the fields of junked cars,
nor my breath that still comes
and comes no matter what I command
and the words that go out
and fall short. I can hear
my heart beating, slowly,
I can feel the blood sliding
behind my eyes, so I close them
first on a known darkness and then
on a red crown forming as from
a dark sea, and I am beginning
once more to rise into the shape
of someone I can be, a man
no different from my father
but slower and wiser. What could be
better than to waken as a man?

I began as you did, smaller
than the wren who circled three times
and flew back into the darkness
before sleep. I was born
of the promise that each night
made and each day broke, out
of the cat's sullen wish to remain
useless and proud and the sunlight's
to find a closed face to waken.
Out of just that and no more.
The tiny stories my grandpa
told in which dogs walked upright
and the dead laughed. I was born

of these and his pocket of keys,
his dresser drawers of black socks
and white shirts, his homilies
of blood and water, all he never
gave me and all he did. Small
and dying he opened his eyes
unto a certain day, unto
stale water and old shoes,
and he never prayed. I could say
that was the finished poem and gather
my few things into a dark suitcase
and go quietly into the streets and wait.
It will be Sunday, and no one will pass.
In the long shadows of the warehouses
it's cool and pleasant. A piece of paper
skips by, but I don't bend to it
or tip my hat.

                    I hear the shouts
of children at play. Sunday afternoon
in August of '36, and the darkness
falls between us on the little island
where we came year after year
to celebrate the week. First I can't
see you, my brother, but I can hear
your labored breathing beside me,
and then my legs vanish, and then
my hands, and I am only a presence
in long grass. Then I am grass
blowing in a field all night, giving
and taking so many green gifts
of the earth and touching everything.
I never wakened from that evening.
The island still rides the river
between two countries. The playground—
yellowed and shrunken—, the rotunda
falling in upon itself, the old
huddled at separate tables and staring
off into the life they've come to.
In this place and at this time,

which is not time, I could take
the long road back and find it all.
I could even find myself. (Writing
this, I know it's not true.)

On Monday morning across the way
the trucks load up with parcels
of everything. This is New York City
in mid-May of 1981, and I am too old
to live that life again, packing
the van with frozen fish, household
goods, oriental vegetables, wristwatches,
weightless cartons of radium. That was
thirty years ago in another town,
and I still recall the mixture
of weariness and excitement as I beheld
the little mound of what was mine
to take into the world. (They had given
me a cap with a shining badge
and a huge revolver to guard
"the valuables." I hid them both
under the seat.) On the near West Side
in a two-room walk-up apartment
a dazed couple sat waiting for weeks
for a foot locker full of clothes
and kitchen utensils. They stood back
when I entered, pretending to be busy,
and they tried to keep me there,
but they had nothing to say. They were
neither young nor old, and I couldn't
then imagine their days in which little
or nothing was done, days on which it
seemed important to smoke before
dressing and not to go out until
late afternoon. I couldn't imagine
who they were and why they'd come
from all the small far-off places
to be homeless where I was homeless.
In another house an old man summoned
me to a high room. There before us

was a massive steamer trunk full
of books he could take back home
to Germany now he could return.
Tolstoi, Balzac, Goethe, all
in the original. Oh yes, I knew
the names, and he called down
to his wife, how wonderful!
This boy knows the names. He brought
the top down carefully, turned the key,
and stepped back, waiting for me
to carry it down three flights
by myself and offered me money
when I couldn't budge it, as though
I'd been pretending. This boy,
this American, in his pressed
work clothes, surely he could do it,
surely there was a way, if only
I would try. I left him shaking
his great head and passed his wife
on the stairs, a little brown mouse
of a woman laughing at such folly.

The memory of rain falling slowly
into the dark streets and the smell
of a new season rising above
the trucks parked in silent rows.
Even without earth or snow melting
or new grass rising into moonlight,
the year is turning, and the streets
can feel it. I dreamed this,
or I lived it for a moment, waking
in the night to no bird song
or wind pull, waking to no one
beside me asking for water
or a child calling from another room.
Awake now for a second or a lifetime,
I'm once again stepping out onto
the tiny veranda above the railyards
of Sevilla. In the room next door
a soldier has dressed a chair

with his uniform and leaned his rifle
against the glass door. A woman's clothes
are scattered on the floor. I look away.
Christmas, 1965. The halls of this hotel
are filled with sleeping peasants.
Each of my three sons is alone
in a narrow room with no windows,
asleep in a darkness beyond darkness,
and I feel their loneliness and fear.
Below the window, the lights
of the railyard flash this way
and that, and an old engine is firing up.
Distant voices speak out, but I can't
understand their words. I am falling
toward sleep again. For a moment
I feel my arms spread wide to enclose
everyone within these walls whitewashed
over and over, my own sons, my woman,
and all the other sons and daughters
stretched out or curled up in bad beds
or on bare floors, their heads
pillowed on their own hard arms
their cheeks darkened by cheap newsprint.
There is a song, bird song or wind song,
or the song old rooms sing when no one
is awake to hear. For a moment I
almost catch the melody we make
with bare walls, old iron sagging beds,
and scarred floors. There is one
deep full note for each of us.
This is the first night of my life
I know we are music.

                    Across the world
in the high mountains of the West,
I had gone one Sunday
with my youngest son, Teddy.
We parked the car and climbed
from the road's end over a rise
of young pines and then descended

192

slowly for a mile or more
through a meadow of wild flowers
still blooming in July. The yellow
ones that reached to his shoulders
stained my legs with pollen.
As we walked he spoke of animals
with the gift of speech. Bears,
he told me, were especially fond
of young people, and the mother bears
were known for coming into towns
like ours to steal boys and girls
and bring them back up here and teach
them hunting, and the children
grew into animals and forgot
their homes and their brothers.
A slight rise, and we entered
a thick forest. The air was still
and damp, and there was no longer
any trail. Soon I lost my way.
In a small clearing we stopped
to have our sandwiches, and I cooled
the soda pop in a stream whose rushing
we'd heard from far off. His head
pillowed on his jacket, he lay out,
eyes closed, the long dark lashes
quivering in sunlight, the cheeks
brown and smooth. When I awoke
he was throwing rocks as large
as he could manage into the stream
where they banged down a stairway
of stone and came to rest. The sun
had shifted, the shadows fell
across our faces, and it was cooler.
He was building a house, he said,
below the water, dark now, and boiling.
I bet him he couldn't lead us back
the way we'd come through the dark
bear woods and across the great plain
and up and down these hills.
A dollar? he said. Yes. And talking

all the way, he took the lead,
switching a fallen branch before him
to dub this little tree as friend
or a tall weed as enemy, stopping once
to uproot a purple wildflower for me.

I reenter a day in a late summer,
the heat going from the streets
and the cramped downriver flats, a day
of departures and farewells, for I
too am going, packing my box
of books and my typewriter and heading
West this time. So it seems
that all of us are on the move,
giving up these jobs that gave us
just enough and took all we had.
Going back to the little hollows
we'd come away from when the land
gave out or going back
to the survivors left in Alabama
or farther back to the villages
of Greece and Italy. From all
of these people I take a drink,
a pastry, and a coin to insure
a safe voyage, and we shake hands
around the battered kitchen tables.
Sometimes the old ones turn away
before I leave and cry without sound
or sometimes a man touches
his wife, but more often each stands
alone and silent in the old pain.

How many lives were torn apart
in those years? How many young men
went off as ours did but never
came back. It was still dark when we
drove into the great harbor and found
the ship to Sweden and said goodbye
not knowing what it was we said.
We saw him climb the gangplank

loaded down with duffle bags
and a guitar he scarcely played.
We turned back to the city
unable to face each other,
unable to face the coming day.
The sun shone on trams and markets,
and until late afternoon I tramped
the streets no longer looking for
the face I sought in childhood,
for now that face was mine, and I
was old enough to know
that my son would not suddenly
turn a corner and be mine
as I was my father's son.
A woman came out of a bar
screaming at her man, and he
hurried silently beside me
and darted quickly down an alley.
When I turned the woman's face
was smeared with tears. She shook
a finger at me and damned me
in her tongue. That night I
slept alone and dreamed of finding
my way back to the house where I
was born. It was quiet when I
entered, for no one has risen yet,
and I climbed the steps to my room
where nothing stirred in all
the rooms beneath me. I slept
fully dressed, stretched out
on a tiny bed, a boy's bed,
and in that dream more vivid
than the waking from it, the rooms
were one and I was home at last.

To get west you go east.
You leave in the dark
by car and drive until you
can't and sleep by the road

for an hour or a moment.
If the windshield is crystalled
when you waken you know
the days will be getting
colder and shorter. If you
wake soaked with sweat
then the year is turning
toward summer. None of
it matters at all, the towns
you travel through, plunging
down hills and over the cobbles
and the twisting tight passageways
and breaking for the open fields,
the apple orchards and the barns
rotting and fallen, none of it
matters to you. No one
you know dreams these houses
or hides here from the rain.
When the long day turns
to dark and you're nowhere
you've ever been before, you
keep going, and the magic eyes
that gleam by the roadside
are those of animals come
down from the invisible hills.
Yes, they have something to tell
or something to give you
from the world you've lost.
If you stopped the car and let
the engine idle and walked
slowly toward them, one hand
held out in greeting, you
would find only a fence post
bullet-scarred and deckled with
red-eyed reflectors. None
of it matters, so just keep going,
forward or back, until you've
found the place or the place
doesn't matter. They were only

animals come down to stand
in silent formation by a road
you traveled.

                    Early March.
The cold beach deserted. My kids
home in a bare house, bundled up
and listening to rock music
pirated from England. My wife
waiting for me in the bar, alone
for an hour over her sherry, and none
of us knows why I have to pace
back and forth on this flat
and birdless stretch of gleaming sand
while the violent air shouts
out its rags of speech. I recall
the calm warm sea of Florida
30 years ago, and my brother
and I staring out in the hope
that someone known and loved
would return out of air and water
and no more, a miracle a kid
could half-believe, could see
as something everyday and possible.
Later I slept alone and dreamed
of the home I never had and wakened
in the dark. A silver light sprayed
across the bed, and the little
rented room ticked toward dawn.
I did not rise. I did not go
to the window and address
the moon. I did not cry
or cry out against the hour
or the loneliness that still
was mine, for I had grown
into the man I am, and I
knew better. A sudden voice
calls out my name or a name
I think is mine. I turn.
The waves have darkened; the sky's

descending all around me. I read
once that the sea would come
to be the color of heaven.
They would be two seas tied
together, and between the two
a third, the sea of my own heart.
I read and believed nothing.
This little beach at the end
of the world is anywhere, and I
stand in a stillness that will last
forever or until the first light
breaks beyond these waters. Don't
be scared, the book said, don't flee
as wave after wave the breakers rise
in darkness toward their ghostly crests,
for he has set a limit to the sea
and he is at your side. The sea
and I breathe in and out as one.
Maybe this is done at last
or for now, this search for what
is never here. Maybe all that
ancient namesake sang is true.
The voice I hear now is
my own night voice, going out
and coming back in an old chant
that calms me, that calms
—for all I know—the waves
still lost out there.

WILDERNESS

by VERN RUTSALA

from BROWN JOURNAL OF THE ARTS

We invented these trees and mountains, that long gash
of gulley tumbling toward the lake.
By main force we brought each rock into being,
each of a different size and shape, each carved
into its dim life by us. We squinted that mica
from nothingness through our eyelashes and pulled
each giant fir from the ground with tweezers—
each beginning thinner than a hair but we
nursed them up with curiosity and the weak strength
of our thin fingers. Before we came
none of this was here—all the ferns and brush
were made with pinking shears. We shoveled
every lake and compelled water
to bear the fruit of fish. With our pens we drew
the creeks and nudged bear and deer from deep shadows.
None of this was here before we came.
We invented these trees and mountains,
conjured each pebble and boulder, shaped
those rough peaks with our hands, nursed those great trees
up and up from the near nothingness
of hairs. A whiskbroom and moonlight
made cougar and wildcat, dry sticks and dust
the snake and mole, with rain and mud we made
beaver, wood chips formed eagle and hawk we whittled
so fast! We needed all this, you see,
not for you but for us. We needed

a wilderness but had found none. Which is why
we invented this lovely one just here
between Thompson and Brazee in Northeast Portland.
Our love, you see, demanded such a setting.

XI

TURTLE, SWAN

by MARK DOTY

from CRAZYHORSE

Because the road to our house
is a backroad, meadowlands punctuated
by gravel quarry and lumberyard,
there are unexpected travelers
some nights on our way home from work.
Once, on the lawn of the Tool

and Die Company, a swan;
the word doesn't convey the shock
of the thing, white architecture
rippling like a pond's rain-pocked skin,
beak lifting to hiss at my approach.
Magisterial, set down in elegant authority.

he let us know exactly how close we might come.
After a week of long rains
that filled the marsh until it poured
across the road to make in low woods
a new heaven for toads,
a snapping turtle lumbered down the center

of the asphalt like an ambulatory helmet.
His long tail dragged, blunt head jutting out
of the lapidary prehistoric sleep of shell.
We'd have lifted him from the road
but thought he might bend his long neck back
to snap. I tried herding him; he rushed,

though we didn't think those blocky legs
could hurry—then ambled back
to the center of the road, a target
for kids who'd delight in the crush
of something slow with the look
of primeval invulnerability. He turned

the blunt spearpoint of his jaws,
puffing his undermouth like a bullfrog,
and snapped at your shoe,
vising a beakful of—thank God—
leather. You had to shake him loose. We left him
to his own devices, talked on the way home

of what must lead him to a new marsh
or old home ground. The next day you saw,
one town over, remains of shell
in front of the little liquor store. I argued
it was too far from where we'd seen him,
too small to be his . . . though who could tell

what the day's heat might have taken
from his body. For days he became a stain,
a blotch that could have been merely
oil. I did not want to believe that
was what we saw alive in the firm center
of his authority and right

to walk the center of the road,
head up like a missionary moving certainly
into the country of his hopes.
In the movies of this small town
I stopped for popcorn while you went ahead
to claim seats. When I entered the cool dark

I saw straight couples everywhere,
no single silhouette who might be you.
I walked those two aisles too small
to lose anyone and thought of a book
I read in seventh grade, *Stranger than Science,*
in which a man simply walked away,

at a picnic, and was,
in the act of striding forward
to examine a flower, gone.
By the time the previews ended
I was nearly in tears—then realized
the head of one half the couple in the first row

was only your leather jacket propped in the seat
that would be mine. I don't think I remember
anything of the first half of the movie.
I don't know what happened to the swan. I read every week
of some man's lover showing
the first symptoms, the night sweat

or casual flu, and then the wasting begins
and the disappearance a day at a time.
I don't know what happened to the swan;
I don't know if the stain on the street
was our turtle or some other. I don't know
where these things we meet and know briefly

as well as we can or they will let us
go. I only know that I do not want you
—you with your white and muscular wings
that rise and ripple beneath or above me,
your magnificent neck, eyes the deep mottled autumnal colors
of polished tortoise—I do not want you ever to die.

THE THRONE OF THE THIRD HEAVEN OF THE NATIONS MILLENNIUM GENERAL ASSEMBLY

by DENIS JOHNSON

from THE PARIS REVIEW

James Hampton, 1909, Elloree, S.C.—1964, Washington, D.C.
Custodian, General Services Administration
Maker of The Throne

I

I dreamed I had been dreaming,
And sadness did descend.
And when from the first dreaming
I woke, I walked behind

The window crossed with smoke and rain
In Washington, D.C.,
The neighbors strangling newspapers
Or watching the TV

Down on the rug in undershirts
Like bankrupt criminals.
The street where Revelation
Made James Hampton miserable

Lay wet beyond the glass,
And on it moved streetcorner men
In a steam of crossed-out clues
And pompadours and voodoo and

Sweet Jesus made of ivory;
But when I woke, the headlights
Shone out on Elloree.

Two endless roads, four endless fields,
And where I woke, the veils
Of rain fell down around a sign:
FRI & SAT JAM W/ THE MEAN

MONSTER MAN & II.
Nobody in the Elloree,
South Carolina, Stop-n-Go,
Nobody in the Sunoco,

Or in all of Elloree, his birthplace, knows
His name. But right outside
Runs Hampton Street, called probably
For the owners of his family.

God, are you there, for I have been
Long on these highways and I've seen
Miami, Treasure Coast, Space Coast,
I have seen where the astronauts burned,

I have looked where the Fathers placed the pale
Orange churches in the sun,
Have passed through Georgia in its green
Eternity of leaves unturned,

But nothing like Elloree.

II

Sam and I drove up from Key West, Florida,
Visited James Hampton's birthplace in South Carolina,
And saw The Throne
At The National Museum of American Art in Washington.
It was in a big room. I couldn't take it all in,
And I was a little frightened.
I left and came back home to Massachusetts.
I'm glad The Throne exists:
My days are better for it, and I feel
Something that makes me know my life is real
To think he died unknown and without a friend,
But this feeling isn't sorrow. I was his friend
As I looked at and was looked at by the rushing-together
    parts
Of this vision of someone who was probably insane
Growing brighter and brighter like a forest after a rain,
And if you look at the leaves of a forest,
At its dirt and its heights, the stuttering mystic
Replication, the blithering symmetry,
You'll go crazy, too. If you look at the city
And its spilled wine
And broken glass, its spilled and broken people and hearts,
You'll go crazy. If you stand
In the world you'll go out of your mind.
But it's all right,
What happened to him. I can, now
That he doesn't have to,
Accept it.
I don't believe that Christ, when he claimed
The last will be first, the lost life saved—
When he implied that the deeply abysmal is deeply
    blessed—
I just can't believe that Christ, when faced
With poor, poor people hoping to become at best
The wives and husbands of a lonely fear,
would have spoken redundantly.
Surely he couldn't have referred to some other time

Or place, when in fact such a place and time
Are unnecessary. We have a time and a place here,
Now, abundantly.

III

He waits forever in front of diagrams
On a blackboard in one of his photographs,
Labels that make no sense attached
To the radiant, alien things he sketched,
Which aren't objects, but plans.
Of his last dated
Vision he stated:
"This design is proof of the Virgin Mary descending
Into Heaven . . ."
The streetcorner men, the shaken earthlings—
It's easy to imagine his hands
When looking at their hands
Of leather, loving on the necks
Of jugs, sweetly touching the dice and bad checks,
And to see in everything a making
Just like his, an unhinged
Deity in an empty garage
Dying alone in some small consolation.
Photograph me photograph me photo
Graph me in my suit of loneliness,
My tie which I have been
Saving for this occasion,
My shoes of dust, my skin of pollen,
Addressing the empty chair; behind me
The Throne of the Third Heaven
Of the Nations Millennium General Assembly.
i AM ALPHA AND OMEGA THE BEGiNNiNG
AND THE END,
The trash of government buildings,
Faded red cloth,
Jelly glasses and lightbulbs,
Metal (cut from coffee cans),
Upholstery tacks, small nails

And simple sewing pins,
Lightbulbs, cardboard,
Kraft paper, desk blotters,
Gold and aluminum foils,
Neighborhood bums the foil
On their wine bottles,
The Revelation.
And I command you not to fear.

DON'T GO TO THE BARN

by TOM SLEIGH

from ANTAEUS

for Rosamund Sleigh

The brick of the asylum shimmered in the sun
As I watched the black hood of your depression
Lower down across your face immobile
But for the eyes staring off into the crystal

Blue bracing the scorched mountain.
Fire like a razor had swept the rock face clean. . . .
Cut off from your despair, I stared across the lawn
To your drug-blinkered gaze staring down

The shivering, flashing eyes of the aspen:
Blinking back that glare, I saw your heart eaten
By the gloom of the weather-warped barn
Off behind the orchard alleys convulsing

Into bloom, saw you walk into the shudder
Of blossoms rippling down in spasms
Of cool wind, the weeds you tread under
Springing back bristling, the tough, fibrous green

Closing in behind you, the chill brushings
Of the leaves feathering dew across your skin.
The barn like a grey flame burns above the bloom,
The hoof-cratered mud, glistening in the sun,

Squelching as you slog across the yard.
And now you enter into the raftered
Damp of lofty spaces cut by the veer
And slice of scaly wings, knot the knot hard,

Loop the rope around the beam, the zero
Of the noose dangling down: Your gaze swings
To mine, and I see your chances narrow:
Sprawled on the table, the volts axing

Through your skull, you jerk and shake,
Your body drugged to flab trembling and trembling,
Your teeth clenching jolt after jolt until crackling
In your brain a voice of fire speaks,

Divinely disapproving: "Don't go to the barn
And try to hang yourself. Don't go to the barn
And try to hang yourself. Don't go to the barn
And try to hang yourself. Rose, don't go to the barn."

THE NOISE THE HAIRLESS MAKE

by STEPHEN DOBYNS

from SONORA REVIEW

How difficult to be an angel.
In order to forgive, they have no memory.
In order to be good, they're always forgetting.
How else could heaven be run? Still,
it needs to be full of teachers and textbooks
imported from God's own basement, since only
in hell is memory exact. In one classroom,
a dozen angels scratch their heads as their teacher
displays the cross-section of a human skull,
saying, Here is the sadness, here
the anger, here's where laughter is kept.
And the angels think, How strange, and take notes
and would temper their forgiveness if it weren't
all forgotten by the afternoon. Sometimes
a bunch fly down to earth with their teacher
who wants them to study a living example and
this evening they find a man lying in a doorway
in an alley in Detroit. They stand around
chewing their pencils as their teacher says,
This is the stick he uses to beat his wife,
this is the bottle he drinks from when he
wants to forget, this is the Detroit Tigers

T-shirt he wears whenever he's sad, this is
the electric kazoo he plays in order to weep.
And the angels think, How peculiar, and wonder
whether to temper their forgiveness or just
let it ride which really doesn't matter since
they forget the question as soon as it's asked.
But their muttering wakes the man in the doorway
who looks to see a flock of doves departing
over the trash cans. And because he dreamed
of betrayal and pursuit, of defeat in battle,
the death of friends, he heaves a bottle at them
and it breaks under a streetlight so the light
reflects on its hundred broken pieces with such
a multi-colored twinkling that the man laughs.
From their place on a brick wall, the angels
watch and one asks, What good are they? Then
others take up the cry, What good are they,
what good are they? But as fast as they articulate
the question it's forgotten and their teacher,
a minor demon, returns with them to heaven.
But the man, still chuckling, sits in his doorway,
and the rats in their dumpsters hear this sound
like stones rattling or metal banging together,
and they see how the man is by himself without
food or companions, without work or family
or a real bed for his body. They creep back
to their holes and practice little laughs
that sound like coughing or a dog throwing up
as once more they uselessly try to imitate
the noise the hairless make when defeated.

DELFINA FLORES AND HER NIECE MODESTA

by HERBERT MORRIS

from SHENANDOAH

Delfina Flores, named for flowers, poses
through the afternoon with the child, Modesta,
named for modesty, squirming in her lap.
Why the painter should want them to pose for him
eludes her, will, it seems, always elude her,
but she will not dwell too long on that aspect.
She does what she is told now, will attempt to
have the child do the same, or very nearly.
Santiago is beautiful, she thinks.
It is he she would paint, if she could paint,
his face and body, if she were a painter
and knew where to make a mark on the canvas,
where, in that field of absence, to begin.

How could anyone think her more than plain?,
she wonders, with these braids (too coarse, too black),
a nose and mouth not small or fine, a look
with too much of the Indian, perhaps
and little enough of the Mexican.
The child, she thinks, is worthy of a portrait,
will be a beauty when she is fourteen.
With those eyes, with such dainty hands and feet
(Señor Rivera asked that they sit shoeless;

dressed in their Sunday church frocks, it seemed fitting
that they wear shoes, as well, but he assured them
his instincts could be trusted in such matters),
she will have any young man that she chooses.
Tía Dolores sewed these blouses for them,
hers and the child's, awoke, these last two mornings,
long before dawn, to baste the final stitches,
the appliqué embroidered at the neckline,
and have them done by the time they would sit.
Let the painter see you both at your best,
she told Delfina Flores; we must show him
those who have little still retain their pride.
It is an honor that this man, Rivera,
has you to sit for him and paints your portrait.
You will become, if you are not already,
the envy of the young girls of this village.

She thinks she would prefer, given the choice,
that Santiago, once, tell her he loves her
to the honor the sitting represents.
Santiago has never told her that,
though he has told her other things, things young men
always, so she has heard, tell those they court,
or hope to court, or dream one day of courting.
Wait, Modesta, wait for a boy to want you
who never brings himself to say he loves you.
But I expect you will know nothing of that;
with such fine hair, and with those hands and feet
as delicate as flowers, what young man
will not feel love for you, when it is time,
will not need to tell you of it himself,
the pain is so intense, so overwhelming.
Be still, Modesta; in this straight-back chair
he has posed us in, how do you expect me
to hold you in my arms if you keep twisting?
It cannot be much longer; we have been here
all afternoon, the sun has set, and Señor
Rivera seems himself ready to quit—
see the sweat on his forehead, see him squint,
see how he rubs his fingers? If, tomorrow,

you behave for the length of the whole sitting,
I will give you a toffee, cinnamon,
your favorite, or almond. Would you like that?
Tía Dolores made these blouses for us;
try not to wrinkle yours. Señor Rivera
says this picture he paints will be a mirror
where we will see our images exactly,
even these cross-stitches Tía Dolores
embroidered here in front, wanting to please us.

Here, take my chain and locket. See the light
catch in the links? See the medallion spinning
in the wind when I breathe on it, like this?
That's Our Lady of Guadeloupe, remember?,
Our Lady of the Sorrows. Every Sunday
the candle which we light we light for her.
We leave it at her feet so that she knows
we have been there and we have not forgotten.
You'll show your nieces how, when it is time;
you'll tell them not to lean into the flame
when you stand at the altar, as I tell you;
you'll hold their hand, as I hold yours, you'll touch
your candle to their candle, as I do;
you'll teach them what the words are, what they mean;
you'll sew their blouses, as our aunts sew ours.
When I was nine I asked Tía Dolores
what sorrow is, or what the sorrows are.
She took a long, deep breath before she spoke
and, when the words came, they came with such passion,
such heat, I looked to see whether her teeth
had split beneath the hammer of her answer:
Another name for Mexico, she whispered.
It seemed she'd always known how she'd respond,
known precisely what she would say, if asked,
and had been waiting only to be asked.

It may be best not to expect too much,
Tía Dolores tells me in the evening,
when she brushes my hair, or mends my skirt.
It is better not to be disappointed.

When I speak to her about Santiago,
what I feel for him, what I wish he felt,
she says it may be unwise to entrust
hope for one's future to another person.
God and the earth are all one can depend on,
and not always even the earth, she says.
I know how hard it is, and has been, for her;
yet, when the time comes that you understand
such things, little Modesta, when, at evening,
I let down your black hair, undo the braids,
begin slowly to brush it, I could never
bring myself to tell you what she tells me.
(Love, I might tell you, if you can; if not,
if, for some reason, feeling is closed to you,
hope in time your life opens you to that,
hope one day for the courage necessary).

Señor Rivera has, in fact, grown weary.
The light begins to go and the wrists ache.
It may be the heat or a combination
of factors: heat, exhaustion, the toll beauty
exacts of vision, darkness slowly falling.
It may be time to stop now, to resume
tomorrow, should the family agree.
The older child (fourteen?), Delfina Flores,
has a look which wholly intrigues him, not quite
Mexican and yet not quite Indian;
Oriental, perhaps, chiseled from marble,
some great, dark marble, veined and streaked with light.
Part of her beauty, too, he thinks, must be
that she does not know she is beautiful,
thinks the reverse, in fact, and so her features
have not had time to recognize themselves,
to settle into mere self-satisfaction.
Her niece, Modesta, is, like any child
her age, two, he would guess, possibly three,
available to what the future stamps
across her face, available, no more.
All of it, all, remains to be decided
and, though conclusions are impossible

218

at this point, one at least can say the makings
of a woman of splendor (hands, feet, eyes)
are already in evidence, it seems.
Nothing more can be said of her than that.

Delfina Flores is another matter.
What she might have become she has become.
Her years already tell us who she is.
Nothing remains to be decided, nothing.
Oh, there will be a wedding one day, children
of her own, hair to brush at evening, births
and deaths, the rituals, time passing, nights,
labor in sun-bleached fields, but the essentials,
that on which it all lies, stands now in place.
Looking into her face, he thinks, is like
looking, for the first time, at Mexico
directly, all at once, face to full light.
Though the artist is not quite brash enough
to make such claims, he would not be displeased
if the viewer, seeing the finished portrait,
Delfina Flores and Her Niece Modesta,
might be moved to cry out one word, just one,
standing before it, one word: Mexico!,
Mexico!, with that sense of recognition
overtaking us when we know the name
of something but not how we come to know it.

The girl, Delfina Flores, at the outset
confided to him her uncertainty,
if she were painting pictures, where to start,
where, in that "field of absence", to begin,
to make one's presence known, and with what stroke.
Though, each day, he confronts the canvas, he knows
no more about the process than Delfina.
Some mornings, entering the studio,
he will not know what first move he might make
(and he thinks it shall all lie with first moves);
the canvas on the easel will assail him
with the burden of emptiness it bears,
with the depth of the silences it shrieks with,

the possibilities it opens to,
could open to, given the gift, luck, or technique
that knows what can be done with emptiness,
that understands what can be worked with silence.
Then, too, one's subject rises, if it rises,
to meet you, singles you as its accomplice,
leaps out at you, seems to insist, *insist,*
everything must be laid aside for this,
implying that this moment, this grand courtship,
if you will, this romance, this pure seduction
of painter by his subject, at first sight,
presents itself, and this intensely, once.
Returning "later" will, of course, be futile.
"Tomorrow", in this case, is unavailing.
You have only to be accessible,
now, at this moment, here, rapt, undivided,
only to learn to resist not at all,
should the moment be at hand and resistance
seems to you the most logical defense
by one who stands there silent, overwhelmed,
besieged, so taken by surprise, so taken
off guard, late, unprepared, now touched beyond
any formerly adequate, if useless,
definition of touched, made obsolete
by these two girls who, Mexican and shoeless,
sit in a straight-back chair where he has placed them,
faces to light, to what remains of light,
patient, obedient, doing as asked,
like Mexico itself ready to please
(how many hours have they been sitting?; evening
already moves down from the hills, the stars rise,
the dogs begin their barking, the wrists ache),
the one whom someone thought to name for flowers,
whom Santiago will not tell he loves
(Santiago of the dark brows and head,
whose darkness she would paint, if she could paint,
bending shirtless in fields beneath those suns
too punishing not to be Mexican),
thinking all afternoon of games, distractions,
both for herself and for her niece, Modesta

(chain and medallion, riddles, revelations
wholly lost on the child, all in a Spanish
equal to music as she hums it, croons it,
the Spanish one is born to and will die with),
so that the child be still, not lose the look
Señor Rivera claims to want, or finds,
or holds to through the afternoon; the other,
the one who has been named for modesty,
delicate even to her feet and hands,
a beauty in the making, for the moment
fascinated by the tears of Our Lady
of the Sorrows (gold leaf staining tin cheeks),
enchanted by the spinning of that figure
dangling before her from thin, beaten links,
turning slowly, slowly now, in the wind
Tía Delfina, out of tenderness,
has devised for her, turning in a way
not unlike the way the continent turns
beneath them, as they sit there (all of it,
forest, lagoon, swamp, cordillera, salt flat,
pasture, scrub, mesa), turning in the only
direction it can turn, downward to evening,
the mountains plunging fiercely to the sea
and the sea slipping underneath the mountains
where the darkness accumulates, or blindness,
or the thing, not yet named, Tía Dolores
calls Mexico, our Mexico, our sorrow.

221

I SEND MAMA HOME

by MARILYN NELSON

from THE SOUTHERN REVIEW

I send you down the road from Paden
scaring bobwhites and pheasants
back into the weeds;
a jackrabbit keeps pace
in front of your headlights
if you drive there at night.
I send you to Boley
past a stand of post oaks
and the rolling blackjack hills.

On Pecan Street
a brown rectangle outlines the spot
where King's Ice House used to be.
The Farmer's and Merchant's Bank
is closed, grizzled boards
blind its windows.
The ghosts of Mister Turner,
the murdered banker,
and Floyd Birdwell,
the right hand of Pretty Boy Floyd,
spill like shadows
over the splintering floor.

This was the city of promise,
the town where no white man
showed his face after dark.

The *Progress* extolled it
in twice weekly headlines
as "Boley, the Negro's Dream."

Mama, I give you this poem
so you can drive past
Hazel's Department Store,
Bragg's Barber Shop,
the Truelove Cafe,
the Antioch Baptist Church,
the C.M.E. church and school,
the Creek-Seminole college.

I deliver you again
to your parents' bedroom
where the piano gleamed
like a black pegasus,
to the three-room farmhouse,
to the Oklahoma plains.
I give you the horses, Prince and Lady,
and the mules. I give you your father's car,
a Whippet, which you learned to drive
at a slow bounce through the pasture.
I give you the cows and calves
you and your brother played rodeo on,
the full smokehouse, the garden,
the fields of peanuts and cotton.

I send you back
to the black town you missed
when you were at college
and on the great white way.
I let you see
behind the mask you've worn
since the fifty-year-ago morning
when you waved goodbye from the train.

XII

POLAND OF DEATH

by ALLEN GROSSMAN

from THE BRIGHT NAILS SCATTERED ON THE GROUND (New Directions)

I

I hear my father underground scratching with a nail. And I say,
"Father, here is a word." He says, "It does not help. I am
Scratching my way with a nail ever since you dug me down
In the grave, and I have not yet come to Poland of death."
And I hear my mother saying, "Sing me something about the
Forest primeval." So I say, "Mother, here is a story."
And she says, "I have a pain in the blind eye, the left one
Which is dead."
             I hear my father scratching with a nail again,
And I offer him the words of a song, first one word and then
Another, and he refuses them. He says, "It is not a word," or
"It is just a word," or "It is not what you feel." "What
Do you feel?" Poland of death! Ever since I put my father
In the grave he has been scratching a way, and has not yet
Got under the sea, and mother has a pain in her blind eye.

So I tell her the story of a woman named Irene: How when she
Walked into a hayfield behind her house the animals shrieked.
How when she crossed over to the other side of the field
The clothes in the bluing froze, and all the yeast died
In the potato water. How when she reached the edge of the forest
Everything went up in flames in the farm she had left behind.
Then my father underground says, "Do not be bewildered by

227

The surfaces. In the depths, everything is law." And I say,
"My true love in the grave-deep forest nation is a forester."
And mother says, "This is the forest Primeval." Poland of death!

II

As not in life my father appeared to me
Naked in death and said, "This is my body."
So I undressed and faced him, and we were
Images of one another for he

Appeared to me at the same age I am.

Then he said, "Now I am in Death's country."
And I saw behind him in the dogmatic
Mirror of our death a forest of graves
In morning light. The smoky air was full
Of men and women sweeping the stone sills.
"Since you dug me down in America,"
He said, "I've been scratching a way with a nail,
And now I have come to Poland of Death."

And I saw the keepers of the graves moving
Among the shadows and the lights like lights.

Then he said to me—and not for the first time—
"Give me a word." And again, "Who are you?"
And then, after a long silence, "Write me
The Black Book of the world." And I replied,
"Louis, here is my body." And then one
Of us grew erect, and the cries began—
Like the weak voices of disembodied children
Driving crows from the cornfields.
                                        —He showed me
The severed head of a mother in her tears
Kissing and eating the severed head of a child;
And one familiar spirit like a snarled hank
Of somebody's black hair. And he showed also
A bloody angle of the wires where groans

228

Of men and women drowned the roar of motors
And mounted to a prophecy. Then he gave me
A sharp look and said, "Thank God, I have no children,"
And ran off with a cry down an alley of
That place like one who remembered suddenly
The day of his own death—

A short, pugnacious man, but honest and reliable.

Night fell and the mirror was empty for a while.
Then appeared, or half-appeared, Beatrice, my mother,
In the bed of her great age.
When she sleeps her human eye closes, and rests:
But her blind eye—the dead one—stares out
As if to say, "This is the forest primeval.
This is Death at last."

And I saw again the keepers of the graves
Moving among the shadows and the lights.

THAT THEY WERE AT THE BEACH

BEACH

—AEOLOTROPIC SERIES

by LESLIE SCALAPINO

from AMERICAN POETRY REVIEW

Playing ball—so it's like paradise, not because it's in the past, we're on a field; we are creamed by the girls who get together on the other team. They're nubile, but in age they're thirteen or so—so they're strong.

(No one knows each other, aligning according to race as it happens, the color of the girls, and our being creamed in the foreground—as part of it's being that—the net is behind us).

—————————

A microcosm, but it's of girls—who were far down on the field, in another situation of playing ball—so it was an instance of the main world though they're nubile but are in age thirteen or so.

My being creamed in the foreground—so it's outside of that—by a girl who runs into me, I returned to the gym.

—————————

It's in the past—yet is repressed in terms of the situation itself, poor people who're working, the division is by color. We're not allowed to leave the airport on arriving—others not permitted to stop over—we're immature in age, so it's inverted.

(Therefore receded—we get on the bus going to the city and look around, seeing people dressed shabbily).

A man—I was immature in age—was a stowaway so not having been active, taken from the ship we're on in a row boat.

'A sailor had fallen out of the row boat then, was embarrassed. So it's like paradise—the embarrassment, therefore it's depressed— seen by his waving at us as the other sailors are coming to him).

The class period ending—it's evanescence not because it's in the past, they'd stamped their feet while seated since the teacher hadn't been able to discipline them. She's old—the red hair coloring had been mocked—they're inactive.

(So it's evanescent because they're inactive. Though I am as well. She'd asked me to pull on her hair to indicate it was her real hair, which I do—them being unaware of this—as the class is disbanding, composed of girls and boys).

It is also an instance in the past, so it's depressed—yet the people on the bus aren't nubile, rather are mature.

We're girls—have to urinate which is unrelated to immaturity— refusing to do so in front of others; we require the bus to leave us. Therefore there aren't other people, we urinate, and then look around.

(So it's inactive—is depressed).

Tall, though they are nubile—playing leap frog is out of place; we're required to do so. It's contemporary in time so it's not depressed—I was immature, thirteen in age or so; responding to the other girls kicking as they jumped over some of us.

(So it's not depressed—but not as being active. I'm creamed, until the crowd of girls is pulled off by an instructor who's in the gym).

Attending a funeral—it's contemporary in time, not being in itself depressed; taking a ridiculous aspect—birds that sing loudly in the

231

chapel where the funeral service is being held. The birds are mechanical—so it's being creamed.

(Like in the earlier episode of playing ball. Our being creamed in the foreground of the field by the other girls).

A microcosm, but it's of sailors—though I'm given attention standing in pictures with one or two of the men. They've come into a port at one time—I'm immature in age—it doesn't occur for that reason but is inverted, the sailors flirted with girls.

(Which is contemporary in time therefore. And being mechanical since I'm interested in the sailors, then merely interest).

A boy was actually at the funeral—so it's inverted—was later playing ball, really occurring.

(Inverted also because of being at the funeral, mechanical birds part of it; so it isn't creamed in the future—not because of that).

The boy who was actually at the funeral—corresponds to work as a chimney sweep which I had for a short time—is inverted.

(I didn't take the job seriously since it was in the past—I was supposed to do it awhile, was contemporary. So it's related to the boy; I got sick from the soot—so my leaving after working only two days stemmed from that).

Someone else driving—the funeral having taken place—is getting speeding tickets, with us in the car—we're older than he

So we don't say anything because we're older. Not about the police stopping him, the drive is several hundred miles at night—which is like him later going below the border

•

Him not being sentient

232

A man whoring—it's from the standpoint of a girl, is a situation of trying to finance going below the border to whore and staying down there as long as he can before having to return to get some job.

(It's a microcosm, is also inverted—not retroactive).

We're thirteen in age or so—they're nubile—so I wouldn't say that ever in describing myself

We're bicycling as are they. Other girls who come on us from a side road. There are fields around, they race us—almost sarcastic seen while bicycling (so it's retroactive; isn't just in relation to their being nubile—contemporary in time)

—so it's mechanical birds though it's in the past

Not really being ill, but thinking he is, (it's also the mechanical birds), the man's deeply embarrassed—he's not old—at it turning out to be viewed this way after having others take him to hospitals.

(So it's the mechanical birds because he isn't old. Nor is there a funeral—but not related to one he's taken from a swimming pool, goes in an ambulance).

Not really being ill—corresponds to the man who mugged me, not the one I mistook for him—it's depressed.

The real thief running away from the telephone booth is in my side vision, I don't realize it while blaming a boy standing in front of me. They're boys really—so it's inverted—though the one who'd stayed behind for a minute while I cursed him flirted with me.

A man mugging me—therefore inverted, not just in relation to maturity—seeing I'm frightened is almost considerate by not hitting me when I struggle with him, though finally giving him the purse.

The naiveté—on my part—he's depressed

He's depressed—by mugging me—corresponds to my having a job

Having an employer, I'd make jokes seen by him to be inappropriate, had offended him—I make jokes because it's in the past (is therefore sentient—I'm fairly immature in age and my offending him is unintentional).

Winos were lying on the sidewalk, it's a warehouse district; I happen to be wearing a silk blouse, so it's jealousy, not that they're jealous of me necessarily.

They're not receded, and are inert—as it happens are bums—so it's being creamed; because it's contemporary in time—jealousy because of that.

The bums happen to be lying in the street, it really occurs that I wear a silk blouse.

So it's mechanical—because of the winos being there—not from the blouse which I'd happened to wear though going into the warehouse district.

Stevedores—I'm immature in age—who are now made to live away from their families to work, the division is by color; they're allowed to form unions but not act—so it's evanescent.

(Because it's inactive—not just in the situation itself. Or in their later not coming to the docks—so they were striking, regardless of them being fired which occurs then).

The man having been in government—it's evanescent because it's inactive, our being immature in age—he's assassinated at an airport where we happen to come in that morning. We get on a bus which goes to the ocean—it's also beefcake but not because of the man already having died, is mature.

(We haven't seen him—as with the sailors it's contemporary in time).

A microcosm, but it's of sailors—so it's in the foreground, is beefcake—is in the past

(Therefore is contemporary in time while being seen then—so beefcake is in the past—similar to the situation of the other girls also refusing as I had to walk out onto the field, my then being immediately required to—not just in relation to them cooperating then).

It's the mechanical birds because of my having gone out on the field then—is the men

So it's sexual coming—anyone—but corresponds to the floating world, seeing men on the street

---

not in relation to there being too many of them standing around on a job

●

It's hot weather—so it's recent—corresponds to them

(though the floating world was in the past). To others as well—is in the setting of me being on a boardwalk seeing crowds of people walking or rollerskating. Some happening to be immature in age— it's not retroactive

●

Being in the past—is jealousy on my part—in general

Not in relation to the people I happened to see who were immature in age—on the boardwalk—necessarily

●

Their not being sentient

The reserves—they weren't using the police, so it's inverted—
were wearing battle-gear, it's beautiful weather—they were old—
is crowded

not occurring now—and their being frightened of the crowd, so it's
inverted because of that—I'm there but jealousy on my part, in
general—stemming from that

I'm not retroactive—corresponds to making jokes because it's in
the past

(Not retroactive because of the beautiful weather. And taking the
car to be repaired; the mechanic coming out to test drive, its tires
have gone flat in the short time I was in the shop. The man and I
get out of the car, laugh, I walk somewhere else to have its tires
filled, drive away. Buying a dip stick then, I'd done what was
necessary to it myself apparently).

Beginning to honk, because a man in a car behind me looked as if
he were going to take my parking place, it's near shops, is
crowded—I honked before seeing that he's old. And it appearing
he hadn't wanted the parking place.

(His being old not mattering because it's crowded—which is
transparent, regardless of there being the one parking place—so it
isn't sentient)

The background had been in the selling of the car—almost giving it
away

though it's not that, but seeing it again sitting by the highway—I'm
weeping because of something, am driving back from the city—so
it's transparent, crowded but my being miserable; which had
occurred anyway. The man who'd bought the car cheating me
though saying it was worthless—it is—having occurred earlier

Corresponding to having a job—and going below the border

On the vacation—I'm fired after I returned though the employer

236

had consented to the vacation—we get to a small town in the desert. There are mines. It's at night. We've driven very fast. A crowd of men are in the store buying liquor who are poor—so it's evanescent (it's evanescent though we're buying liquor as well)

Someone else, who's middle aged—so it's not the man with the boy, getting gasoline

—being miserable, had put his head on the steering wheel, corresponds to there being the one parking place, though he's not going then. So isn't in that one. And weeping unrestrainedly because of his life—isn't necessarily related to his age

---

Other people not being retroactive—because of the beautiful weather—so it's recent

people said to be working for subsistence complimented for being willing to—in a naive way by the plant owner—is then inactive

●

The construction workers whistling or catcalling at women who go by the construction site, at each woman going by—they're not sentient

(We're not—either are they)

It's hot weather—so it's reversed, is contemporary as with the sailors

(beefcake is in the foreground)

---

is naive—corresponds to the floating world

---

isn't knowledgeable of myself therefore—is the boys—who happen to be standing on a street corner, they're unemployed though it's Sunday anyway. It's necessary that they not have jobs. We're downtown driving—so there's no one else there

(is not sentient—but which is the mechanical birds, because of the weather)

---

so it would be transparent in the past, crowded but my being miserable

—as it happens—and have it not occur now

●

Their not being sentient

Seeing a crowd of people—we'd gone to a gallery as it happened—so they're not at their jobs

---

that they were at the beach—aren't retroactive

The floating world was courtesans though

It was in a man's divorce, (he's the father of a man who'd earlier gone below the border)—and him just taking off to the south one day to be near the border for good, not wanting his job anyway—not clarifying

(it's therefore sentient—isn't for him)

isn't for me

taking a cab, the driver seems frightened, seen by him not speaking to me—stemming from his job—unfamiliar because of the streets

---

A crazy, recognized by people around because he is always on the street—staying outside is it being crowded, though the man isn't old.

I'm going by when fraternity boys are shouting at him, making fun—didn't realize he could've shouted first, occurring to me when I saw him shouting by himself one time

Alcohol not enabling someone to be in paradise, being what he was saying

therefore inverted. A man getting out of a car, another transient coming by who begins to shout for some reason, addressed the man by the car (though it's not necessarily to him)—who also shouted, but not making fun of him

---

It having to be some time ago—was related to the bus driver, we're in school. The driver is surly, in general—turning a corner driving he hits a girl because she's not out of the way, thinking she should run

he hasn't drunk anything—so it isn't dislike

●

and isn't dislike for him—so afterwards we'd always make the sound in the bus of it hitting her at that corner

---

which is their wanting to take the money I might have on me

two muggers—though they were not together—who both followed me for a time aware of each other and that I see them. I was walking quickly with my suitcase which would mean to them that I'd just arrived in the city, it's crowded with passers-by (so not enabling someone to be in paradise—is regardless of the money I might have on me).

A transient—so it's not necessary to be it—the other men in the restaurant throw him out

because he's noisy, being drunk—but having no arms so removing him is inverted, another transient comes in who has arms, is also drunk—and therefore thrown out as well (that man had reentered carrying a cat before being thrown out again).

The floating world was courtesans though

●

A girl at the time—the insects which is inverted, in a situation in

239

which she's on the deck of a boat on the Nile, there was a swarm of locusts, coming on her suddenly—she's a friend

really the friend of a relative

●

It'd have to be some time ago—I got cake on me, handed to me by my mother, we're in a taxi. Men in another car—beside me, I'm somewhat immature in age—whistled and called to me customary stemming from seeing me eating the cake

(so I'm embarrassed)

Climbing a mountain—it's Fuji—there are marines having to climb it for exercise; easily able to get far ahead of us, which we don't realize, we're girls, they wait when we have to rest—

it isn't creamed for us—though dissolution not occurring. And not occurring in the situation with the marines.

---

it's regardless—I was immature in age, so that is mechanical

Holding one end of a jump rope, the other end is tied to a tree—a boy who was a bully riding his bicycle is going to ride across the jump rope; I pull the rope slightly as it's lying on the sidewalk before he gets to it so he sees that and knows I can do it—so it isn't mechanical in that sense

---

is so our being fairly immature in age, we're students—the man who's discovered in the crowd—he's there to observe it, is in the F.B.I., had been in it in my childhood living nearby since he was a neighbor

Though the people in the crowd don't call to him saying they know who he is because of that—but it's mechanical because of that

---

it being reversed

●

It's obvious—occurring recently

The checkers falling behind—after chasing a man out shouting that he has stolen, he ran far away from the supermarket—a woman I know rode after him on a bicycle (for the reason given by the checkers)

●

I went on up the street, seeing a transient who had his things with him sitting near-by—there are men pouring cement in a site, he's watching them—so isn't sentient

because of occurring recently

---

stemming from that—

I take her to the hospital—meaning the landlady who's in her nineties—to visit a tenant who's fallen down having been drunk

We walk a block, the street flooding since it's raining. It isn't creamed—in the sense of her age

as it is being caught in the rain with bags of groceries—no one's around

It's pouring, I'm on the street corner unable to carry them further—it's funny because I should have known better. But though taxis are never in the neighborhood, one goes by and I go home in it

---

So it's the bicyclist, cursing—which occurs when I almost hit a bicyclist, he says so following my car for a block afterwards—

So I'm sentient—he is not

I'm in a packed courtroom, a crowd is outside; the man sitting there—having been informed on as communist in a ridiculous situation—the other members of the cell had been F.B.I. So there not having been understanding on his part, he was embarrassed—in expression—

Therefore dissolution not occurring—my being fairly immature in age. Not creamed for me afterwards.

I'd gotten into the hearing—of the man—because of the crowd's pushing and the police admitting me into the courtroom

though my friends had been left outside, were more aware than I—so it's the landlady because of them being amidst the crowd

---

as it is working for a lawyer only slightly older than I, I'm fairly immature in age—I offend him unintentionally by making a joke when he says he'd like to get into working for trusts

It's dumb work, temporary for me—so that is the landlady

---

it's temporary work—he's the lawyer who's slightly older than I, I was fairly immature in age

He doesn't speak to me for a week once, we're in the car mostly— because I'd made jokes; I hadn't meant to offend him—so it's the landlady in that sense

●

which is like selling my car—having an ad

I have the feeling I wouldn't have luck without the car, though it won't run—but nevertheless sell it to a man who puts the money on the grass. I'd bent down to get it giving him the chance to grab me—picking me up in his arms isn't the reason he buys the car— it's to repair it

---

Seeing my old car parked on the street—I'm driving by and had

already been unhappy—regardless of the feeling that I wouldn't have luck without the car, so that is then the landlady

●

The lawyer and I, he's only slightly older than I—working have to have dinners; though I've unintentionally offended him—

which is the landlady for that reason. We're in expensive restaurants, he and I fairly immature in age

---

my being fairly immature in age—we dock, there are lines of stevedores, men coming onto the ship—we can't get off in that port, it's the port's authority, because a few people on the ship had become sick

but the stevedores can

—making jokes

was making fun of the lawyer, our both being fairly immature in age—though I didn't realize it

●

We're—the lawyer and I—in the car, I had made the jokes before this, he's gotten beer

but we hadn't opened it yet; he backed into a tree, driving away from the grocery

●

The thought that there is no riot—isn't going to be any

is connected to the stevedores

There is no riot—associated with the stevedores—the man to whom I sold my car, he'd taken me for a drive in the hills deciding on it, had driven it recklessly

he's trying to frighten me so I'll give him the car—which I do, though I realize it

---

THE GARDEN
OF EARTHLY DELIGHTS

by CZESLAW MILOSZ

from UNATTAINABLE EARTH (Ecco Press)

1/Summer

In the July sun they were leading me to the Prado,
Straight to the room where *The Garden of Earthly Delights*
Had been prepared for me. So that I run to its waters
And immerse myself in them and recognize myself.

The twentieth century is drawing to its close.
I will be immured in it like a fly in amber.
I was old but my nostrils craved new scents
And through my five senses I received a share in the earth
Of those who led me, our sisters and lovers.

How lightly they walk! Their hips in trousers, not in trailing
   dresses,
Their feet in sandals, not on cothurni,
Their hair not clasped by a tortoiseshell buckle.
Yet constantly the same, renewed by the moon, Luna,
In a chorus that keeps praising Lady Venus.

Their hands touched my hands and they marched, gracious,
As if in the early morning at the outset of the world.

2/A Ball

It is going on inside a transparent ball
Above which God the Father, short, with a trimmed beard,
Sits with a book, enveloped in dark clouds.
He reads an incantation and things are called to being.
As soon as the earth emerges, it bears grasses and trees.
We are those to whom green hills have been offered
And for us this ray descends from opened mists.
Whose hand carries the ball? Probably the Son's.
And the whole Earth is in it, Paradise and Hell.

3/Paradise

Under my sign, Cancer, a pink fountain
Pours out four streams, the sources of four rivers.
But I don't trust it. As I verified myself,
That sign is not lucky. Besides we abhor
The moving jaws of crabs and the calcareous
Cemeteries of the ocean. This, then, is the Fountain
Of Life? Toothed, sharp-edged,
With its innocent, delusive color. And beneath,
Just where the birds alight, glass traps set with glue.
A white elephant, a white giraffe, white unicorns,
Black creatures of the ponds. A lion mauls a deer.
A cat has a mouse. A three-headed lizard,
A three-headed ibis, their meaning unknown.
Or a two-legged dog, no doubt a bad omen.
Adam sits astonished. His feet
Touch the foot of Christ who has brought Eve
And keeps her right hand in his left while lifting
Two fingers of his right like the one who teaches.
Who is she, and who will she be, the beloved
From the Song of Songs? This Wisdom-Sophia,
Seducer, the Mother and Ecclesia?
Thus he created her who will conceive him?
Where then did he get his human form
Before the years and centuries began?
Human, did he exist before the beginning?
And establish a Paradise, though incomplete,

So that she might pluck the fruit, she, the mysterious one,
Whom Adam contemplates, not comprehending?
I am these two, twofold. I ate from the tree
Of knowledge. I was expelled by the archangel's sword.
At night I sensed her pulse. Her mortality.
And we have searched for the real place ever since.

4/Earth

Riding birds, feeling under our thighs the soft feathers
Of goldfinches, orioles, kingfishers,
Or spurring lions into a run, unicorns, leopards,
Whose coats brush against our nakedness,
We circle the vivid and abundant waters,
Mirrors from which emerge a man's and a woman's head,
Or an arm, or the round breasts of the sirens.
Every day is the day of berry harvest here.
The two of us bite into wild strawberries
Bigger than a man, we plunge into cherries,
We are drenched with the juices of their wine,
We celebrate the colors of carmine
And vermillion, as in toys on a Christmas tree.
We are many, a whole tribe swarming,
And so like each other that our lovemaking
Is as sweet and immodest as a game of hide-and-seek.
And we lock ourselves inside the crowns of flowers
Or in transparent, iridescent bubbles.
Meanwhile a flock of lunar signs fills the sky
To prepare the alchemical nuptials of the planets.

5/Earth Again

They are incomprehensible, the things of this earth.
The lure of waters. The lure of fruits.
Lure of the two breasts and long hair of a maiden.
In rouge, in vermillion, in that color of ponds
Found only in the Green Lakes near Wilno.
And ungraspable multitudes swarm, come together
In the crinkles of tree bark, in the telescope's eye,
For an endless wedding,

246

For the kindling of the eyes, for a sweet dance
In the elements of the air, sea, earth and subterranean caves,
So that for a short moment there is no death
And time does not unreel like a skein of yarn
Thrown into an abyss.

LE PETIT SALVIÉ

by C. K. WILLIAMS

from THE PARIS REVIEW

for Paul Zweig
1935–1984

1.

"The summer has gone by both quickly and slowly.
It's been a kind of eternity, each day spinning
out its endlessness, and yet with every look
back, less time is left . . ."

So quickly, and so slowly . . . In the tiny elevator of the flat you'd
    borrowed on the Rue de Pondicherry,
you suddenly put your head against my chest, I thought to show
    how tired you were, and lost consciousness,
sagging heavily against me, forehead oiled with sweat, eyes
    ghastly agape . . . so quickly, so slowly.
Quickly the ambulance arrives, mewling at the curb, the
    disinterested orderlies strap you to their stretcher.
Slowly at the clinic, waiting for the doctors, waiting for the
    ineffectual treatments to begin.
Slowly through that night, then quickly all the next day, your last
    day, though no one yet suspects it.
Quickly those remaining hours, quickly the inconsequential tasks
    and doings of any ordinary afternoon.

Quickly, slowly, those final silences and sittings I so regret now
  not having taken all of with you.

2.

"I don't think we'll make the dance tonight," I mumble
  mawkishly. "It's definitely worse," you whisper.
Ice-pack hugged to you, you're breathing fast; when you stop
  answering questions, your eyes close.
You're there, and then you slip away into your meditations, the
  way, it didn't matter where,
in an airport, a café, you could go away into yourself to work, and
  so we're strangely comforted.
It was dusk, late, the softening, sweetening, lingering light of the
  endless Paris evening.
Your room gave on a garden, a perfect breeze washed across your
  bed, it wasn't hard to leave you,
we knew we'd see you again: we kissed you, Vikki kissed you,
  "Goodbye, my friends," you said,
lifting your hand, smiling your old warming smile, then you went
  into your solitude again.

3.

We didn't know how ill you were . . . we knew how ill but hid it
  . . . we didn't know how ill you were . . .
Those first days when your fever rose . . . if we'd only made you go
  into the hospital in Brive . . .
Perhaps you could have had another year . . . but the way you'd
  let death touch your life so little—
the way you'd learned to hold your own mortality before you like
  an unfamiliar, complex flower.
Your stoicism had become so much a part of your identity, your
  virtue, the system of your self-regard.
If we'd insisted now, you might have given in to us, when we
  didn't, weren't we cooperating
with what wasn't just your wish but your true passion never to be
  dying, sooner dead than dying?

You did it, too: composed a way from life directly into death, the ignoble scribblings between elided.

4.

It must be some body-thing, some species-thing, the way it comes to take me from so far,
this grief that tears me so at moments when I least suspect it's there, wringing tears from me
I'm not prepared for, had no idea were even there in me, this most unmanly gush I almost welcome,
these cries so general yet with such power of their own I'm stunned to hear them come from me.
Walking through the street, I cry, talking later to a friend, I try not to but I cry again,
working at my desk I'm taken yet again, although, again, I don't want to be, not now, not again,
though that doesn't mean I'm ready yet to let you go . . . what it does mean I don't think I know,
nor why I'm so ill-prepared for this insistence, this diligence with which consciousness afflicts us.

5.

I imagine you rising to something like heaven: my friend who died last year is there to welcome you.
He would know the place by now, he would guide you past the ledges and the thorns and terror.
Like a child I am, thinking of you rising in the rosy clouds and being up there with him,
being with your guru Baba, too, the three of you, all strong men, all partly wild children,
wandering through my comforting child's heaven, doing what you're supposed to do up there forever.
I tell myself it's silly, all of this, absurd, what we sacrifice in attaining rational mind,
but there you are again, glowing, grinning down at me from somewhere in the heart of being,
ablaze with wonder and a child's relief that this after all is how astonishingly it finishes.

6.

In my adult mind, I'm reeling, lost—I can't grasp anymore what I
    even think of death.
I don't know even what we hope for: ecstasy? bliss? or just release
    from being, not to suffer anymore.
At the grave, the boring rabbi said that you were going to eternal
    rest: rest? why rest?
Better say we'll be absorbed into the "Thou," better be consumed
    in light, in Pascal's "Fire!"
Or be taken to the Godhead, to be given meaning now, at last,
    the meaning we knew eluded us.
God, though, Godhead, Thou, even fire: all that is gone now,
    gone the dark night arguments,
gone the partial answers, the very formulations fail; I grapple for
    the questions as *they* fail.
Are we to be redeemed? When? How? After so much disbelief,
    will something be beyond us to receive us?

7.

Redemption is in life, "beyond" unnecessary: it is radically
    demeaning to any possible divinity
to demand that life be solved by yet another life: we're
    compressed into this single span of opportunity
for which our gratitude should categorically be presumed; this is
    what eternity for us consists of,
praise projected from the soul, as love first floods outward to the
    other then back into the self . . .
Yes, yes, I try to bring you to this, too; yes, what is over now is
    over, yes, we offer thanks,
for what you had, for what we all have: this portion of eternity is
    no different from eternity,
they both contract, expand, cast up illusion and delusion and all
    the comfort that we have is love,
praise, the grace not to ask for other than we have . . . yes and
    yes, but this without conviction, too.

8.

What if after, though, there is something else, will there be
    judgement, then, will it be retributive,

251

and if it is, if there is sin, will you have to suffer some hellish
    match with what your wrongs were?
So much good you did, your work, your many kindnesses, the
    befriendings and easy generosities.
What sort of evil do we dare imagine we'd have to take into those
    awful rectifications?
We hurt one another, all of us are helpless in that, with so much
    vulnerable and mortal to defend.
But that vulnerability, those defenses, our belittling jealousies,
    resentments, thrusts and spites
are the very image of our frailty: shouldn't our forgiveness for
    them and our absolution be assumed?
Why would our ultimate identities be burdened with absolutes,
    imperatives, lost discordant hymns?

9.

How ambiguous the triumphs of our time, the releasing of the
    intellect from myth and magic.
We've gained much, we think, from having torn away corrupted
    modes of aggrandizement and gigantism,
those infected and infecting errors that held sway over us and so
    bloated our complacencies
that we would willingly inflict even on our own flesh
    the crippling implications of our metaphysic.
How much we've had to pay, though, and how dearly
    had to suffer for our liberating dialectic.
The only field still left to us to situate our anguish and
    uncertainty is the single heart,
and how it swells, the heart, to bear the cries with which we used
    to fill the startled heavens.
Now we have the air, transparent, and the lucid psyche, and
    gazing inwards, always inwards, to the wound.

10.

The best evidence I have of you isn't my memory of you, or your
    work, although I treasure both,
and not my love for you which has too much of me in it as
    subject, but the love others bore you,

bear you, especially Vikki, who lived out those last hard years
    with you, the despairs and fears,
the ambivalences and withdrawals, until that final week of fever
    that soaked both your pillows.
Such a moving irony that your last days finally should have seared
    the doubt from both of you.
Sometimes it's hard to tell exactly whom I cry for—you, that last
    night as we left you there,
the way you touched her with such solicitude, or her, the
    desolation she keeps coming to:
*"I've been facing death, touched death, and now I have a ghost I
love and who loves me."*

11.

Genevieve, your precious Gen, doesn't quite know when to cry,
    or how much she's supposed to cry,
or how to understand those moments when it passes, when she's
    distracted into games and laughter
by the other kids or by the adults who themselves don't seem to
    grasp this terrible non-game.
At the cemetery, I'm asked to speak to her, to comfort her: never
    more impossible to move beyond cliché.
We both know we're helplessly embedded in ritual: you wanted
    her, I tell her, to be happy,
that's all, all her life, which she knows, of course, but nods to,
    as she also knows what I don't say,
the simplest self-revealing truths, your most awful fear, the brutal
    fact of your mortality:
how horribly it hurt to go from her, how rending not to
    be here as father and friend.

12.

Nothing better in the world than those days each year with you,
    your wife, my wife, the children,
at your old stone house in the Dordogne, looking over valleys one
    way, chestnut woods the other,
walks, long talks, visits to Lascaux and Les Eyzies,
    listening to each other read.

Our last night, though, I strolled into the moonless fields, it
    might have been a thousand centuries ago,
and something suddenly was with me: just beyond the boundaries
    of my senses presences were threatening,
something out of childhood, mine or man's; I felt my fear,
    familiar, unfamiliar, fierce,
might freeze me to the dark, but I looked back—I wasn't here
    alone, your house was there,
the zone of warmth it made was there, you yourself were there,
    circled in the waiting light.

13.

I seem to have to make you dead, dead again, to hold you in my
    mind so I can clearly have you,
because unless I do, you aren't dead, you're only living
    somewhere out of sight, I'll find you,
soon enough, no need to hurry, and my mind slips into this other
    tense, other grammar of condition,
in which you're welded to banalities of fact and time, the reality
    of what is done eluding me.
If you're accessible to me, how can you be dead? You are
    accessible to me, therefore . . . something else.
So what I end with is the death of death, but not as it would have
    been elaborated once,
in urgencies of indignation, resignation, faith: I have you neither
    here, nor there, but not not-anywhere:
the soul keeps saying that you might be here, or there—the
    incessant passions of the possible.

14.

Here's where we are: out behind the house in canvas chairs,
    you're reading new poems to me,
as you have so often, in your apartment, a park in
    Paris—anywhere: sidewalk, restaurant, museum.
You read musically, intensely, with flourishes, conviction: I might
    be the audience in a hall,
and you are unimaginably insecure, you so want me to admire
    every poem, every stanza, every line,

just as I want, need, you, too, to certify, approve, legitimize, and
all without reservation,
and which neither of us does, improving everything instead,
suggesting and correcting and revising,
as we knew, however difficult it was, we had to, in our barely
overcome but overcome competitiveness.
How I'll miss it, that so tellingly accurate envy sublimated into
warmth and brothership.

15.

Here's where we are: clearing clumps of shrub and homely brush
from the corner of your yard,
sawing down a storm-split plum tree, then hacking at the dozens
of malevolently armored maguey:
their roots are frail as flesh and cut as easily, but in the August
heat the work is draining.
Now you're resting; you're already weak although neither of us
will admit it to the other.
Two weeks later, you'll be dead, three weeks later, three months,
a year, I'll be doing this,
writing this, bound into this other labor that you loved so much
and that we also shared,
still share, somehow always will share now as we shared that
sunny late summer afternoon,
children's voices, light; you, pale, leaning on the wall, me tearing
at the vines and nettles.

16.

"A man's life cannot be silent; living is speaking, dying, too, is
speaking," so you wrote,
so we would believe, but still, how understand what the finished
life could have meant to say
about the dying and the death that never end, about potential
gone, inspiration unaccomplished,
love left to narrow in the fallacies of recall, eroding down to
partial gesture, partial act?
And we are lessened with it, amazed at how much our selfworth
and joy were bound into the other.

There are no consolations, no illuminations, nothing of that long
    awaited flowing toward transcendence.
There is, though, compensation, the simple certainty of having
    touched and having been touched.
The silence and the speaking come together, grief and gladness
    come together, the disparate fuse.

17.

Where are we now? Nowhere, anywhere, the two of us, the four
    of us, fifty of us at a *fête*.
Islands of relationships, friends and friends, the sweet, normal,
    stolid matrix of the merely human,
the circles of community that intersect within us, hold us, touch
    us always with their presence,
even as, today, mourning, grief, themselves becoming memory,
    there still is that within us which endures,
not in possession of the single soul in solitude, but in the
    covenants of affection we embody,
the way an empty house embodies elemental presences, and the
    way, attentive, we can sense them.
Breath held, heart held, body stilled, we attend, and they are
    there, covenant, elemental presence,
and the voice, in the lightest footfall, the eternal wind, leaf and
    earth, the constant voice.

18.

"The immortalities of the moment spin and expand; they seem to
    have no limits, yet time passes.
These last days here are bizarrely compressed, busy, and yet full
    of suppressed farewells . . ."
The hilly land you loved, lucerne and willow, the fields of
    butterfly and wasp and flower.
Farewell the crumbling house, barely held together by your
    ministrations, the shed, the pond.
Farewell your dumb French farmer's hat, your pads of yellow
    paper, your joyful, headlong scrawl.
The coolness of the woods, the swallow's swoop and whistle, the
    confident call of the owl at night.

Scents of dawn, the softening all night fire, char, ash, warm
embers in the early morning chill.
The moment holds, you move across the path and go, the light
lifts, breaks: goodbye, my friend, farewell.

Four from the Baudelaire series

by MICHAEL PALMER

from ACTS

A man undergoes pain sitting at a piano
knowing thousands will die while he is playing

He has two thoughts about this
If he should stop they would be free of pain

If he could get the notes right he would be free of pain
In the second case the first thought would be erased

causing pain

It is this instance of playing

he would say to himself
my eyes have grown hollow like yours

my head is enlarged
though empty of thought

Such thoughts destroy music
and this at least is good

* * *

Words say, Misspell and misspell your name
Words say, Leave this life

From the singer streams of color
but from you

a room within a smaller room
habits of opposite and alcove

Eros seated on a skull as on a throne
Words say, Timaeus you are time

A page is edging along a string
Never sleep never dream in this place

And altered words say
O is the color of this name

full of broken tones
silences we mean to cross one day

* * *

Desire was a quotation from someone.

Someone says, This this. Someone says, Is.

The tribe confronts a landscape of ice.

He says, I will see you in the parallel life.

She says, A miser has died from the cold; he spoke all
his sentences and meant no harm.

My voice is clipped, yours a pattern of dots.

Three unmailed ones have preceded this, a kind of illness.

Now I give you these lines without any marks, not even
a breeze

dumb words mangled by use

like reciting a lesson or the Lord's Prayer.

How lovely the unspeakable must be. You have only to say
it and it tells a story.

A few dead and a few missing

and the tribe to show you its tongue. It has only one.

* * *

There is much that is precise
between us, in the space

between us, two of this
and three of that

(after Vallejo)

LAMENT FOR THE MAKERS

by ROBERT PINSKY

from THE PARIS REVIEW

What if I told you the truth? What if I could?
The nuptial trek of the bower apes in May:
At night in the mountain meadow their clucking cries,

The reeking sulphur springs called Smoking Water,
Their skimpy ramparts of branches, pebbles and vines—
So slightly better than life, that snarl of weeds,

The small town bank by comparison is Rome,
With its four-faced bronze clock that chimes the hours,
The six great pillars surmounted by a frieze

Of Cronus eating his children—or trying to,
But one child bests him because we crave to live,
And if that too means dying then to die

Like Arthur when ladies take him in his barge
Across the misty water: better than life,
Or better than truly dying. In the movies

Smoking and driving are better, a city walk.
Grit on the sidewalk after a thaw, mild air.
I took the steps along the old stone trestle

Above the station, to the part of town
I never knew, old houses flush to the street
Curving uphill. Patches of ice in the shade.

What if I found an enormous secret there
And told you? We would still feel something next
Or even at the same time. Just as now. In Brooklyn,

Among the diamond cutters at their benches
Under high Palladian windows full of a storm,
One wearing headphones listens to the Talmud.

What if he happens to feel some saw or maxim
Inwardly? Then the young girl in her helmet,
An allegorical figure called The Present,

Would mime for us the action of coming to life:
A crease of shadow across her face, a cross,
And through the window, washing stumps of brick,

Exuberant streaks and flashes—literal lightning
Spilling out into a cheery violent rain.
Worship is tautological, with its Blessed

Art thou O Lord who consecrates the Sabbath
Unto us that we may praise it in thy name
Who blesses us with this thy holy day

That we may hallow it unto thy holy blessings . . .
And then the sudden curt command or truth:
God told him, Thou shalt cut thy foreskin off.

Then Abraham was better than life. The monster
Is better when he startles us. Hurt is vivid,
Sincerity visible in the self-inflicted wound.

Paws bleeding from their terrible climb, they weave
Garlands of mountain creeper for their bed.
The circle of desire, that aches to play

Or sings to hear the song passing. We sense
How much we might yet make things change, renewed
As when the lovers rise from their bed of play

And dress for supper and from a lewd embrace
Undress again. Weeds mottle the fissured pavement
Of the playground in a net of tufted lines

As sunset drenches a cinematic honey
Over the stucco terraces, copper and blue,
And the lone player cocks wrist and ball behind

His ear and studies the rusty rim again.
The half-ruined city around him throbs and glows
With pangs of allure that flash like the names of bars

Along San Pablo Avenue: Tee Tee's Lounge,
The Mallard Club, Quick's Little Alaska, Ruthie's,
Chiquita's, and inside the sweet still air

Of tobacco, malt and lime, and in some music
But in others only voices or even quiet,
And the player's arm pauses and pumps again.

CHEER

by LAURA JENSEN

from IRONWOOD

The nights are restless, days
are noise right into night.

That was not what I wanted
ever to say. I waited

until the day said *cheer.*
That moment, *cheer,* I had begun

picking a few things up
and was running a bath

and the thought
was the robin's song

the clay birds in the chimes
on the porch, saying *cheer up.*

It all came together, every part
so intimate and right

that the song is a song
without words. I waited some more

and remembered Marilyn Monroe
who died alone, a suicide.

*

Trim.

Rick-rac.
Lace
with a ribbon
latticed.

Just lace.
Edging
made with a ruffle.
Braid.

Quilting.
Smocking.

Lace daisy.
Child
needs the emblem
appliqued.

Make it all
small.
Doll
needs its soul

said
and decorated.
And
embroidered.

*

My little friends
were blonde
or dark and some
were remarkable in their
cleanliness, brushed
so that was their essence.

The fairness of us
was unmistakable.
Marilyn Monroe—
all of us knew she was
beautiful. A girl named
Marilyn had the same
name as she.
We knew her, she
was like one of us
and any of us
could believe. She made it
seem real, and fun.
We may look at old photos,
almost a photo
of someone we knew,
although we were not
someone she knew, and say
she was so pretty, so
small, her hair like a
beautiful flower, why—
and the pictures stay,
a loveliness about us.

But Katherine Hepburn
is still just
as lovely, Greta Garbo
is still just
so in the photos,
they are still lovely,
their names are still
lovely to us.

                    *

We may say,
I suppose, and I suppose.
And, what happened?
Someone should have
eased her, we say, when. Was she
cheated, did someone

cheat her? Did we?
We suppose, and we suppose
and that loveliness did
not stay alive
to stay with us, just
the loveliness alive.
But the child
she was, complete
and completed?

What was
does not have to be
what had to happen.

                    *

A leaf flies off
the tree.
It hits the house
like a rubber glove.

Little frail thing
that is a house—
please do not fall
during the winter.

I go and put on socks.

Yellow light
falls through the trees.

JUSTICE WITHOUT PASSION

by JANE HIRSHFIELD

from ZYZZYVA

My neighbor's son, learning piano,
moves his fingers through the passages
a single note at a time, each lasting an equal interval,
each of them loud, distinct,
deliberate as a camel's walk through sand.
For him now, all is dispassion, a simple putting in place;
and so, giving equal weight to each mark in his folded-back book,
bending his head towards the difficult task,
he is like a soldier or a saint: blank-faced, and given wholly
to an obedience he does not need to understand.
He is even-handed, I think to myself,
and so, just. But in what we think of as music
there is no justice, nor in the evasive beauty of this boy,
glimpsed through his window across the lawn,
nor in what he will become, years from now,
whatever he will become.
For now though, it is the same to him:
right note or wrong, he plays only for playing's sake
through the late afternoon, through stumbling and error,
through children's songs, Brahms,
long-rehearsed, steady progressions,
as he learns the ancient laws—that human action is judgment,
each note struggling with the rest.
That justice lacking passion fails, betrays.

TENDERNESS

by STEPHEN DUNN

from POETRY

Back then when so much was clear
   and I hadn't learned
young men learn from women

what it feels like to feel just right,
   I was twenty-three,
she thirty-four, two children, a husband

in prison for breaking someone's head.
   Yelled at, slapped
around, all she knew of tenderness

was how much she wanted it, and all
   I knew
were back seats and a night or two

in a sleeping bag in the furtive dark.
   We worked
in the same office, banter and loneliness

leading to the shared secret
   that to help
National Biscuit sell biscuits

was wildly comic, which led to my body
    existing with hers
like rain water that's found its way

underground to water it naturally joins.
    I can't remember
ever saying the exact word, tenderness,

though she did. It's a word I see now
    you must be older to use,
you must have experienced the absence of it

often enough to know what silk and deep balm
    it is
when at last it comes. I think it was terror

at first that drove me to touch her
    so softly,
then selfishness, the clear benefit

of doing something that would come back
    to me twofold,
and finally, sometime later, it became

reflexive and motiveless in the high
    ignorance of love.
Oh abstractions are just abstract

until they have an ache in them. I met
    a woman never touched
gently, and when it ended between us,

I had new hands and new sorrow,
    everything it meant
to be a man changed, unheroic, floating.

EPITHALAMIUM

by LESLIE ADRIENNE MILLER

from OPEN PLACES

I have seen them introduce the silver
twisted bits, spikes and wires into the mouths
of horses with the skill and care
the young learn in love. There is little
or no philosophy to this act. The horse will
take the bit. The girl will rise over him
like a moon because she is beautiful
and he does not care if she can or cannot stay.
I've watched these girls for days in the barn,
passing their knowing fingers over the bodies
of the animals, chiding the neurotic
and most beautiful one called Incomparable
who rocks for hours against his stall, silent
and closed as an autistic child. I have seen
the smallest girl stand before a chest
wide and hard as a truck bumper, and shove
the creature off balance for some slight
misconduct. She is intimate with every
muscle and bone that longs to crush her;
she will marry the back of the beast
because it is the only way to be with him in this world.

When it is my turn to ride, the young flutter
around me as if I am going to ascend.
They towel my boots and stirrup irons,
say I am happy, he is happy, if we leave

the ground for a moment, it will be joy
that throws his head, joy that rings
the silver bits and chains, throws the clods
of earth above the dreaming bleachers.
It is part of the art for horse and rider
to move out looking haughty and pained
as martyrs. I look down at the meaty shoulders
that take us forward, two creatures
pursued by something we can't stop to think about—
what we have in common now is our wish to exceed
time, that scream or storm behind us
far more complicated than death. I can almost
believe we are ahead of it, seeing ourselves
with those eyes that are not the heart's eyes,
not the soul's eyes or even the intellect's,
but the eyes in our flesh that see,
without mirror or word, that beauty lifts itself
ever so slightly and moves ahead of its own end.

MAY, 1968

by SHARON OLDS

from POETRY

The Dean of the University said
the neighborhood people could not cross campus
until the students gave up the buildings
so we lay down in the street,
we said The cops will enter this gate
over our bodies. Spine-down on the cobbles—
hard bed, like a carton of eggs—
I saw the buildings of New York City
from dirt level, they soared up and stopped,
chopped off cleanly—beyond them the sky
black and neither sour nor sweet, the
night air over the island.
The mounted police moved near us
delicately. Flat out on our backs
we sang, and then I began to count,
12, 13, 14, 15, I
counted again, 15, 16, one
month since the day on that deserted beach when we
used nothing, 17, 18, my
mouth fell open, my hair in the soil,
if my period did not come tonight
I was pregnant. I looked up at the sole of the
cop's shoe, I looked up at the
horse's belly, its genitals—if they
took me to Women's Detention and did the
exam on me, jammed the unwashed

speculum high inside me, the guard's
three fingers—supine on Broadway, I looked
up into the horse's tail like a
dark filthed comet. All week, I had
wanted to get arrested, longed to
give myself away. I lay in the
tar, one brain in my head and another
tiny brain at the base of my tail and I
stared at the world, good-luck iron
arc of the gelding's shoe, the cop's
baton, the deep curve of the animal's
belly, the buildings streaming up
away from the earth. I knew I should get up and
leave, stand up to muzzle level, to the
height of the soft velvet nostrils and
walk away, turn my back on my
friends and danger, but I was a coward so I
lay there looking up at the sky,
black vault arched above us, I
lay there gazing up at God, at his
underbelly, till it turned deep blue and then
silvery, colorless, *Give me this one*
night, I said, *and I'll give this child*
the rest of my life, the horses' heads
drooping, dipping, until they slept in a
dark circle around my body and my daughter.

A LITTLE DEATH

by ARTHUR SMITH

from CRAZYHORSE

Anyone almost anywhere on the walkway could have
   heard it—I did—
That boom-like, intermittent grunting
   pained with effort, resonating suddenly like a foghorn
Through the late-summer, Sunday afternoon drowse
   of the Knoxville City Zoo.

Here, I thought, was an animal
   so overwhelmed
The most it could hope for was to bellow into being
   that intensity—those waves mounting, even then
Bearing it away. A group already ringed
   the tortoise pen,

Where earlier, leaning over a barrier of logs, patting,
   and then more boldly
Stroking the larger of the two, his fatherly, reptilian neck
   craning—distended, really, upward,
Tolerantly, it seemed—I had reckoned
   him old,

So old, in fact, that crowding
   back around the pen,
I expected to find him dead or, worse, still living,
   convulsed
With those horribly irreversible last spasms for air.

He was "dying," to be sure, clambered up
   and balanced—to say the least—precariously on
The other's high-humped shell,
   his stump-like front feet extended forward,
Grasping, as they were able, the other's weathered carapace,
   for leverage,

His own neck dangling, gaze floating
   vacantly downward,
And his mouth agape, saliva
   swaying on short, thick threads only inches
From the other's bony face. And,
   all along,

The noise. It wasn't pretty
Though it was soon over—
This "little death" referred to in our youth,
   snickeringly,

As "makin' bacon," back when all knowledge
Belonged, by fiat, to the young, but here witnessed
   in the frank
Generation of matter, all amenities
   beside the fact—

The male beached on his own bulk, panting, less than
   tolerant, now,
Of the heavy-handed petting,
And the female, unencumbered again,
   scooting rather

Indifferently toward the mud-bracketed pond
   tattered with froth-pads
Of algae, immersing herself as far as the shallow water
Would allow.

SEQUENCE

by MARILYN NELSON

from NEW VIRGINIA REVIEW

HIS MOTHER

For months the letters from his mother came,
that first year of our lawful wedded life.
She didn't even want to know my name,
much less what I was like, his nightmare wife.
He wouldn't read them to me, but I knew
her letters told him that she'd been betrayed
by his transgression of her worst taboo.
She begged him to renege the vows he'd made.
Dumbstruck with pain, he struggled toward a choice
between love for his mother and for me,
turning from both of us without a voice
to ask either of us for sympathy.
Its tongue cut out by my guilt and his loss,
our love hung silent on his mother's cross.

HOW DID I LOVE HIM?

I loved him with a passion put to use
in childhood's longing for identity.
I loved him for his detailed and profuse
remembered past: It gave a past to me.
I loved him for the thin potato soup,
the push-meat sandwiches after the war,

his mother's sneaking up on him, to swoop
him up and wrestle him to the floor.
I loved his college and his army days,
his trips to capitols I'd never seen;
the operas and concerts, films and plays
I saw as he described them, with a keen
and narcissistic vision: With what grace
I bent to kiss his sky, and saw my face!

FROGS

That spring I dreamed incessantly of frogs.
Their silly croaking lulled me every night;
sometimes they swam through me as polliwogs
or sperm bearing the chromosome for blight.
They wanted me to kiss their ugliness,
beseeching me with staring, swollen eyes.
Caught in the dream, I had to acquiesce:
My children, in dream-logic's weird disguise,
they wanted me to love them and conceive.
In autumn when the test read positive,
he told me if I had it, he would leave.
I loved him: That's the thing I can't forgive.
Feet in the stirrups, riding on my back,
I loved him. Even as my world went black.

THE CIRCUS

The woman whom I hoped to make my friend
invited us to meet her and her kids
three hours' drive away, so we could spend
an evening at the circus. There, amid
the awe and shouts of laughter, I forgot
how miserable I'd been an hour before.
Like Guinevere in love in Camelot,
I was enchanted by the lions' roar,
the trained pigs, and this woman's youngest son
whose giggle was a melody of bells

284

which shivered joy through every ganglion
of my unhappy body, made me swell
almost to bloom. Then he said he'd prefer
if I drove her kids home: He'd ride with her.

WHAT I KNEW

The clash of cultures—of my ignorance
and his clear, European intellect—
embarrassed and enraged me. What a dunce
I thought I was. My fledgling self-respect
disintegrated daily. He was shocked
by my miseducation, so I'd shrink
when he made any overture to talk,
because I was afraid of what he'd think.
The insecurity I'd felt at school—
where I got A's, I thought, for being black
when all the time I knew I was a fool—
and deeply buried in myself, came back.
My habit of surrender grew so strong
he never knew when I knew he was wrong.

EVERYDAY

I never felt the ordinary rage
my friends confess to over coffee cups.
I never had to go on a rampage
as they do, when their husbands won't clean up
the bathroom, when they don't take out the trash,
when they leave dirty laundry on the floor.
My husband whipped up dinners with panache;
he gladly tackled any household chore.
We went for months without an argument,
without a missed beat in our clockwork life,
with nothing to take ill, or to resent:
my perfect husband and his perfect wife.
For months, I could have nothing to complain
to him about, except my constant pain.

SISTERS

The schoolbus drove us home from highschool, where
we got off in the Negro neighborhood
and several times a week there was a fight:
One sister called another sister "hoe,"
pulled out black handfuls of her straightened hair,
clawed at her face and hands, and ripped her shirt.
I walked home. I believed in sisterhood.
I still do, after thirty years, although
I'll never understand why several white
sisters walked on me as if I was dirt.
We were all sisters, feminists, I thought,
forgetting what those cat-fights should have taught.
I was too well brought-up, too middle class
to call a heifer out, and whup her ass.

BY THE TRACK

We came home to our lives, and home to all
the friends we'd half-forgotten. Home to her.
She was unhappy; at midnight, she'd call
to talk with him. I listened: a voyeur.
I saw her notes to him, counted her gifts,
and plotted routes by which I could escape.
It wasn't her fault: She'd been set adrift,
and had no sextant other than her shape.
One day, we walked beside the railroad track.
I thinking *murder, lawyers, money, death.*
He reached his goal, decided to turn back,
and mused, "I think, before my fortieth
birthday, I might like to have a child . . ."
He didn't understand why I ran wild.

COLOR

For him, I gave away my father's name.
He gave away his mother's love for me.

286

So each of us was partially to blame
for the other's lost, and found identity.
I tried to find myself, in our old car,
by looking at his profile as he drove
to see if we were somehow similar,
had more in common than the kitchen stove
and our Breughel print, which only shared a room.
I asked him once what he was thinking of;
I should have known his answer spelled our doom,
for nothing I could think of sounded duller:
He said, "Of Goethe's writings about color."

RECURRENT DREAM

My father came back regularly, to see
how I was doing, long after he died.
He came in dreams in which he lovingly
explained that he'd returned to be my guide
through the important shadows. I awoke
and all day saw day's light intensified.
The last time, in an aureole of smoke
that somehow shone, he stood outside the door.
I didn't open it. Instead, I spoke:
"I'm grown up; I don't need you any more."
He smiled and nodded, saying, "Yes, I know."
Last night I had another visitor:
Love's ghost, as though compelled by need, as though
it knew the way. My love, I'm grown. Let go.

INTERPRETATION OF A POEM BY FROST

by THYLIAS MOSS

from EPOCH

A young black girl stopped by the woods,
so young she knew only one man: Jim Crow
but she wasn't allowed to call him Mister.
The woods were his and she respected his boundaries
even in the absence of fence.
Of course she delighted in the filling up
of his woods, she so accustomed to emptiness,
to being taken at face value.
This face, her face eternally the brown
of declining autumn, watches snow inter the grass,
cling to bark making it seem indecisive
about race preference, a fast-to-melt idealism.
With the grass covered, black and white are the only options,
polarity is the only reality; corners aren't neutral
but are on edge.
She shakes off the snow, defiance wasted
on the limited audience of horse.
The snow does not hypnotize her as it wants to,
as the blond sun does in making too many prefer daylight.
She has promises to keep,
the promise that she bear Jim no bastards,
the promise that she ride the horse only as long
as it is willing to accept riders,

the promise that she bear Jim no bastards,
the promise to her face that it not be mistaken as shadow,
and miles to go, more than the distance from Africa to Andover,
more than the distance from black to white
before she sleeps with Jim.

FOR YOU

by JIM MOORE

from THE FREEDOM OF HISTORY (Milkweed Editions)

I know it sounds too much like poetry,
but it was dusk that made me a felon,
a winter evening in Moline, Illinois.
The next day I quoted Whitman
to my draft board, "Dismiss
whatever insults your own soul,"
and sent my draft card back to them.
I can still feel the cold metal
on the mailbox, see the park
with its oaks, the black winter sky
so close, so distant,
as I dropped the letter inside
and turned quickly away.

For two years I'd argued the War,
drinking instant coffee with a man
who wore the same blue velour shirt so often
it's all I remember of him now.
We took turns arguing one way,
then another about "what to do."
We sat in the basement kitchen
of a boarding house.
Sometimes we yelled,
sometimes we sat silently, our hands
around our mugs of coffee,
our hearts confused. Deferments

from the draft meant we were the men
who could afford to choose a future.
And we had so wanted to go on drifting,
floating on the moment's shifting current
as we learned to give the poems we tried to write
a chance to rise, waveringly,
into their own shapes, existences
born of dreams, not arguments. I didn't want
to chant slogans. I didn't want
to be "right." To judge.
And these were more than choices,
these were entire lives, futures
that could never be redeemed—
or so we felt then in the midst
of a slaughtering time.
Back and forth we went, the guy
in the blue velour shirt and I,
all of us who read Emerson and Thoreau,
ate frozen dinners, drank
3.2 beer, played pinball or pool—
any game at all that would give us
a few hours away from ourselves,
those of us who underlined
CIVIL DISOBEDIENCE and wrote excited comments
in the margins late at night,
rather than actually take to the streets.

I lived alone in Moline, Illinois,
one dusty and dimly lit flight
above a greeting card shop
run by a likeable red-faced
John Bircher. It was the first year
I got paid for teaching, paid
for being excited
about what I believed in,
for having opinions
I couldn't give away
to my friend in the velour shirt.
Then two students quit school
and within months were dead

in Vietnam. A working class
college, our basement classroom
was in an old pentecostal church.
The mix of Sunday School
and poverty was too much
on Monday mornings, the students
almost asleep, sprawled
on the freshly waxed floor,
huddled near their classrooms
like refugees waiting for their morning soup
rather than for classes to begin.

I was the razzle dazzle guy
from the Big U
in Iowa City. I didn't
own a tie, I lived
in a VW bus all fall,
I had opinions that gave off
the glitter of newly minted
funny money. To the students
I was a classy eccentric
and I had them with me from the first,
those future postal clerks
and nurses, mechanics
and would-be writers
with their mixed bag of Sartre
and letter jackets, hickeys
and acid and—finally—
of life and death.

The second student who died
had sat in the back of the room,
chair tilted against the wall,
his long hair spread out behind him
like a scraggly fan. He often
brought his guitar to class
in a black case, and wrote his poems
on cheap yellow paper. He wanted
to know about mileage
from my bus: these

were the only details I remembered
when his girlfriend told me he had been killed.

It was winter by then
and I was living alone
above the greeting card shop.
After that second student's death
I spent the week-end by myself.
I was reading Suzuki at the time
and wanted to believe in something,
even if it was only the pull
and release of my own breath
as I sat cross-legged, meditating
best I knew how. I liked Zen.
For someone raised an Anglican
it seemed the closest thing
to all that upper class tastefulness, so
lovely, so earnest in its own careful way.
While I sat, meditating, I felt
even lonelier: all my enthusiasm
in the classroom, my voluble
and spontaneous love of poetry
that fit itself so nicely
into the 50 minute school hour,
my a la mode hiking boots.
I thought of that dead boy
with his guitar and his questions,
and the careful but wasted economy
of his cheap yellow paper
and I felt sick to my soul,
for all my talk of Thoreau and Whitman.
I wanted to be a citizen again, to Pledge
Allegiance to something with the faith
I'd felt in 4th grade, facing
the flag behind Miss Rodger's desk.
It was my country, too,
not just the John Bircher's downstairs
with his saccharine greeting cards
and his private gun collection.
That weekend I drank green tea,

believing it more Japanese than Lipton Orange.
I stared at the gray clouds
of dust under the bed, I followed
the flow of my breath
in and out of my stomach—
like a golden river, Suzuki said.
For two days I did nothing
but alternately sit and then hobble
on legs permanently sore
from being crossed so much.
I quit thinking about everything: the draft,
my dead students,
the future, the past. Was it
a spiritual state? I don't know,
but I felt as if I'd grown 3 inches overnight
and everything I saw
looked slightly different,
smaller and further away,
the way a dream does
as you wake up
and it begins to leave you.
Towards evening of the second day
I'd had enough of the hush,
pause, hush, of my own breath
and the shooting pain of ankles
and knees. I wanted out
and away from those motionless dust balls.
It felt wonderful to walk into evening
alone in Moline, Illinois,
in the middle of America,
the weightless center
of a centerless country.

I walked and I looked.
I saw some men sitting at a bar.
I stood outside, staring
through the small pane of glass
at the top of the door.
Everything moved so slowly:
my breath still deep

and even, holding me rooted
in the evening air like an anchor
when men fish from a boat and seem to drift,
but are only rocking back and forth
between one known place and another.
I saw the men, heads bent
toward the neon light of a beer sign
behind the bar: a man with a lasso
in one hand and a beer in another.
The lasso was red, the beer golden.
A bartender stood beside the sign,
white-aproned, holding
a pencil.
I watched as he gestured
towards the bent heads of the men
sitting before him. One of them
nodded up and down and that simple,
barely noticeable sign of agreement
brought tears to my eyes
and an assent of my own
where I stood anchored
by my own steady breath.
I walked on, went up the hill
that rose steeply away from the river
near where I lived. A sled
had been left out for the night
on a front yard's thin crust of snow.
I saw this ordinary sight
framed in a deepening gray
like a letter in a phrase,
still undeciphered, but so important
that once I understood it
it would change the meaning of all other words.

As I walked slowly up the hill,
other objects I saw seemed part
of the same phrase:
a porch swing drawn up on its two chains
waiting near the roof for spring;
a car with a broken windshield

295

glittering under a streetlight
like the traces of a phosphorescent map;
the corner of an old newspaper
frozen into an iced-over sidewalk.

"For you," I found myself saying
over and over as I neared the top of the hill.
My breath came in short gasps now,
"For you, for you."
It became a kind of greed.
I couldn't get enough
of the men with their bent heads in the bar,
the sled, the swing. They gave
and I took.
I wanted it to go on forever,
this greed for the world. I knew
that it was for the sake of a sled
left behind in the moment of impatience
for dinner that I would go to prison.
Not just for political reasons,
not even for moral ones:
not for reasons at all,
or not the kind I could explain
to a draft board. For you,
sled. For you, bent heads.
For you, for you.

If, in a moment of peace, the world
could yield up such signs,
then I wanted an inner peace,
both permanent and casual.
But I could not begin
until I settled with the War.
It was that dusk, that walk, that sled
that convinced me their world could sustain me
if only I could abandon my soul-searching
and endless arguments over what to do,
like a character in a Chekhov story
so busy talking outside
on a cold winter's night

he almost dies of frostbite
while trying to prove the existence of God.
If it meant going to prison,
so be it. There, too, there would be
ordinary sights that would sustain me.
Or so I told myself
in that moment when I believed so deeply
in the strangely calming power
that came from seeing clearly
into the heart of everyday life.
I stood at the top of the hill, alone,
surrounded by what I loved.
I looked down towards the Mississippi,
black except where a bridge curved
through the night, and I did not know
what the future would bring
or what it was inside me
that would not let go
of my two new words, "For you."

THE LOVE OF TRAVELLERS

(Doris, Sandra and Sheryl)

by ANGELA JACKSON

from CALLALOO

At the rest stop on the way to Mississippi
we found the butterfly mired in the oil slick;
its wings thick
and blunted. One of us, tender in the finger tips,
smoothed with a tissue the oil
that came off only a little;
the oil-smeared wings like lips colored with lipstick
blotted before a kiss.
So delicate the cleansing of the wings
I thought the color soft as watercolors would wash off
under the method of her mercy for something so slight
and graceful, injured, beyond the love of travellers.

It was torn then, even after her kindest work,
the almost-moth exquisite charity could not mend
what weighted the wing, melded with it,
then ruptured it in release.
The body of the thing lifted out of its place
between the washed wings.
Imagine the agony of a self separated by gentlest repair.

"Should we kill it?" One of us said. And I said yes.
But none of us had the nerve.
We walked away, the last of the oil welding the butterfly
to the wood of the picnic table.
The wings stuck out and quivered when wind went by.
Whoever found it must have marveled at this.
And loved it for what it was and
had been.
I think, meticulous mercy is the work of travellers,
and leaving things as they are
punishment or reward.

I have died for the smallest things.
Nothing washes off.

FURIOUS VERSIONS

by LI-YOUNG LEE

from IRONWOOD

1.

These days I waken in the used light
of someone's spent life, to discover
the birds have stripped my various names of meaning entire:
the sparrow by quarrel,
the dove by grievance.
I lie
dismantled. I feel
the hours. Do they veer
to dusk? Or dawn?
Will I rise and go
out into an American city?
Or walk down to the wilderness sea?
I might run with wife and children to the docks
to bribe an officer for our lives
and perilous passage.
Then I'd answer
in an oceanic tongue
to *Professor, Capitalist, Husband, Father.*
Or I might have one more
hour of sleep before my father
comes to take me
to his snowbound church,
where I dust the pews, and he sets candles

out the color of teeth.
That means I was born in Bandung, 1958;
on my father's back, in borrowed clothes,
I came to America.
And I wonder
if I imagined those wintry mornings
in a dim nave, since
I'm the only one
who's lived to tell it,
and I confuse
the details: was it my father's skin
which shone like teeth?
Was it his heart that lay snowbound?
But if I waken to a jailor
rousting me to meet my wife and son,
come to see me in my cell,
where I eat the chocolate
and smoke the cigarettes they smuggle,
what name do I answer to?
And did I stand
on the train from Chicago to Pittsburgh
so my fevered son could sleep? Or did I
open my eyes
and see my father's closed face
rocking above me?
Memory revises me.
Even now a letter
comes from a place
I don't know, from someone
with my name,
and postmarked years ago,
while I await
injunctions from the light,
or the dark;
I wait for shapeliness
limned, or dissolution.
Is paradise due, or narrowly missed,
until another thousand years?
I wait

in a blue hour
and faraway sound of hammering,
and on a page a poem begun, something
about to be dispersed,
something about to come into being.

2.

I wake to black
and one sound—
neither a heart
approaching, nor one shoe
coming, but something
less measured, never
arriving. I wander
a house I thought I knew,
I walk the halls as if the halls
of that other
mansion, my father's heart.
I follow the sound
past a black window
where a bird sits like a blacker
question: *To where? To where? To where?*
Past my mother's room where her
knees creak, *Meaning, Meaning.*
While a rose
rattles at my ear, *Where
is your father?*
And the silent house
booms, *Gone. Long gone.*

A door jumps
out from shadows,
then jumps away. This
is what I've come to find:
the back door, unlatched.
Tooled by an insular wind, it
slams and slams
without meaning
to and without meaning.

3.

Moonlight and high wind.
Dark poplars toss, insinuate the sea.
The yard heaves, perplexed
with shadows massed
and shadows falling away.
Before me a tree, distinct
in its terrible
aspects, emerges, reels, sinks,
and is lost.
At my feet, shapes
tear free, separate darknesses
mingle, then crawl to the common
dark, lost.
At the brink
of my own now-here-now-gone
shadow stand three flowers,
or two flowers,
and one's shade.
Impatients? Alyssum?
Something forbids me to speak
of them in this
upheaval of forms and
voices—voices
now, plaintive, anxious.
Now I hear
interrogation in vague tongues.
I hear ocean sounds and a history of rain.
Somewhere is a streetlamp
and my brother never coming.
Somewhere a handful of hair and a lost box of letters.
And everywhere, fire,
corridors of fire, brick and barbed wire.
Soldiers sweep the streets
for my father. My mother
hides him, haggard,
in the closet.
The booted ones herd us
to the sea.

Waves furl boats
lovingly, and bodies
going out, farther out.
Now my father holds my hand, he says
Don't forget any of this.
A short, bony-faced corporal
asks him politely, deferring to class,
*What color suit, Professor, would you like
to be buried in? Brown or blue?*
A pistol butt turns my father's spit to blood.
It was a tropical night.
It was half a year of sweat and fatal memory.
It was one year of fire
out of the world's diary of fires,
flesh-laced, mid-century fire,
teeth and hair infested,
napalm-dressed and skull-hung fire,
and imminent fire, an elected
fire come to rob me
of my own death, my damp bed
in the noisy earth,
my rocking toward a hymn-like night.
How, then, may I
speak of flowers
here, where
a world of forms convulses,
here, amidst
drafts—yet
these are not drafts
toward a future form, but
furious versions
of the here and now . . .

Here, now, one
should say nothing
of three flowers,
only enter with them
in silence, fear, and hope,
into the next nervous one hundred human years.

4.

But I see these flowers, and they seize
my mind, and I
can no more un-see
them than I can un-dream
this, no more than
the mind can stop
its wandering over the things
of the world, snagged on the world
as it is.
The mind is
a flowering
cut into time,
a rose,

the wandering rose
that scaled the red brick
of my father's house in Pennsylvania.
What was its name?
Each bloom, unsheathed
in my mind, urges, *Remember!*
The Paul's Scarlet!
Paul, who promised the coming
of the perfect and the departing of the imperfect,
Else why stand we in jeopardy every hour?

I thought of Paul
the morning I stepped out my door
and into an explosion of wings,
thudding and flapping, heavenly blows.
Blinded, I knew the day
of fierce judgement and rapture
had come. I thought
even the dooryard rose,
touched by wind, trembling
in anticipation
of first petal-fall,
announcement of death's commencement,
would take back

305

its flowering, claim glory.
So the rose and I
stood, terrified, at the beginning
of a new and beloved era.

It was pigeons, only pigeons
I'd startled from the porch rafters.
But the dread and the hope
I carry with me
like lead and wings
let me momentarily believe otherwise.

True, none of this
has to do with heaven since the sight
of those heavy birds flying away
reminded me
not so much of what's to come
as of what passes
away: birds,
hours, words, gestures, persons,
a drowned guitar in spring,
smell of lacquered wood
and wax when I prayed as a boy,
a pale cheek cut
by a green leaf,
the taste of blood
in a kiss,
someone whispering into someone's ear,
someone crying behind a door,
a clock dead at noon.
My father's hand
cupping my chin, weighing
tenderness between us,
pressing my mother's hip, weighing desire,
and cleaving a book open.
On the right of his hand the words:
The Song of Songs, which is Solomon's.
Let him kiss me with the kisses of his mouth.
On the left of his hand the words:
For God shall bring every work

into judgement with every secret thing,
whether it be good,
or whether it be evil.
Outside his window, his
rose, aphid-eaten, bad-weather-wracked,
stem and thorn,
crook and bramble groping,
gripping brick, each sickly
bloom uttering, *I shall not die!*
before it's dispersed.

5.

My father wandered,
me beside him, human,
erect, unlike
roses. And unlike
Paul, we had no mission,
though he loved Paul, read him continually
as republic to republic,
oligarchy to anarchy to democracy we arrived.

Once, while I walked
with my father, a man
reached out, touched his arm, said, *Kuo Yuan?*
The way he stared, and spoke my father's name,
I thought he meant to ask, *Are you a dream?*
Here was the sadness of ten thousand miles,
of an abandoned house in Nan Jing,
where my father helped a blind man
wash his dead wife's newly dead body,
then bury it, while bombs
fell, and trees raised
charred arms and burned.
Here was a man who remembered
the sound of another's footfalls
well enough to call to him
after twenty years,
on a sidewalk in America.
America, where, in Chicago, Little Chinatown,

who should I see
on the corner of Argyle and Broadway
but Li Bai and Du Fu, those two
poets of the wanderer's heart.
Folding paper boats,
they sent them swirling
down little rivers of gutter water.
Gold-toothed, cigarettes rolled in their sleeves,
they noted my dumb surprise:
What did you expect? Where else should we be?

6.

It goes on and it goes on,
the ceaseless inventions, incessant
constructions and deconstructions
of shadows over black grass,
while, overhead, poplars
rock and nod,
wrestle *No* and *Yes*, contend
moon, no moon.

To think of the sea
is to hear in the sound of trees
sound of the sea's work,
the wave's labor to change
the shore, not for shore's sake, nor wave's,
certainly not for me,
hundreds of miles from sea,
unless you count
my memory, my traverse
of sea one way to here.
I'm like my landlocked poplars; far
from water, I'm full of the sound of water.

But sea-sound differs from the sound of trees
in that it owns
a rhythm, almost
a meaning, but
no human story,

and so is like
the sound of trees,
tirelessly building
as wind builds, rising
as wind rises, steadily gathering
to nothing, quiet, and
the wind rising again.
The night grows
miscellaneous in the sound of trees.
But I own a human story,
whose very telling
remarks loss.
The characters survive through the telling,
the teller survives
by his telling; by his voice
brinking silence does he survive.
Yet, no one
can tell without cease
our human
story, and so we
lose, lose.

Yet, behind the sound
of trees is another
sound. Sometimes, lying
awake, or standing
like this in the yard, I hear it. It
ties our human telling
to its course
by momentum, and ours
is merely part
of its unbroken
stream, the human
and otherwise simultaneously
told. The past
doesn't fall away, the past
joins the greater
telling, and is.
At times its theme seems
murky, other times clear. Always

death is a phrase, but just
a phrase, since nothing is ever
lost, and lives
are fulfilled by subsequence.
Listen, you can hear it: indescribable,
neither grief nor joy, neither mine nor yours . . .

But I'll not widow the world.
I'll tell my human
tale, tell it against
the current of that vaster, that
inhuman telling.
I'll measure time by losses and destructions.
Because the world
is so rich in detail, all of it so frail;
because all I love is imperfect;
because my memory's flaw
isn't in retention but organization;
because no one asked.
I'll tell once and for all
how someone lived.
Born on an island ruled by a petty soldier,
he was wrapped in bright cloth
and bound to his mother's hip,
where he rode until he could walk.
He did not utter a sound his first three years,
and his parents frowned.
Then, on the night of their first exile,
he spoke out in complete sentences
a Malaysian so lovely it was true song.
But when he spoke again
it was plain, artless, and twenty years later.
He wore a stranger's clothes,
he married a woman who tasted of iron and milk.
They had two sons, the namesakes
of a great emperor and a good-hearted bandit.
And always he stood erect to praise or grieve,
and knelt to live a while
at the level of his son's eyes.

7.

Tonight, someone, unable
to see in one darkness,
has shut his eyes
to see into another.
Among the sleepers, he is one
who doesn't sleep.
Know him by his noise.
Hear the nervous
scratching of his pencil,
sound of a rasping
file, a small
restless percussion, a soul's
minute chewing,
the old poem
birthing itself
into the new
and murderous century.

INCIDENT AT IMURIS

by ALBERTO RÍOS

from THE LIME ORCHARD WOMAN (Sheep Meadow Press)

Mr. Aplinio Morales has reported this:
They were not after all
Watermelons, it was not the wild
Fruit patch they at first had thought;
In the manner of what moths do,
These were cocoons, as every child has
Picked up and squeezed,
But from in these came and they saw
Thousands of green-winged half moths,
Half moths and not exactly butterflies,
Not exactly puppies—
A name for them did not exist here.
Half this and some of that,
What was familiar and what might be European.
And when the fruit rotted, or seemed to rot—
Almost all of them on the same day—
From out of each husk the beasts flew
Fat, equipped, at ease
So that they were not so much
Hungry as curious.
The watermelons had been generous homes.
These were not begging animals,
Not raccoons, nor rats,
Not second or third class;
These were the kind that if human
They would have worn dinner jackets

And sniffed, not at anything in particular,
Just as general commentary.
Animals who had time for tea.
Easily distracted and obviously educated
In some inexplicable manner,
The beasts of the watermelons left
The same day, after putting their heads
In windows, bored already
From chasing the horses
And drinking too much from the town well.

XV

MILES WEEPING

by MICHAEL WATERS

from AMERICAN POETRY REVIEW

To hear Miles weep
    for the first time, the notes bent
        back into his spent frame to keep
    them from soaring away—
I had to click the phonograph off
    and hug myself to stop the shaking.
        I'd recognized a human cry
    beyond any longing given a name.
If ever he let go that grief
    he might not touch his horn again.
        That cry rose in another country,
    full-throated in awkward English.
I still have the envelope, unstamped,
    addressed to "Mother/Father," its oily
        scrap of paper torn from a primer,
    the characters like the inky
root-hairs scrawling the washed-out soil.
    Lek—every boy's nickname—
        wrote he was "to be up against,"
    meaning, I guess, that his future
was end-stopped, one unbroken line
    of tabletops waiting to be wiped.
        He'd walked miles along the coast
    to find us combing the beach, then
stood, little Buddhist, with bowed head
    while we read his letter, composed

with the help of the schoolmaster.
How could we deny the yearning
ambition to abandon the impossible
land of his fathers, to begin again?
We could only refuse in a silent way.
When someone asked Miles Davis
why he wouldn't play ballads anymore,
he replied, "Because I love them too much."
All that we never say to each other.
The intimacies we can't complete.
Those ineluctable fragments. To be up against.

Koh Samui Thailand

LISTENING

by DAVID MURA

from CRAZYHORSE

And from that village, steaming with mist, riddled with rain,
from the fishermen in the bay hauling up nets of silver flecks;
from the droning of the Buddhist priest in the morning,

incense thickening his voice, a bit other-wordly, almost sickly;
from the oysters ripped from the sea bottom by half-naked women,
their skin darker than the bark in the woods, their lungs

as endless as some cave where a demon dwells
(soon their harvest will be split open by a blade, moist
meaty flesh, drenched in the smell of sea bracken, the tidal winds);

from the *torrii* half way up the mountain
and the steps to the temple where the gong shimmers
with echoes of bright metallic sound;

from the waterfall streaming, hovering in the eye, and in illusion, rising;
from the cedars that have nothing to do with time;
from the small mud-cramped streets of rice shops and fish mongers;

from the pebbles on the riverbed, the aquamarine stream
floating pine-trunks, felled upstream
by men with *hachimaki* tied round their forehead

and grunts of *o-sha* I remember from my father in childhood;
from this mythical land of the empty sign and a thousand-thousand manners,
on the tip of this peninsula, far from Kyoto, the Shogun's palace,

in a house of *shoji* and clean cut pine, crawling onto a straw futon,
one of my ancestors lay his head as I do now on a woman's belly
and felt an imperceptible bump like the bow of a boat hitting a swell

and wondered how anything so tiny could cause such rocking unbroken joy.

POST-LARKIN TRISTE

by MARY KARR

from TRIQUARTERLY

The day you died a cold New England wind
stung the air I breathed, and on the street
faces erased themselves as I approached.
For several blocks, I shadowed a big

round-shouldered man built like a pear,
plaid scarf and tweedy overcoat.
Sir, I almost said a hundred times,
but he escaped as you escaped:

my one, careful fan letter returned
unopened; the night I'd hitched
the length of England under thunderheads
your window glowed pure rose.

There you stood wiping off a plate,
the last romantic, a blade of fire
flickering in your eye. I didn't knock
or climb your stair. When you carried

your milk bottles to the stoop,
you briefly stared my way as if you knew
I crouched there in the mud,
my vision starry with the sleet,

your old sad music streaming through my head.
Then stepping through the door,

you sank from view, and later from our lives.
What might I have said to you?

That you were loved perhaps; that love's
a cure. I wanted to hold
your large white hands in mine
and say I understood until you yielded

all your pent-up hurt and wept
as you once said you did alone
safe in the bubble of your car
hearing Wordsworth read on the radio.

Instead, I watched you glower at the night.
The cloudy, dread-locked moon reflected
in your spectacles was a face
I didn't dare to meet, the face of someone

rushing to tell us something terrifying, true.

ASCENSION ON FIRE ISLAND

by HENRI COLE

from ANTAEUS

No octopus-candelabra
    or baby Jesus adorns
the summerhouse we gather in
    to sing a hymn of forgiveness.
No churchbells bronzed overhead
    ring and set our little mob free
when the service is said.
    Only curtains in a strong wind,

billowing like spinnakers
    upon us, seem a godly sign,
or almost so. Sharp as a new pin,
    the day begins around us,
a speckled doe nibbling
    petunias as we pray,
an excess of elementals
    piloting us forward, like Polaris,

into the gospel's verbal cathedral.
    As when Jesus appeared
to the eleven as they sat at meat
    and upbraided them with their
unbelief and hardness of heart,
    our congregation seems unknowing

at first of goodness yet to come:
      Is there a god unvexed to protect us?

What pious groups wouldn't have it so!
      The floor creaks beneath us
like the hull of a ship,
      and the surf purrs in the distance,
confounding us with place,
      till a cardinal alights, twig-flexing,
anchoring us with his featherweight.
      Listen for the passing stillness . . .

In the harbor a man floats
      portside of his sloop, his purple
windbreaker flashing in a sunburst.
      Let him be forgiven, this once,
who put him there. The family squabble,
      the bruised cranium, piece by piece,
will face up to the light of day.
      And the body, its brief

unimmaculate youth, will be hoisted
      from the water's patina of calm.
The nervous deer, the cardinal,
      our perfect citizen, even invisible
bells aloft, press in upon us
      with sheltering mystery,
as in the distance a throng gathers
      and the yellow death-blanket unfolds.

A VACANT LOT

by GIBBONS RUARK

from YARROW

One night where there is nothing now but air
I paused with one hand on the bannister
And listened to a film aficionado's
Careless laughter sentence poetry to death.

It's twenty gone years and a few poems later,
The house demolished, the film man vanished,
The friend who introduced us to him dead.

I side with one old master who loves to tell
His film buff friends that film is *like* an art form,
And yet my eyes keep panning the empty air
Above the rubble, as if, if I could run

The film back far enough, I might still start
For home down the darkened street from the newsstand
And turn a corner to the house still standing,

A faint light showing in an upstairs window.
Is someone reading late? Or is it the night
Our newborn lies burning up with fever,
And all the doctor can say is plunge her

In cold water, wrap her up and hold her,
Hold her, strip her down and plunge her in again
Until it breaks and she is weak but cooling?

Is it the night they call about my father
And I lay the mismatched funeral suit
In the back seat with the cigarettes and whiskey
And drive off knowing nothing but Death and South?

Somewhere a tree limb scrapes at a gutter.
The wind blows. Late trucks rattle the windows.
Never you mind, I say out loud to the girls

Away at school, there's nothing there to hurt you.
The sky is thickening over a vacant lot,
And when I leave there is a hard rain drumming
With the sound of someone up in the small hours,

Thirsty, his palm still warm from a sick child's
Forehead, running the spigot in the kitchen
Full force till the water's cold enough to drink.

DYING IN MASSACHUSETTS

by DONALD W. BAKER

from THE DAY BEFORE (Barnwood Press)

I think I should like to die in Massachusetts,
wading Parker's River in sneakers at slack water,
my wire basket a quarter full of blue crabs,
and I easing my long-handled net towards a big one.

The sun is shining as hard as it can, for it is August.
Clamshell clouds are crowding over the western horizon.
I mash a green-head fly against the nape of my neck,
and the big crab scuttles away under the peat.

No matter. Because I am thinking of what I read
last night in Van Gogh's letters: *I am in it*
with all my heart. I must become more skilled than I am
before I can be ever so slightly satisfied with myself.

And so at that moment the sun collapses into the river,
the crabs are spilled, the net, the fly, the collecting storm
plunge through a canvas of reds and yellows and blues
into the still, cool, clouded poem my life has written.

I'm the old white-bearded geezer they find,
floating face-down, two guys in a rented skiff,
with beer and sub sandwiches and Saturday off,
who on Sunday read about themselves in the Boston *Globe*,

and at night tell their wives about it in Worcester,
and on Monday their buddies down at the station-house.
So the rumor of Donald Baker's death ripples
into the neighborhoods where he was born and grew up.

It passes 14 Reed Street, riding no-hands on a blue bicycle,
and Red Logan's mother peers through her parlor curtains,
saying: *all that expensive college education.*
It rings a doorbell at 282 Chandler Street,

and Alice Crowe's father takes his pipe out of his mouth,
saying: *a good thing you married the dentist.*
And for about ten seconds the streets light up
with the glances and ball games and arguments nobody remembers.

Now the tide turns, a cold stream flooding in
from Nantucket Sound nudges the body upriver,
and the majestic voyage begins, through the grief
of sister and daughters and wife, across the promotion,

with tenure, of junior colleagues, beyond Life Insurance
and Supplemental Retirement Annuity, to a Free
Government Marker and Eternal Care in the plot
in Pine Grove Cemetery behind the Tastee Freeze on Route 28.

My friends, there's a lot of genetic dignity here.
Those oaks are rooted in great-aunts and great-uncles,
that headstone shadows the secrets of my mother's bed,
and my father's electrons waver forever in this loam.

It is March 26th. I am in it with all my heart.
I must try to become more skilled than I am before I die.
For the titles of a thousand unwritten lives
are circling overhead on the gray sails of the gulls.

SESAME

by JACK MARSHALL

from ZYZZYVA

Delectable little seeds
freckling the round cookies' crown—
kaa-iik, in Arabic, strands of skin-
smooth dough pinched together
end to end, each a circle
fitting in the palm of the hand;
speckled with anise seeds, baked
in the oven, golden brown.

Weeks later, I still have the shoebox
filled with them you left for me.
These last years, each new batch made
smaller, thinner,
by your hands that near the end
had to see for you
instead of your eyes that saw,
you said, "only smoke."

After each visit I'd bring my stash
on the plane back to San Francisco
and in my kitchen dip one,
then another into coffee, lingering
over them—hard, edible
chunks of dust; inside, a horizon
taste of anise, after-
taste of the black licorice

we were addicted to as kids. Daily
dust we used to munch on
for hours, without their giving out,
kept in the battered tin can on the stove.

Over dishes piled with them,
women gossiped, planned weddings;
men discussed business and argued
the minutest variations of religious law.

Now I ration and savor
each one, since they're growing scarce,
and the recipe has disappeared
along with the maker.

*

Her cooking pots and pans—dented,
discolored, burnt black—
over the years took on
character, each taking on
a different face and shape,
like friends I'd recognize
in her small apartment. Kitchen folk,
who'd served her more than 50 years.
Friends of the family, in
and out of the fire.

*

Having arrived too late,
coffin already closed,
I missed seeing you
a last time.
Later, took a keepsake
from your dresser—
the old pair of scissors,
handles' black enamel
wearing off—I now use
to cut the manuscripts

you never saw, and trim
the beard you made a face at
on first seeing.

Make another face. Any
of your many mocking ones . . .
I wouldn't mind.

*

Laid in ground, July's end
evaporating, in slow-
motion recall: her never asking
"What's on your mind?"
but "Ish fee elbak?" Arabic for
"What's in your belly?"—question
whose grasp of the real
does not depend on any answer.

"Phish elbak" ("Satisfy your belly.")
she'd urge me to
go out into the street
when she'd find me poring over
my microscope and slides,
staining an insect wing, or after
one of my successful chemistry experiments
which stunk up the house . . .

                    But I was already
happy, like the roaches
inside the walls
with a little garbage.

*

Excess honey
crystallized in the aluminum foil
lining the can of baklava
she'd urged on me and I'd protest, having

too much luggage for the plane-ride back . . .
and now, late as usual, remorse
a near miss,
am glad I brought it.

             Shaved slivers, thick
sugar chunks like coarse silver-streaked
quartz, sticky, fragrant with rose-water . . .
I pinch out
and melt under the hot tap
from the kitchen sink.

I have no use now
for so much sweetness.

*

Long distance
calls I used to make to you Sundays . . .
I'll miss them,

and, as they say, regret
my lower phone bill.

*

She used to tease me:
"If you lost your mind
you wouldn't be losing much."

*

At the cemetery, nodding
toward the expensive pink marble
headstones among rows of grey slabs,
Louie says, "When you're alive
people are not so good to you,
but after you're dead
they're very good. In death,
they're terrific."

*

September sun, lower
earlier each day,
and a hard soughing
wind high in the trees . . .

Summer, which did not come,
is not going to.

*

After 80 years, she still cannot read
nor write a word in English or Arabic,
not having been to school, neither
in Beirut or Brooklyn.

In more than 50 years, she absorbs
a few simple words in English in the way sand
absorbs water, and peppers her Arabic
with mockeries of the language
in which she feels herself a reluctant
refugee.

Mimicking Pop's "Don't give me a lecture,"
with "Don't give me a rupture."

*

Another moon shot.
After the first man was landed,
she said, "Let's see them land a man
on the *sun!*"

*

After managing to scratch her name
in English (lower case, predating e.
e. cummings), a painstaking
scrawl, barely

legible enough to qualify
for citizenship papers back when,
she promptly put pen and paper down
ever after.

Her illiteracy, a kind of stubborn
immobility.
                    Obstinate
power of the old
                    to say *No*.

*

Sad, the way old faces change so much
we can no longer detect in them
any similarity to our own.

*

In the absence of a tape, impossible to reproduce her speech.
Spoken Arabic comes from far deeper
in the throat than English, or what she often scornfully referred
        to as
"Frenjy": all that is quaint, mannered, and ultimately
worthless.

Hawked, gargled, spit: Arabic,
arid and vivid at once. Desert parched
down to a mineral grit where dryness hones things to an edge.
Gutturals and consonants grind stones,
pulverize enemies into a pinch of snuff;
the stuff old Arab men stick up their noses.

*

Odd, from that place you did not see to here,
but from this place you see to there. If so, where
go to be seen

here?

*

In the Koran, "Paradise
is under the feet
of your mother."
Paradise may be
all lust. If so, then aren't we al-
ready in paradise . . .

*

At times now, absently turning on the afternoon TV soaps
and game shows. Like you, watching without seeing,
listening without watching, leaving on without listening,
colored flicker, canned laughter.

At your grave we joked
about putting in with you your beloved
TV.

*

You keep coming back
to her whom you came from and fed on
and left.

        She herself is gone. Now
you are not *from* any more, but *to*.

*

Passed on. But not gone? O.K. then,
withdrawn—as God
is that which we have
to do without. For the faithful, God
becomes all
the dreams one
never acted on.

All fresh grows
old. God

or word, what-
ever you cannot live or face,
you're told.

*

Pop used to chide me: "You want things easy
and want to find things out for yourself."
Both true.
And what I have found out for myself is that
things are not easy.

*

Curses in Arabic are like a secret weapon,
incendiary
burrs attaching to the hated one and burning
through the genetic
channel of assholes descending in time
back to his ancestors.

Founded not on feast or famine,
Islam is a fire in the bowels,
extinguishment of the senses.
No wonder, Rimbaud's
headlong
rush into that inferno.

Curses' portable
stream of fire
to annihilate
an enemy's traces
as surely as the desert
wipes out footprints.

We ought to study curses
to know what lies in store for us.

What would have become of Rimbaud in reverse?—
After Africa, poetry . . .

*

How tired of speaking, how exhausted
from appearing you must have been.

The older people become, the more their faces have
to carry the weight
of their entire body.

*

Ike telling about his father:
how in the hospital after a massive heart attack,
the old man (an avid cardplayer) in a coma
kept repeating, "Give me an ace, give me
a king, a queen,
give me a heart, give me a heart . . . "

an hour later, gone.

*

A certain logic of feeling?—
that what we hear leads us to want to hear more?
Forms a pattern oddly familiar
yet alluringly strange; leaps on us
in welcome
surprise or fearful dread, words that must be
made to flow as easily as water; aqua
architecture, going through
you back to the beginning
before taking a next step forward.
Words that can sometimes rescue
if you're lucky
enough to be surprised by them.

*

On TV, the young woman in Istanbul,
after terrorists had gunned down worshippers in a synagogue,

quips, "My mother is Jewish, my father is Muslim;
we have our own Mideast
crisis at home."

*

Yehudi Arabi.
Arabic Jew.
Ox-
      ymoron.

*

In the future
slum or kingdom
come, never
mind the doves, the
wolves will do
fine.

Only let
streets and alleys
not be just wide
enough for one,
in which no two
can meet.

*

Lately am getting practice in peering
into people's eyes at 8 in the morning
at the clinic, putting in Mydriacil drops
to dilate their pupils.

Patients call me "Doctor."
I don't correct them.

Most people squirm in their seats, flinch at the drops
that sting. But the old Asian women from Vietnam and Laos,
slender as young girls in their long, flower-print skirts,

are quiet and still when I lean forward with the dropper;
not blinking, they stare straight ahead.

Photos of the eyes' interior
show light pockets of fluid and dark craters,
nerve webs, blood vessels, like the moon's surface.
Or solar coronas, helical patterns like the rings of Saturn.

Any of them could be your
cataract eyes.

*

Passing the cemetery, an elderly woman on the street
greets a neighbor and her two small boys.
Passing them, croons, "My, my, how you boys are growing fast!"
then turns away, muttering under her breath, "To what,
I don't know."

*

Under blue sky, red-breasted robin standing on funereal land-
    scaped grass . . .
as if these colors, day's variation of the rainbow, delectable
little seeds, could heal once.
And for all.

WHITE BOOT

by MICHAEL McCLURE

from NEW YORK QUARTERLY

In Golden Gate Park After the Storm

for Sterling Bunnell

STERLING BELIEVES THAT CHAOS ARISES FROM DEEP
INTRINSIC
ORDER
and is merely a quality of energy
in the scene that surrounds.
ORDER, he asserts, is earlier
than this universe,
preceding what a finger
or tongue touches on now;
order enhances and shapes
the buttercup and the moss
stirring on the storm-soaked ground
as well as the shark-colored jay that flies
to take popcorn from my hand.
Even the junco
there by my white boot
on the dripping flagstones
knows it.
The hail intermingling in silvery stripes
with the downrush of rain,
is the same structure as thought.
The flesh of the resonating psyche is free

342

and cannot be bought.
—BUT
ALL
SOME
KNOW
of such things
is the nuggetlike gold of hunger,
the rippling muscle of ongoing love,
and light that flashes
from a wild eye.

SUN SPOTS

by CHRISTOPHER BUCKLEY

from THE IOWA REVIEW

Every eleven years they appear
like dark pores beneath the floating
photosphere, the atomic skin that makes
up the surface. The *auroras* erupt then too,
the irrepressible fiery hair of the sun torn loose and
thrown into space at us, a welter of flaming astral birds
lifting off the *limb*, that visible edge and hard limit of the star.
The magnetic whorls, paired anywhere from two to fifty, are then
several times larger than earth, and strain and pull at fission's invisible frame,
setting out against the rotation of burning equatorial seas, hovering above the blue-
hot center like a sickness in gravity. Yet, when the ocellated torrents and latitudinal drifts
are graphed, the *penumbras* echo the winged patterns of butterflies rather than some matrix of sinking
anti-matter. And after all our spinning about this source, this seething theme and variation, we have nothing new
to say about the spots outside of the old tales that still flare up and forebode havoc in the distant atmosphere of our lives.
So last winter when auroras blazed and the black fields swelled, it was no wonder that broadcasts were interrupted
with blank bursts. "Live from the Met," waffled out and in with a certain nothing on the air—
a soundless hiss and drop-out from the blue. And just weeks before, the opera at the Met
went, a first time ever, unfinished—and the stage turned dark after one un-
balanced soul threw himself mid-aria from a balcony to a break-
neck death. And so, the dread forecasts must have held
sway over at least one man as his will sparked
out and reason fumed in on itself.

It was reported he'd recently
been observed storming around
the mezzanine, stalking some absent
space—and with the house lights down he slipped
into the empty box and pitched himself head-long over
into the dark. He did not stand out in tuxedo and black tie
they said—there was no sound, no note. Only the lovely and loveless
Turandot, waiting high and star-white on the stage, with her riddle for the hero
who was confident as any tenor despite the heads of other suitors who'd been unable to answer
staggered about her on poles like disjunct planets, like moons bruised beyond all aspects of the light . . .
Is it coincidence then, that this year they discover the hole in our ozone to be much larger than first supposed,
that melanoma is on the rise, that the clear-cut Amazon is leaving us with thin air, a simmering rain?
Where on the scale finally are we—Galactic to Sub-Atomic? Our cells cluster and spiral

like galaxies, to or from what effect? Yet we're most open to what lies beyond us—
astronomers have now abandoned our own solar system in favor of great radio
telescopes fixed on the obfuscated heart of space—steely petals of the dishes
unfolding, like camera lenses, like slow and awkward flowers
craning toward sound instead of light. And anchored
firmly in those white sands and eroding shoals
of time, they focus toward some innuendo
sung down in dim, binomial bleeps—
too far away ever to be of use
to the future hanging fire.

SEEING YOU

by JEAN VALENTINE

from AMERICAN POETRY REVIEW

1. MOTHER

I was born under the mudbank
and you gave me your boat.

For a long time
I made my home in your hand:

your hand was empty, it was made
of four stars, like a kite;

you were afraid, afraid, afraid, afraid,
I licked it from your finger-spaces

and wanted to die.
Out of the river sparks rose up:

I could see you, your fear and your love.
I could see you, brilliance magnified.

That was the original garden:
seeing you.

2. LOVER

Your hand was empty, it was made
of four stars, like a kite;

blessed I stood my fingers
in your blue finger-spaces, my eyes' light in

your eyes' light,
we drank each other in.

I dove down my mental lake fear and love:
first fear then under it love:

I could see you,
Brilliance, at the bottom. Trust you

stillness in the last red inside place.
Then past the middle of the earth it got light again.

Your tree. Its heavy green sway. The bright male city.
Oh that was the garden of abundance, seeing you.

MIGHTY FORMS

by BRENDA HILLMAN

from ZYZZYVA

The earth had wanted us all to itself.
The mountains wanted us back for themselves.
The numbered valleys of serpentine wanted us;
that's why it happened as it did, the split
as if one slow gear turned beneath us . . .
Then the Tuesday shoppers paused in the street
and the tube that held the trout-colored train
and the cords of action from triangular buildings
and the terraced gardens that held camellias
shook and shook, each flower a single thought.

Mothers and children took cover under tables.
I called out to her who was my life.
From under the table—I hid under the table
that held the begonia with the fiery stem,
the stem that had been trying to root, that paused
in its effort—I called to the child who was my life.
And understood, in the endless instant,
before she answered, how Pharaoh's army, seeing
the ground break open, seeing the first fringed
horses fall into the gap, made their vows,
that each heart changes, faced with a single awe
and in that moment a promise is written out.

However we remember California later
the earth we loved will know the truth:

that it wanted us back for itself
with our mighty forms and our specific longings,
wanted them to be air and fire but they wouldn't;
the kestrel circled over a pine, which lasted,
the towhee who loved freedom, gathering seed
during the shaking lasted, the painting released
by the wall, the mark and hook we placed
on the wall, and the nail, and the memory
of driving the nail in, these also lasted—

WOMAN WHO WEEPS

by ELLEN BRYANT VOIGT

from THE ANTIOCH REVIEW

Up from the valley, ten children working the fields
and three in the ground, plus four who'd slipped like fish
from a faulty seine, she wept to the priest:
      Father, I saw the Virgin on a hill,
      she was a lion, lying on her side,
      grooming her blonde shoulders with her tongue.

Six months weeping as she hulled the corn,
gathered late fruit and milked the goats,
planted grain and watched the hillside blossom,
before she went to the Bishop, kissed his ring.
      Father, I saw Our Lady in a tree,
      swaddled in black, she was a raven,
      on one leg, on one bent claw
      she hunched in the tree but she *was* the tree,
      charred trunk in a thicket of green.

After seven years of weeping,
not as other stunned old women weep,
she baked flat bread, washed the cooking stones,
cut a staff from a sapling by the road.
The Holy Father sat in a gilded chair:
      Father, I saw Christ's Mother in a stream,
      she was a rock, the water
      parted on either side of her,
      from one stream she made two—

two tresses loosened across her collarbone—
until the pouring water met at her breast
and made a single stream again—

Then from the marketplace, from the busiest stall
she stole five ripened figs
and carried her weeping back to the countryside,
with a cloth sack, with a beggar's cup,
village to village and into the smoky huts,
her soul a well, an eye, an open door.

XVII

FROM THE MEADOW

by PETER EVERWINE

broadside from ARALIA PRESS

It isn't that you were ignorant:
star thistle, bloodroot, cruciform . . .
beautiful words, then as now,
unlike pain with its wooden alphabet,
its many illustrations, which are redundant.

You had imagined vistas, an open meadow:
on the far side, water trembles its lights;
cattle come down to their shadow lives
beneath the trees;
the language of childhood is invented anew.

But now you know, right? what lies ahead
is nothing to the view behind?
How breathtaking these nostalgias rising
like hazy constellations overhead!—

little to go by, surely,
though from the meadow where you stand looking
over your shoulder, that tiny figure you see
seems to be calling someone,
you perhaps.

TO A WREN ON CALVARY

by LARRY LEVIS

from THE MISSOURI REVIEW

> *"Prince Jesus, crush those bastards . . . "*
> —*François Villon, Grand Testament*

It is the unremarkable that will last.

As in Brueghel's camouflage, where the wren's withheld,
While elsewhere on a hill, small hawks (or are they other birds?)
Are busily unraveling eyelashes & pupils
From sunburned thieves outstretched on scaffolds,
Their last vision obscured by wings, then broken, entered.
I cannot tell whether their blood spurts, or just spills,
Their faces are wings, & their bodies are uncovered.

The twittering they hear is the final trespass.

*

And all later luxuries—the half-dressed neighbor couple
Shouting insults at each other just beyond
Her bra on a cluttered windowsill, then ceasing it when
A door was slammed to emphasize, like trouble,

The quiet flowing into things then, spreading its wake
From the child's toy left out on a lawn
To the broken treatise of jet-trails drifting above—seem
Keel scrapes on the shores of some enlarging mistake,

A wrong so wide no one can speak of it now in the town
That once had seemed, like its supporting factories

That manufactured poems & weaponry,
Like such a good idea. And wasn't it everyone's?

Wasn't the sad pleasure of assembly lines a replica
Of the wren's perfect, camouflaged self-sufficiency,
And of its refusal even to be pretty,
Surviving in a plumage dull enough to blend in with

A hemline of smoke, sky, & serene indifference?

*

The dead wren I found on a gravel drive
One morning, all beige above and off-white
Underneath, the body lighter, no more than a vacant tent

Of oily feathers stretched, blent, & lacquered shut
Against the world—was a world I couldn't touch.
And in its skull a snow of lice had set up such
An altar, the congregation spreading from the tongue

To round, bare sills that had been its eyes, I let
It drop, my hand changed for a moment
By a thing so common it was never once distracted from
The nothing all wrens meant, the one feather on the road.

No feeding in the wake of cavalry or kings changed it.
Even in the end it swerved away, & made the abrupt
Riddle all things come to seem . . . irrelevant:
The tucked claws clutched emptiness like a stick.

And if Death whispered as always in the language of curling
Leaves, or a later one that makes us stranger,
"Don't you come *near* me motherfucker";
If the tang of metal in slang made the New World fertile,

Still . . . as they resumed their quarrel in the quiet air,
I could hear the species cheep in what they said . . .
Until their voices rose. Until the sound of a slap erased
A world, & the woman, in a music stripped of all prayer,

357

Began sobbing, & the man become bystander cried *O Jesus*.

*

In the sky, the first stars were already faint
And timeless, but what could they matter to that boy, blent
To no choir, who saw at last the clean wings of indifferent

Hunger, & despair? Around him the other petty thieves

With arms outstretched, & eyes pecked out by birds, reclined
Fastened forever to scaffolds which gradually would cover
An Empire's hills & line its roads as far
As anyone escaping in a cart could see, his swerving mind

On the dark brimming up in everything, the reins
Going slack in his hand as the cart slows, & stops,
And the horse sees its own breath go out
Onto the cold air, & gazes after the off-white plume,

And seems amazed by it, by its breath, by everything.
But the man slumped behind it, dangling a lost nail
Between his lips, only stares at the swishing tail,
At each white breath going out, thinning, & then vanishing.

For he has grown tired of amazing things.

I WOULD CALL IT DERANGEMENT

by GERALD STERN

from THE SOUTH FLORIDA POETRY REVIEW

I cut a stick for my love. It is too early
to clear the yard. I pick some lilac. I hate them
dying on the vine. I plan my assault
on the dead maple. I will tie some rope
to the rotting side and I will pull it down so I can
cut it limb from limb without destroying
the phone connections from one state to another
or smashing the new tomato plants and ruining
the asters. She is walking from place to place
and wrapping herself in sheets. If the wind
were free up there it would lift the curtains
just as it bends the poppies and the yearning
iris. I am setting a table. I
am smiling at the Greeks next door. I put
an old gardenia in the center, something
that has some odor. We are in the flowery
state now. I spill half the petals over
her watermelon; only here are flowers
good for eating, here and India
where they are sprinkled over colored ice
and onto the half-cooked fish. I have a system
for counting bricks but this one day I study

the clouds that move from left to right and the swallows
hunting for food. They seem to fly in threes
and alternately flap their wings, then skim
the roofs; they even make a sound, some brief
chipping; I hear it when they come in range,
maybe when they fight for space. One cloud
is black, it goes from a simple skeleton
to a bloated continent. Given my inclination,
I will turn it into a blowfish before
breakfast is over—or an uprooted tree.
Upstairs she sings—she chips—I know she's dancing
with something or other. When she comes down she'll have
the static of the radio on her tongue,
she understands the *words*, she actually sings
those songs—her voice is a high soprano—I
love it going up and down. My voice is ruined
but I can do a kind of quaver. I have
unearthed the wisdom from my second decade,
and though it did the world little good and even
served as a backdrop to our horrors I don't
blame the music, I can't blame the music
if the horrors grow stronger every year.
She listens to me with one hand, eating sugary
pineapple with the other. I listen too,
under the washrag and the dead maple,
hearing the words for the first time, making her scream
with laughter at my words, almost lucid
compared to hers, as hers are labyrinthian
compared to mine. There is this much music
in eastern Pennsylvania and this much love
and this much decadence. I would call it
derangement—the swallows twice a day
have it, and the white delphiniums
turning to blue again and the orange snapdragons.
If we could lie down for a minute we would let
the bastardy of our two decades take over
just as we let the songs do; there is nothing
that doesn't belong with love; we can't help it
if anguish enters; even leaving the world
as we do there is no disgrace, that is

another kind of anguish—just as it was
following a band of swallows, just as it was
bending down to taste the flowers or turning
the clouds into overturned trees or smiling in Greek.

MY FATHER'S BODY

by WILLIAM MATTHEWS

from THE GETTYSBURG REVIEW

First they take it away,
for now it belongs to the state.
Then they open it
to see what may have killed it,
and it had arteriosclerosis
in its heart, for this was an inside job.
Now someone must identify it
so that the state may have a name
for what it will give away,
and the funeral people come in a stark car
shaped like a coffin with a hood
and take it away,
for now it belongs to the funeral people
and its family buys it back,
though it lies in a box at the crematorium
while the mourners travel and convene.
Then they bring it to the chapel, as they call it,
of the crematorium and it lies in its box
while the mourners enter and sit
and stare at the box, for the box
lies on a pedestal where the altar would be
if this were a chapel.
A rectangular frame with curtains at the sides
rises from the pedestal,
so that the box seems to fill a small stage,
and the stage gives off the familiar

illusion of being a box with one wall torn away
so that we may see into it,
but it's filled with a box we can't see into.
There's music on tape and a man in a robe
speaks for a while and I speak
for a while and then there's a prayer
and then we mourners can hear the whir
of a small motor and curtains slide
across the stage. At least for today,
I think, this is the stage that all the world is,
and another motor hums on
and we mourners realize that behind
the curtains the body is being lowered,
not like Don Giovanni to the flames
but without flourish or song
or the comforts of elaborate plot,
to the basement of the crematorium,
to the mercies of the gas jets
and the balm of the conveyor belt.
The ashes will be scattered,
says a hushed man in a mute suit,
in the Garden of Remembrance,
which is out back.
And what's left of a mild, democratic man
will sift in a heap with the residue of others,
for now they all belong to time.

READING WITH THE POETS

by STANLEY PLUMLY

from ANTAEUS

FOR STANLEY KUNITZ

Whitman among the wounded, at the bedside,
kissing the blood off boys' faces, sometimes stilled
faces, writing their letters, writing the letters
home, saying, sometimes, the white prayers, helping,
sometimes, with the bodies or holding the bodies
down. The boy with the scar that cuts through his speech,
who's followed us here to the Elizabeth
Zane Memorial and Cemetery, wants
to speak nevertheless on the Civil War's
stone-scarred rows of dead and the battle here
just outside of Wheeling equal in death to
Gettysburg because no doctor between the war
and Pittsburgh was possible. Boys dressed like men

and men would gangrene first before the shock of
the saw and scalpel. Three days between this part
of the Ohio River and Pittsburgh. He
knows, he is here since then a child of history
and knows Elizabeth Zane saved all she could.
Keats all his wounded life wanted to be a healer,
which he was, once at his mother's bedside, failed,

364

once at his brother's, failed. Whitman in Washington
failed: how many nights on the watch and it broke
him, all those broken boys, all those bodies blessed
into the abyss. Now the poem for Lincoln,
now the boy with the scar almost singing, now

the oldest surviving poet of the war
reading one good line, then another, then
the song of the hermit thrush from the ground cover.
Lincoln's long black brooding body sailed in a train,
a train at the speed of the wind blossoming,
filling and unfilling the trees, a man's slow
running. Whitman had nowhere to go, so I
leave thee lilac with heart-shaped leaves, he says at
last, and went to the other side with the corpses,
myriads of them, soldiers' white skeletons,
far enough into the heart of the flower
that none of them suffered, none of them grieved, though
the living had built whole cities around them.

Keats at his medical lectures drew flowers.
Not from indifference, not from his elegance:
his interest couldn't bear the remarkable
screams of the demonstrations. He sat there, still
a boy, already broken, looking into the living
body, listening to the arias of the spirit
climbing. So the boy at the graves of the Union
singing, saying his vision, seeing the bodies
broken into the ground. Now the poem for Lincoln.
Now the oldest surviving poet still alive
weaving with the audience that gossamer,
that thread of the thing we find in the voice again.
Now in the night our faces kissed by the healer.

RAY

by HAYDEN CARRUTH

from AMERICAN POETRY REVIEW

How many guys are sitting at their kitchen tables
   right now, one-thirty in the morning, this same
time, eating a piece of pie?—that's what I
   wondered. A big piece of pie, because I'd just
finished reading Ray's last book. Not good pie,
   not like my mother or one of my wives
could've made, an ordinary pie I'd bought at the
   Tops Market in Oneida two hours ago. And how
many had water in their eyes? Because of Ray's
   book, and especially those last poems written
after he knew: the one about the doctor telling
   him, the one where he and Tess go down to
Reno to get married before it happens and shoot
   some craps on the dark baize tables, the one
called "After-Glow" about the little light in the
   sky after the sun sets. I can just hear Ray,
if he were still here and this were somebody
   else's book, saying, "Jesus," saying, "This
is the saddest son of a bitch of a book I've
   read in a long time," saying, "A real long time."
And the thing is, he *knew* we'd be saying this
   about his book, he could just hear us saying it,
and in some part of him he was *glad!* He
   really was. What crazies we writers are,
our heads full of language like buckets of minnows
   standing in the moonlight on a dock. Ray

was a good writer, a wonderful writer, and his
    poems are good, most of them, and they made me
cry, there at my kitchen table with my head down,
    me, a sixty-seven-year-old galoot, an old fool
because all old men are fools, they have to be,
    shoveling big jagged chunks of that ordinary pie
into my mouth, and the water falling from my eyes
    onto the pie, the plate, my hand, little speckles
shining in the light, brightening the colors, and I
    ate that goddamn pie, and it tasted good to me.

XVIII

NOTE I LEFT FOR GERALD STERN IN AN OFFICE I BORROWED, AND HE WOULD NEXT, AT A SUMMER WRITERS' CONFERENCE

by WILLIAM MATTHEWS

from NEW ENGLAND REVIEW

Welcome, good heart. I hope you like—I did—
the bust of Schiller, the reproduction
of Casper David Friedrich's painting
of Coleridge, with his walking stick, gazing
over the peaks of German thought (the Grand
Teutons?), and the many Goethe pin-ups.
The life of the mind is celebrated here,

so why's the place so sad? I hate the way
academic life can function as a sort
of methadone program for the depressed,
keeping the inmates steadily fatigued

and just morose enough that a day's full
measure of glum work gets done. Inquilines
like us will have to put in our two weeks' worth

before the studied gloom begins to leak
forth from the files, the books, the postcards sent
back by colleagues from their Fullbright venues,
Tubingen, Dubrovnik, Rome, and Oslo.
Of course our own offices wait for us
and fall is coming on. To teach, Freud warned,
is one of three impossible jobs

(the others are to govern and to cure),
but to teach what you know—laughter, ignorance,
curiosity and the erotic thrall
of work as a restraint against despair—
is as close to freedom as anyone pays
wages for. The classroom's fine. Meetings are not,
those slow afternoons of the living dead,

and to watch academics isolate
some colleague they don't like is to look on
while an oilslick engulfs and coats a gull.
You can witness like torture in most jobs,
though not the drenched-in-sanctimony prose
by which it is excused. The louder they quote
Dr. Johnson, the faster I count the spoons.

Well, the grunts always kvetch about the food
and the scant morals of their officers.
Who'd want to skip that part? In the office,
though, alone with the books, postcards, busts
and sentimental clutter, we feel rage
dim and joy recede. These dusty keepsakes
block from view the very love they're meant to be

an emblem of, the love whose name is books.
It's as if we'd been kidnapped by the space
people and whisked around the galaxies,
whirred past wonders that would render Shakespeare

mute and make poor stolid Goethe whimper
like a beagle. The stellar dust, debris
agleam in the black light, the fell silence,

the arrogant and gratuitous scale of it
all, the speed of attack and decay each
blurred, incised impression made, the sure greed
we'd feel to describe it, and how we'd fail
that greed. . . . And then we're back, alone
not with the past but with how fast the past
eludes us, though surely, friend, we were there.

THE OLD TESTAMENT

by PHILIP LEVINE

from HUDSON REVIEW

My twin brother swears that at age thirteen
I'd take on anyone who called me kike
no matter how old or how big he was.
I only wish I'd been that tiny kid
who fought back through his tears, swearing
he would not go quietly. I go quietly
packing bark chips and loam into the rose beds,
while in his memory I remain the constant child
daring him to wrest Detroit from lean gentiles
in LaSalle convertibles and golf clothes
who step slowly into the world we have tainted,
and have their revenge. I remember none of this.
He insists, he names the drug store where I poured
a milkshake over the head of an Episcopalian
with quick fists as tight as croquet balls.
He remembers his license plate, his thin lips,
the exact angle at which this 17 year old dropped
his shoulder to throw the last punch. He's making
it up. Wasn't I always terrified?
"Of course," he tells me, "that's the miracle,
you were even more scared than me, so scared
you went insane, you became a whirlwind,
an avenging angel."
                    I remember planting
my first Victory Garden behind the house, hauling
dark loam in a borrowed wagon, and putting in

carrots, corn that never grew, radishes that did.
I remember saving for weeks to buy a tea rose,
a little stick packed in dirt and burlap,
my mother's favorite. I remember the white bud
of my first peony that one morning burst
beside the mock orange that cost me 69¢.
(Fifty years later the orange is still there,
the only thing left beside a cage for watch dogs,
empty now, in what had become a tiny yard.)
I remember putting myself to sleep dreaming
of the tomatoes coming into fullness, the pansies
laughing in the spring winds, the magical wisteria
climbing along the garage, and dreaming of Hitler,
of firing a single shot from a foot away, one
that would tear his face into a caricature of mine,
tear stained, bloodied, begging for a moment's peace.

IN THE LAND OF THE LOTUS EATERS

by TONY HOAGLAND

from THE GEORGIA REVIEW

What was the name of that bronze-headed god
in charge of the Temple of Distraction?
Around whose shrine the ancient Greeks
would congregate, like flies, for hours
instead of working in their shops and fields?

I remember dying for a drink
about the time my grandmother was ready
to say her final words into someone's ear.
I remember seeing, in the air above her head,
among the tubes and stainless steel,
a vision of a speedboat

with a laughing girl on board—
a red speedboat with the word
ALOHA stenciled on the bow,
ready tot ake me anywhere. I don't know
I guess I'm the kind of person

who needs to be continually reminded
about love and brevity, about diligence
and loyalty to pain. And maybe my attention
is permanently damaged, never coming back

from too much television,
too much silly talk,

the way Ulysses' men turned into swine
from too much recreation in the Lotus Land,
then ran away because they couldn't stand
to see what they'd become.

That's why the newsreels of Cambodia must be divided into
slices by deodorant commercials,
why the lipstick shades to choose between in drugstores
equal the number of remaining whales.
That's why the disintegration of the ozone
is directly proportionate to the number of couples
entering therapy in Kansas City.

It is as if, in another version of *The Odyssey*,
Ulysses' men forgot to tie him to the mast,
and he abandoned ship
to chase the luscious a cappella voices of the sexy siren sisters.
To chase and chase and chase and chase and chase.

And the archers shot their arrows with their eyes closed.
And the workers in the factory denied any knowledge
of what the weapons would be used for.
And the name of the one in charge was forgotten.
And the boat sailed on without a captain.

A.M.: THE HOPEFUL MONSTER

by ALICE FULTON

from THE AMERICAN VOICE

For John H. Holland

So dawn. A morcellation of the dark, the one
dumb immaculate gives way.
Appetite and breakfast.
    The light is enlarged
to show detail. It strokes the earth
with no boring or fumbling, with just
    enough. So dawn. Like charity it spreads
itself thin, "envieth not, vaunteth not,
beareth all things. . . ."
It circulates
but has no currency;
    it scraps the dark
for fluctuation and rough justice,
puts a lean on the fields,
glittering like insect flesh.
    A vastation, it braces
every thistle, scrub, and burr. Each minnow, morsel,
swimming in its limber glue, each cell
    strung with elation. The dirt dances in yields.
Look at it that way and give
wonder. The light is enlarged to show detail.
    It bareth all things, it maketh all things

naked, a slater, stripping
the flesh from the hide.
It circulates, but has no currency.
    It takes shape from what blocks it,
the obstacles, like criticism, a kind of birth
control. So scathe
the one who made the pus and suffering
of the stray. He has twenty-six toes
and twenty-six claws to break the spines of mice.
Fleas suck his blood
    and that's how he will die. Nice nature,
nice. Kitten is a pretty thing,
bred to pet. "Cute" is a baby
human concept. Toddler in utopia,
    undergulfed by nothing all
the night, give wonder. And give fear.
Everything that knows it lives
is shivering. Everything
that lives predicts.
    Terror is just
the confidence of prophecy:
what from the gut
the nerve emerges—
    step by step and sweat by sweat.

COLEMAN VALLEY ROAD

by GERALD STERN

from BLACK WARRIOR REVIEW

This is where I had my sheep vision,
in the brown grass, under the stars.
I sat there shivering, fumbling with my paper,
losing tobacco. I was a spark at the most,
hanging on to my glasses, trying to hide
from the wind. This is how I bent

my head between my knees, the channels and veins
pumping wildly, one leg freezing, one leg
on fire. That is the saxophone
and those are the cymbals; when it gets up here
the roar of the waves is only a humming, a movement
back and forth, some sloshing we get used to.

That is my cello music and those are my headlights
making tunnels in the grass; those are
the clouds going down and those are the cliffs going out.
I am reaching up. I think I have
a carp's face, I have a round nose
and a large red eye and a ragged white moustache.

The strings are stretched across the sky; one note
is almost endless—pitiless I'd say
except for the slight sagging; one note is
like a voice, it almost has words, it sings
and sighs, it cracks with desire, it sobs with fatigue.
It is the loudest sound of all. A shrieking.

GUILT TRIP

by DAVID LEHMAN

from ANTIOCH REVIEW

Too much coffee. His mind was racing. Relief of tension:
Was fucking no more than this? Love no nobler than parking?
"She specialized in making him feel bad." He wanted her
Anyway. Something other than the law of mimetic desire
("I want you because he does") was at work. He had watched
Enough movies to understand: Vietnam was the product
Of bad grass, a paranoid trip on the IRT, and the garbage
Was growing, a living organism like the monster
In a Japanese movie, c. 1954. What a strange wonderful island
America was, a monument to impermanence and ocean foam.
Old people lived there, arguing noisily in slow elevators
Over 53 cents off for orange juice, minimum purchase $10.
The scar on her belly convinced him she was telling the truth.
He wanted her anyway. "How they could make a six-part
    documentary
About the Sixties, and never once mention the pill,
I don't understand," she said. "I have a better sense of humor
Than you do," said her seven-year-old son, "because I'm more
Serious than you are." He was right. In the fresh green breast
Of the new world, he had sought a compliant nipple. In time
The darkness would overcome him, sweet as the sweat of sex.
"I love you," he lied. "I love you, too," she replied,
Waking beside him in the morning, scaring him with her love.

XIX

SUITE FOR EMILY

by LYNDA HULL

from THE KENYON REVIEW

1. The Letter

Everywhere the windows give up nothing
but frost's intricate veined foliage.
Just engines shrilling pocked and frozen streets
wailing towards some new disaster.
No *bright* angel's ladders going to split
heaven this Chicago instant where the pier's
an iced fantastic: spiked, the glacial floes
seize it greedy like a careless treasure—

marquise diamonds, these round clear globes, the psychic's
crystal world spinning in her corner shop
when I passed, a globe boundaried with turning
silent winds and demons. Out here the pavement's
a slick graffitied strip: *There's more to life
than violence.* Someone's added *Yes, Sex and Drugs.*
Hello, Plague Angel. I just heard your wings
hiss off the letter on my table—Emily's

in prison again, her child's lost to the State,
Massachusetts. Fatigue, pneumonia,
the wasting away. In the secret hungering,
the emptiness when we were young would come
the drug's good sweep like nothing else,

godly almost the way we'd float immune
and couldn't nothing touch us, nothing.
Somehow I'd thought you'd pass her over—

positive yes—but never really sick,
that flayed above her door there'd be some sign
of mercy. But there's only January's
rough ministry peeling my face away.
Light like the cruel light of another century
and I'm thinking of Dickinson's letter
"Many who were in their bloom have gone
to their last account and the mourners go about

the streets." The primer pages yellowing
on her shelf beneath an album of pressed gentian:
"Do most people live to be old? No, one half die
before they are eight years old. But one in four lives
to see twenty-one." She'd known the bitter sponge
pressed to the fevered forehead, the Death Angel's
dark familiar company, how she'd rustle her veils,
how she'd lean over the ewer and basin

blackening the water. This arctic water, this
seething rustle—lamé, sequins, a glitter wrap
trailing from a girl's shoulders so the shadow pimps
go *hey princess, why you so sad tonight,*
let me make you happy, when she's only tired,
up all night and needing a hit to let her sleep.
We know that story, the crest and billow
and foam and fleeting fullness

before the disappearing. Discs of hissing ice,
doors you (I?) might fall through to the underworld
of bars and bus stations, private rooms of
dancing girls numb-sick and cursing the wilderness
of men's round blank faces. Spinning demons.
Round spoon of powder hissing over the flame.
Worlds within worlds, beneath worlds, worlds that flare
and consume so they become the only world.

2. Holy City, City of Night

What is that general rule which tells
    how long a thing will live? The primer answers,
Whatever grows quick decays quick: soon ripe,
    soon rotten. The rust-blown calla gracing
my table, those Boston girls twenty years gone,
    young men in lace and glitter washed alien
        by gasoline sunsets, the burning sphere
lapsing below night's black rim. *Live fast, die . . .*
we know the rest. Reckless anthem.
    The pier cable's ice-sleeved beneath
my hands—miraculous, yes, to be here
    januaried by this lake's barbaric winterscape
Dickinson might read as savage text
and emblem of a deity indifferent. Her embassy lay
    beyond the city of jasper and gold, the beaten
wrought towers scripture promised the saved

would enter. What heaven she found she made.
    And so did we, worlds that sear, consume—earthly,
delirious. *Ignis fatuus.* Strike the match,
    the fizzing cap. But oh Reader, the wild beauty
of it, the whirring rush, blond hiss of aerial
miles, worn stairways in every burning school
    of nodding classrooms, the buzz-snap of
talk blurring hallucinatory fraught

avenues. Illusive inner city, drugged
    majestic residence spiraled with staircases,
balustrades rococoed, lapidary. Invisible empires
    dreamt beneath the witchery of birds
circling the Commons with twilight, their caw
and settle, the patterns as they wheel
    over the pond's reflective mirror bruised
roseate, violet, deeper, the swanboats

darkening into night's charged dazzle,
    Park Square joints gone radiant, the bus station
burnished before the zap, the charge the edge.

387

It was the life wasn't it? Compatriots you'd
just love to die for, who'd jump you
in a New York minute. But the glory
    as the lights went up, torching the air chartreuse,
lipsticked pink, casting embers, seraphic fires

fallen earthward. Fallen, the furious emblems.
    We were so young we'd spend and spend
ourselves as if there'd be no reckoning, then grew
    past caring. All the darkening chapters.
Dream time, the inner time
where towers and battlements erect
    their coruscating glamour and how we'd glide,
celebrities among them, the crowds falling back,

dream deeper, gone and wake to daylight's assault
    knocking another bare room, the alley, the bathroom
you inhabit like the thief you are. *Ignis fatuus*.
    I can follow you there, Emily, we girls
setting out a thousand ruined nights in the splendor
of the torched and reckless hour.
    Who wouldn't trade heaven for that fleet city
when winter beaks the shattered pane,

when summer's a nauseous shimmer
    of sexual heat, though sex is a numb machine
you float above. When the place you walk into
    is a scream in the shape of yourself.
When it makes perfect sense to blow someone away
for twenty bucks beyond even your bleak human universe.
    When the only laughter that falls down
is iron and godless. Here, I—the one who left—

must falter where persists
    this chrome traffic shrill, where the cable's
bitter alloy comes away in my hand,
    this metaled pungence of hair and skin
in wind persists riven as the taste of myself,
the blood blooming healthy

real in my mouth, a future's lavish venues
spread stunned before me. These hands.

3. Combat Zone/War Stories

The district's been demolished, sown with salt.
The dazzling girls, girls, girls in platinum wigs
have been lifted away by some infernal agency,
the queens, exotic Amazons and rough-trade gay boys.

Sometimes I go back to walk the streets all shops
and swank hotels, the office blocks and occasional
burnt out shell. So American, this destruction
and renewal, cities amnesiac where evening's

genesis falls through vast deserted silences,
towers grown otherworldly with light
thrown starlike from some alien world. Gone the Show Bar,
the Mousetrap, the whole gaudy necklace

of lacquer-dark underground lounges, halls
of mirrors, music billowing dancers
clean out of themselves beyond the dead-faced tricks,
the sick voyeurs. The Combat Zone. I can map it

in my mind, some parallel world, the ghost city
beneath the city. Parallel lives, the ones
I didn't choose, the one that kept her.
In all that dangerous cobalt luster

where was safety? home? when we were delirium
on rooftops, the sudden thrill of wind dervishing
cellophane, the shredded cigarettes. We were
the dust the Haitians spit on to commemorate

the dead, the click and slurried fall of beads
across a doorway. In the torn and watered silk
of night, the Zone exploded its shoddy neon orchid
to swallow us in the scent of fear, emergency,

that oily street perfume and weeping brick.
Gossamer clothes, summertime and leaning
against the long dusty cars, cruising siren songs.
Summer? My memory flutters—had I—was there summer?

Dancer, and floor, and cadence
quite gathered away, and I a phantom, to you
a phantom, rehearse the story.
And now it's autumn turning hard to winter,

Thanksgiving, 1990, and all she wants is sweets
so it's apple pie barehanded and Emily's
spinning war stories, how bad she is: *So, I say,*
go ahead and shoot me, put me out of my misery.

Cut me motherfucker—my blood's gonna kill you.
Then she's too tired to sit and in the blue ·
kaleidoscopic TV shift I stroke
her hair, the ruined hands *I didn't know*

how sick I was—if the heroin wanted the AIDS,
or the disease wanted the heroin. She asks me
to line up her collection of matchbox houses
so we can make a street, so we can make a neighborhood.

4. Jail, Flames—Jersey, 1971

The psychic's globe whirls its winds: demons,
   countless futures, the pasts. Only
     thirteen the first time
  I saw you in jail, just a kid looking
up at me, the usual gray detective clamor,

inkpads and sodium flash. Hauled out by the officials,
   exemplary bad-news girl, they shoved
     a lyric sheet at me. Command
  recitation to sway you from straying.
"King Heroin," James Brown pompadoured like nobody's

business and here's Death cartoonishly aloft on a white
    winged horse, grim reaper lording it
        over the shivering denizens
    of a city, exaggerated as any Holy City,
going down, down, down. Just a kid, you, peering out

the jungle of your dark hair, greasy jeans a tangle
    of beads at your throat. Ludicrous,
        I know, me declaiming within
    the jail gleam that never sleeps all over us,
that effluvium of backed-up plumbing. On my palm,

the bar's iron taint lingered for hours after.
    It didn't mean that much to me, seventeen,
        my practiced sangfroid
    chilling the terror, that long drop
inside, the way you collapse to fall in flames.

I might have said you'll pay for the wild and reckless hour,
    pay in the currency of sweat and shiver,
        the future squandered, the course
    of years reconfigured, a relinquishment so
complete it's more utter than any falling in love. Falling

instead in flames, burning tiles spiraling to litter
    the courtyards of countless places that will
        never be yours, the fingerprints,
    tossed gloves and glittering costumes, flared
cornices and parapets, shattering panes, smoked out

or streaked with embers, the tinder of spools, such
    a savage conflagration, stupid edge-game,
        the way junkies tempt death,
    over and over again, toy with it. I might have
told you that. Everything you ever meant to be, *pfft*,

out the window in sulfured match-light, slow tinder
    and strike, possession purely ardent as worship
        and the scream working its way out

391

of your bones, demolition of wall and strut
within until you're stark animal need. That *is*

love, isn't it? Everything you meant to be falls
    away so you dwell within a perfect
        singularity, a kind of saint,
        Pearl of great price. Majestic, searing,
the crystal globe spins futures unimaginable, that

crucible you know so well, Emily, viral fever refining
    you to some essence of pain more furious
        than these winter trees
        stripped to black nerves above
the El's streaked girders, a harsh equation, some

god's iron laughter combing down time's blind
    and hush. *Hush child, forgive me.*
        Twenty years later, you say
        that night in jail you looked up
at me and wanted to be me. And I didn't care.

5. Address

Hello Death Angel, old familiar, old nemesis.
    In the deepest hours, I have recognized
your floating shape. I've seen your breath
    seduce the torn curtain
masking the empty window, have crouched with you
    in the doorway, curled in the alley
hooded in your essence and shadow, have
    been left blue, heart-stopped
for yours, for yours. Death,
    you are the bead in the raptor's eye,
Death you dwell in the funneling depths
    of the heavens beyond each
star's keening shrill, Death you are the potion
    that fills the vial, the night
the monuments have swallowed. You live
    in the maimed child wrapped in a wreckage

of headlines. Death you center
　　in the fanged oval
of the prison dog's howl. Death you dwell within
　　the necropolis we wake to in nightmare's
hot electric wind. You glint
　　the edge of the boy's razor,
patient in the blasted stairwell. Everywhere
　　you walk deep lawns, TVs pollinating air
with animals wired up to dance
　　for their food, with executions
and quiz shows. You're in the column
　　of subway wind roaring before each
train's arrival. I've seen you drape thoughtlessly
　　a woman's hair over her face
as the shot carried her forward into stop-time
　　and beyond anything she'd lain
her money down for. Death your sliver works
　　swiftly through the bloodstream.
Hello Death Angel, Plague is your sister.
　　I've seen her handiwork, heard
the tortured breath, watched her loosen the hands
　　of the dazzling boys one from each other.
For love, love. I've seen the AIDS hotels
　　and sick ones begging homeless
in the tunnels, the whispered conspiracies.
　　Shameless emissaries with your powders
and wands, your lunar carnivorous flowers.
　　Tricks, legerdemain. I've seen you draw
veined wings over the faces of sleepers,
　　the abandoned, the black feather that sweeps
so tenderly. I've seen the stain you scribe
　　on the pavement, the glossy canopy of leaves
you weave. I've seen waste and ruin, know
　　your kingdom for delirium, the furious thumbprints
you've scored on the flesh of those you choose.
　　I've seen you slow-dance in a velvet mask, dip
and swirl across dissolving parquet.
　　I've seen you swing open the iron gate—
a garden spired in valerian, scullcap, blue vervain.
　　Seen you stir the neat halfmoons, fingernails

left absently in a glazed dish.
   Felons, I've cursed you in your greed, have spat
and wept then acquiesced in your wake. Without rue
   or pity, you have marked the lintels and blackened
the water. Your guises multiply, bewildering
   as the firmament's careless jewelry.
Death I have welcomed you to the rooms
   where Plague has lain when the struggle is passed
and lit the candles and blessed the ash.
   Death you have taken my friends and dwell
with my friends. You are the human wage.
   Death I am tired of you.

6. Dartmouth Women's Prison, 1992

Emily, delirium's your province.
You dwell feverish in prison
voiceless to plead
your need before the agencies
of government who *cannot hear the buildings*
falling and oil exploding, only people walking
and talking, cannon soft as velvet from parishes
that do not know you are burning up,
that seasons have rippled
like a beast the grasses beyond
the prison.

               They cannot hear the strummed harp
of the nerves, black trees swaying winter,
cannot know your child is lost to you.

The human wage that's paid and paid?

Once, we were two girls
setting out towards that city
of endless searing night, the route taking on
the intricacy, the fumes and bafflements
of a life a woman might dream turning
feverish in her prison bunk. Probation violation,

when broke and sick, no way home
from the clinic the detective going
ride with me, just talk, that's all
I want. Twenty bucks and him crowing
we just love to run you little sluts in.
Em, if I could reach you through the dust notes'
spinning, infernoed dreams, I would dwell
in the moon's cool glistering
your cell, the rough cloth, the reflection
of your face given back in the steel basin's
water, in the smooth moan of women loving women,
a cacophony of needs. I am there with you lost
in the chaos of numbers, that nattering PA buzz,
in the guards' trolling clank and threat echoing
walls so eloquent
with all the high-frequency sizzle
of anguish they've absorbed.
Emily, I will bless your child, will
hold for you the bitter sponge,
would give you staff and orb, a firmament
radiant and free.

But these are phantoms, lies—
I cannot follow where you are. On my street,
the psychic's crystal globe whirls pasts, futures
but where you are is timeless.
"Pain—has an Element of Blank—It cannot recollect
when it Began—or if there were
a time when it was not—
It has no Future—but itself. . ."

Off the lake a toothed wind keens
and it's just me here, the one who's left.
Just me helpless to change anything caught
in this ellipsis between traffic, this
fleet human delay, all around
the wind singing like a mechanical ballerina
a girl might hold in her hand, the one
that watched your childhood bed, porcelain
upturned gaze, stiff tutu, dust in the folds

of that spindly piercing music sounding
of voices winged over water, becoming
water, and gone.

7. A Style of Prayer

There is a prayer that goes Lord I am powerless
    over these carnivorous streets, the fabulous
        breakage, the world's ceaseless *perpetuum mobile,*

like some renaissance design, lovely and useless
    to harness the forces of weather, the planet's
        dizzy spin, this plague. A prayer that asks

where in the hour's dark moil is mercy?
    Ain't no ladders tumbling down from heaven
        for what heaven we had we made. An embassy

of ashes and dust. Where was safety? Home?
    Is this love, staff, orb and firmament?
        Parallel worlds, worlds within worlds—chutes

and trapdoors in the mind. Sisters and brothers,
    the same thing's going down all over town, town
        after town. There is a prayer that goes Lord,

we are responsible. Harrow us through the waves,
    the runnels and lace that pound, comb, reduce us so
        we may be vessels for these stories.

Oh, the dazzling men torn one from the other,
    these women taken, these motherless children.
        Perhaps there's no one to fashion such new grace,

the world hurtling its blind proposition
    through space and prayer's merely a style of waiting
        beyond *the Hour of Lead*—

Remembered, if outlived,
  As Freezing persons, recollect the Snow—
    First-Chill—then Stupor—then the letting go . . .

But oh, let Emily become anything
  but the harp she is, too human, to shiver
    grievous such wracked and torn discord. Let her be

the foam driven before the wind over the lakes,
  over the seas, the powdery glow floating
    the street with evening—saffron, rose, sienna

bricks, matte gold, to be the good steam
  clanking pipes, that warm music glazing the panes,
    each fugitive moment the heaven we choose to make.

A PORTRAIT OF THE SELF AS NATION, 1990–1991

by MARILYN CHIN

from ZYZZYVA

Fit in dominata servitus
In servitude dominatus
In mastery there is bondage
In bondage there is mastery
        (Latin proverb)

The stranger and the enemy
We have seen him in the mirror.
        (George Seferis)

Forgive me Head Master
but you see, I have forgotten
to put on my black lace underwear, and instead
I have hiked my slip up, up to my waist
so that I can enjoy the breeze.
It feels good to be *without,*
so good as to be salacious.
The feeling of flesh kissing tweed.
If ecstasy had a color, it would be
yellow and pink, yellow and pink
Mongolian skin rubbed raw.
The serrated lining especially fine
like wearing a hair-shirt, inches above the knee.
When was the last time I made love?
The last century? With a wan missionary.

Or was it San Wu the Bailiff?
The tax-collector who came for my tithes?
The herdboy, the ox, on the bridge of magpies?
It was Roberto, certainly,
high on coke, circling the galaxy.
Or my recent vagabond love
driving a reckless chariot, lost
in my feral country. *Country*, Oh I am
so punny, so very, very punny.
Dear Mr. Decorum, don't you agree?
It's not so much the length of the song
but the range of the emotions—Fear
has kept me a good pink monk and poetry
is my nunnery. Here I am alone in my altar,
self-hate, self-love, both self-erotic notions.
Eyes closed, listening to that one hand clapping—
not metaphysical trance, but fleshly mutilation—
and loving *it*, myself and that pink womb, my bed.
Reading "Ching Ping Mei" in the "expurgated"   (1)
where all the female protagonists were named
Lotus.
Those damned licentious women named us
Modest, Virtue, Cautious, Endearing,
Demure-dewdrop, Plum-aster, Petal-stamen.
They teach us to walk headbent in devotion,
to honor the five relations, ten sacraments.
Meanwhile, the feast is brewing elsewhere,
the ox is slaughtered and her entrails are hung
on the branches for the poor. They convince us, yes,
our chastity will save the nation—Oh mothers,
all your sweet epithets didn't make us wise!
Orchid by any other name is equally seditious.

Now, where was I, oh yes, now I remember,
the last time I made love, it was to *you*.
I faintly remember your whiskers
against my tender nape.
You were a conquering barbarian,
helmeted, halberded,
beneath the gauntleted moon,

whispering Hunnish or English—
so-long Oolong went the racist song,
bye-bye little chinky butterfly.
There is no cure for self-pity,
the disease is death,
ennui, disaffection,
a roll of flesh-colored tract homes crowding my imagination.
I do hate my loneliness,
sitting cross-legged in my room,
satisfied with a few off-rhymes,
sending off precious haiku to some inconspicuous journal
named "left Leaning Bamboo."
You, my precious reader, O sweet voyeur,
sweaty, balding, bespeckled,
in a rumpled rayon shirt
and a neo-Troubadour chignon,
politics mildly centrist,
the *right* fork for the *right* occasions,
matriculant of the best schools—
herewith, my last confession,
(with decorous and perfect diction)
I loathe to admit. Yet, I shall admit it:
there was no Colonialist coercion,
sadly, we blended together well.
I was poor, starving, wartorn,
an empty coffin to be filled,
You were a young, ambitious Lieutenant
with dreams of becoming Prince
of a "new world order," Lord
over the League of Nations.

Lover, destroyer, savior!
I remember that moment of beguilement,
one hand muffling my mouth,
one hand untying my sash—
On your throat dangled a golden cross.
Your god is jealous, your god is cruel.
So, when did you finally return?
And . . . was there a second coming?
My memory is failing me, perhaps

400

you came too late,
(we were already dead).
Perhaps, you didn't come at all,
you had a deadline to meet,
another alliance to secure,
another resistance to break.
Or you came too often
to my painful dismay.
(Oh how facile the liberator's hand.)
Often when I was asleep
You would hover over me
with your great silent wingspan
and watch me sadly.
This is the way you want me—
asleep, quiescent, almost dead,
sedated by lush immigrant dreams
of global bliss, connubial harmony.

Yet, I shall always remember
and deign to forgive
(long before I am satiated,
long before I am spent)
that last pressured cry,
"your little death."
Under the halcyon light
you would smoke and contemplate
the sea and debris,
that barbaric keening
of what it means to be free.
As if we were ever free,
as if ever we could be.
Said the judge,
"Congratulations,
On this day, fifteen of November, 1967,
Marilyn Mei Ling Chin,
application # z-z-z-z-z,
you are an American citizen,
naturalized in the name of God
the father, God the son and the Holy Ghost."
Time assuages, and even

the Yellow River becomes clean . . .

Meanwhile we forget
the power of exclusion
what you are walling in or out—
and to whom you must give offence.
The hungry, the slovenly, the convicts
need not apply.
The syphilitic, the consumptive
may not moor.
The hookwormed and tracomaed
(and the likewise infested).
The gypsies, the sodomists, the mentally infirm.
The pagans, the heathens, the non-
denominational—
The coloureds, the mixed-races and the reds.
The communists, the usurous,
the mutants, the Hibakushas, the hags . . .

(2)

(3)

(4)

Oh connoiseurs of gastronomy and *keemun* tea!
My foes, my loves,
how eloquent your discrimination,
how precise your poetry.
Last night, in our large, rotund bed,
we witnessed the fall. *Ours*
was an "aerial war." Bombs
glittering in the twilight sky
against the Star Spangled Banner.
Dunes and dunes of sand,
fields and fields of rice.
A thousand charred oil wells,
the firebrands of night.
Ecstasy made us tired.

Sir, Master, Dominatrix,
Fall—was a glorious season for the hegemonists.
We took long melancholy strolls on the beach,
digressed on art and politics
in a quaint wharfside cafe in La Jolla.
The storm gazed our bare arms gently . . .

History has never failed us.
Why save Babylonia or Cathay,
when we can always have Paris?
Darling, if we are to remember at all,
let us remember it well—
We were fierce, yet tender,
fierce and tender.

Notes:

1) "Ching Ping Mei"—Chinese erotic novel.

2) Exclusion—refers to various "exclusion acts" or anti-Chinese legislation which attempted to halt the flow of Chinese immigrants to the U.S.

3) Hookworm and tracoma—two diseases which kept many Chinese detained and quarantined at Angel Island.

4) Hibakushas—scarred survivors of the atom bomb and their deformed descendants.

LOST BRILLIANCE

by RITA DOVE

from BLACK WARRIOR REVIEW

I miss that corridor drenched in shadow,
sweat of centuries steeped into stone.
After the plunge, after my shrieks
had diminished and his oars sighed
up to the smoking shore,
the bulwark's gray pallor soothed me.
Even the columns seemed kind, their murky sheen
like the lustrous skin of a roving eye.

I used to stand at the top of the stair
where the carpet flung down
its extravagant heart. Flames
teased the lake into glimmering licks.
I could pretend to be above the earth
rather than underground: a Venetian
palazzo or misty chalet tucked into
an Alp, that mixture of comfort
and gloom . . . nothing was simpler

to imagine. But it was more difficult
each evening to descend: all that marble
flayed with the red plush of privilege
I traveled on, slow nautilus
unwinding in terrified splendor
to where he knew to meet me—

my consort, my match,
though much older and sadder.

In time, I lost the capacity
for resolve. It was as if
I had been traveling all these years
without a body,
until his hands found me—
and then there was just
the two of us forever:
one who wounded,
and one who served.

TWICE REMOVED

by RALPH ANGEL

from VOLT

Not even sleep (though I'm ashamed of that too).
Or watching my sleeping self drift out and kick harder, burst
    awake, and then the nothing,
leaf-shadow, a shave and
black coffee, I know how a dream sounds.

This ease. This difficulty. The brain that lives on a little longer.
    The long
commute (not even what happened back then—this sort of
giving up with no one around and therefore
no charge for anything).

No word. No feeling
when a feeling wells up and is that much further.
Cupola and drumming, from the inside, holes open up a sky no
    thicker than cardboard.
You, the one I'd step over. You, whom I care for

and lie to, who doesn't want to, either, not even this failure
(having grown so used to it), the wreck that still
seeps from a stone, sinks down among the roots and, in their
    perfect darkness, such bloom.
No name for it. No place inscribed with its own grief,

where the grass resists, and I too
resist.

No place to get to. No place to leave from. No place where those
   times,
and times like these, are allowed to die.

SALT

by LINDA GREGERSON
from COLORADO REVIEW

Because she had been told, time and
         again,
                not to swing on the neighbor's high hammock,

and because she had time and again gone
         back, lured
                by the older boys and their dangerous

propulsions, because a child in shock (we
         didn't know
                this yet) can seem sullen or intran-

sigent, and because my father hated his life,
         my sister
                with her collarbone broken was spanked

and sent to bed for the night, to shiver
         through the August
                heat and cry her way through sleep.

And where, while she cried, was the life he
         loved?
                Gone before she was born, of course,

gone with the river-ice stored in sawdust,
         gone with the horses,
                gone with the dogs, gone with Arvid Anacker

up in the barn. 1918. My father was six.
                    His father thought Why
              leave a boy to the women. Ole (like "holy"

without the h, a good Norwegian
                    name)—
              Ole had papers to sign, you see,

having served as county JP for years—
                    you
              would have chosen him too, he was salt

of the earth—and Arvid's people needed to cut
                    the body down.
              So Ole took the boy along, my father

that is, and what he hadn't allowed for was
                    how badly
              Arvid had botched it,

even this last job, the man had no luck.
                    His neck
              not having broken, you see, he'd thrashed

for a while, and the northeast wall of the barn—
                    the near wall—
              was everywhere harrows and scythes.

It wasn't—I hope you can understand—
                    the
              blood or the blackening face,

as fearful as those were to a boy, that forty
                    years later
              had drowned our days in bourbon and dis-

gust, it was just that the world had no
                    savor left
              once life with the old man was

409

gone. It's common as dirt, the story
of ex-
pulsion: once in the father's fair

lost field, even the cycles of darkness cohered.
Arvid swinging
in the granular light, Ole as solid

as heartwood, and tall . . . how
could a girl
on her salt-soaked pillow

compete? The banished one in the story
measures
all that might heal him by all

that's been lost. My sister in the hammock
by Arvid
in the barn. I remember

that hammock, a gray and dirty canvas
thing,
I never could make much of it.

But Karen would swing toward the fragrant
branches, fleshed
with laughter, giddy with the earth's

sweet pull. Some children are like that,
I have one
myself, no wonder we never leave them alone,

we who have no talent for pleasure
nor use
for the body but after the fact.

SONG

from **BRIGIT PEGEEN KELLY**

from **THE SOUTHERN REVIEW**

Listen: there was a goat's head hanging by ropes in a tree.
All night it hung there and sang. And those who heard it
Felt a hurt in their hearts and thought they were hearing
The song of a night bird. They sat up in their beds, and then
They lay back down again. In the night wind, the goat's head
Swayed back and forth, and from far off it shone faintly,
The way the moonlight shone on the train track miles away
Beside which the goat's headless body lay. Some boys
Had hacked its head off. It was harder work than they had
    imagined.
The goat cried like a man and struggled hard. But they
Finished the job. They hung the bleeding head by the school
And then ran off into the darkness that seems to hide
    everything.
The head hung in the tree. The body lay by the tracks.
The head called to the body. The body to the head.
They missed each other. The missing grew large between them,
Until it pulled the heart right out of the body, until
The drawn heart flew toward the head, flew as a bird flies
Back to its cage and the familiar perch from which it trills.
Then the heart sang in the head, softly at first and then louder,
Sang long and low until the morning light came up over
The school and over the tree, and then the singing stopped. . . .
The goat had belonged to a small girl. She named
The goat Broken Thorn Sweet Blackberry, named it after

The night's bush of stars, because the goat's silky hair
Was dark as well water, because it had eyes like wild fruit.
The girl lived near a high railroad track. At night
She heard the trains passing, the sweet sound of the train's horn
Pouring softly over her bed, and each morning she woke
To give the bleating goat his pail of warm milk. She sang
Him songs about girls with ropes and cooks in boats.
She brushed him with a stiff brush. She dreamed daily
That he grew bigger, and he did. She thought her dreaming
Made it so. But one night the girl didn't hear the train's horn,
And the next morning she woke to an empty yard. The goat
Was gone. Everything looked strange. It was as if a storm
Had passed through while she slept, wind and stones, rain
Stripping the branches of fruit. She knew that someone
Had stolen the goat and that he had come to harm. She called
To him. All morning and into the afternoon, she called
And called. She walked and walked. In her chest a bad feeling
Like the feeling of the stones gouging the soft undersides
Of her bare feet. Then somebody found the goat's body
By the high tracks, the flies already filling their soft bottles
At the goat's torn neck. Then somebody found the head
Hanging in a tree by the school. They hurried to take
These things away so that the girl would not see them.
They hurried to raise money to buy the girl another goat.
They hurried to find the boys who had done this, to hear
Them say it was a joke, a joke, it was nothing but a joke. . . .
But listen: here is the point. The boys thought to have
Their fun and be done with it. It was harder work than they
Had imagined, this silly sacrifice, but they finished the job,
Whistling as they washed their large hands in the dark.
What they didn't know was that the goat's head was already
Singing behind them in the tree. What they didn't know
Was that the goat's head would go on singing, just for them,
Long after the ropes were down, and that they would learn to
    listen,
Pail after pail, stroke after patient stroke. They would
Wake in the night thinking they heard the wind in the trees
Or a night bird, but their hearts beating harder. There
Would be a whistle, a hum, a high murmur, and, at last, a song

The low song a lost boy sings remembering his mother's call.
Not a cruel song, no, no, not cruel at all. This song
Is sweet. It is sweet. The heart dies of this sweetness.

XX

SOMETHING LIKE HAPPINESS

by STEPHEN DUNN

from ANTAEUS

Last night Joan Sutherland was nuancing
the stratosphere on my fine-tuned tape deck,
and there was my dog Buster with a flea rash,
his head in his privates. Even for Buster
this was something like happiness. Elsewhere
I knew what people were doing to other people,
the terrible hurts, the pleasures of hurting.
I repudiated Zen because it doesn't provide
for forgiveness, repudiated my friend X
who had gotten "in touch with his feelings,"
which were spiteful and aggressive. *Repudiate*
felt good in my mouth, like someone else's tongue
during the sweet combat of love.
I said out loud, *I repudiate,* adding words
like *sincerity, correctness, common sense.*
I remembered how tired I'd grown of mountaintops
and their thin, unheavenly air,
had grown tired, really, of how I spoke of them,
the exaggerated glamor, the false equation between
ascent and importance. I looked at the vase
and its one red flower, then the table
which Zennists would say existed
in its *thisness*, and realized how wrong it was

to reject appearances. How much more difficult
to accept them! I repudiated myself, citing my name.
The phone rang. It was my overly serious friend
from Syracuse saying *Foucault, Foucault,*
like some lost prayer of the tenured.
Advocates of revolution, I agreed with him, poor,
screwed for years, angry—who can begrudge them
weapons and victory? But people like us,
Joan Sutherland on our tapes and enough fine time
to enjoy her, I said, let's be careful
how we link thought and action,
careful about deaths we won't experience.
I repudiated him and Foucault, told him
that if Descartes were alive and wildly in love
he himself would repudiate his famous dictum.
I felt something like happiness when he hung up,
and Buster put his head on my lap,
and without admiration stared at me.
I would not repudiate Buster, not even his fleas.
How could I? Once a day, the flea travels
to the eye of the dog for a sip of water.
Imagine! The journey, the delicacy of the arrival.

FILM NOIR: TRAIN TRIP OUT OF METROPOLIS

by LYNN EMANUEL

from ANTIOCH REVIEW

We're headed for empty-headedness,
the featureless amnesias of Idaho, Montana, Nevada,
states rich only in vowel sounds and alliteration.
We're taking the train so we can see into the heart
of the heart of America framed in the windows' cool
oblongs of light. We want cottages, farmhouses
with peaked roofs leashed by wood smoke to the clouds;
we want the golden broth of sunlight ladled over
ponds and meadows. We've never seen a meadow.
Now, we want to wade into one—up to our chins in the grassy
welter—the long reach of our vision grabbing up great
handfuls and armloads of scenery, our eyes at the clouds
white sale, our eyes at the bargain basement give away
of clods and scat and cow pies. We want to feel half
of America to the left of us and half to the right, ourselves
like a spine dividing the book in two, ourselves holding
the whole great story together.

And then, suddenly, the train pulls into the station,
and the scenery begins to creep forward—a friendly but timid tribe.
The ramshackle shapes of Main, the old-fashioned cars dozing
at the ribbon of curb, the mongrel hound loping across a stretch

of unpaved road, the medals of the Lions and Chamber of
    Commerce
pinned on the town's chest, the street lights on their long stems,
the little park, the trolley, the faint bric-a-brac of park stuff:
bum on the bench, boy with the ball come closer and closer.
Then the pleasantly sinister swell of the soundtrack tapers
to a long wail. The noise of a train gathers momentum
and disappears into the distance leaving us stranded here,
and our names are strolling across the landscape in the crisply
voluminous script of the opening credits, as though these were
our signatures on the contract, as though we were the authors of this
    story.

.

THE DECONSTRUCTION OF EMILY DICKINSON

by GALWAY KINNELL

from AMERICAN POETRY REVIEW

The lecture had ended when I came in,
and the professor was answering questions.
I do not know what he had been doing with her
poetry, but now he was speaking of her
as a victim of reluctant male publishers.
When the questions dwindled, I put up my hand,
said the ignorant meddling of the Springfield *Daily Republican*
and the hidebound response of literary men,
and the gulf between the poetic wishfulness
then admired and her own harsh knowledge
had let her see that her poems
would not be understood in her time;
and therefore, passionate to publish,
she vowed not to publish again. I said
I would recite a version of her vow.

      Publication—is the Auction
      Of the mind of Man—

But before I could, the professor broke in.
"Yes," he said, " 'the Auction'—'auction,' from *augere, auctum,* to
    augment, to author . . . "
"Let's hear the poem!" "The poem!" several women,

who at such a moment are more outspoken than men, shouted,
but I kept still and he kept going.
"In *auctum* the economy of the signifier is split, revealing an
   unconscious collusion in the bourgeois commodification of
   consciousness.
While our author says 'no,' the unreified text says 'yes,' yes?"
He kissed his lips together and turned to me
saying, "Now, may we hear the poem?"
I waited a moment for full effect.
Without rising to my feet, I said,
"Professor, to understand Dickinson
it may not always be necessary to uproot her words.
Why not, first, try *listening* to her?
Loyalty forbids me to recite her poem now."
No, I didn't say that—I realized
she would want me to finish him off with one wallop.
So I said, "Professor, I thought you
would welcome the words of your author.
I see you prefer to hear yourself speak."
No, I held back—for I could hear her
urging me to put outrage into my voice
and substance into my argument.
I stood up so that everyone might see
the derision in my smile. "Professor," I said,
"you live in Amherst at the end of the twentieth century.
For you 'auction' means a quaint event
where somebody coaxes out the bids
on a butter churn on a summer Saturday.
Forget etymology, this is history.
In Amherst in 1860 'auction' meant
the slave auction, you dope!"
Well, I didn't say that either,
although I have said them all,
many times, in the middle of the night.
In reality, I stood up and recited
like a schoolboy called upon in class.
My voice gradually weakened, and the women
who had called out for the poem
now looked as though they were thinking
of errands to be done on the way home.

422

When I finished, the professor smiled.
"Thank you. So, what at first some of us may have taken as a simple
   outcry, we all now see is an ambivalent, self-subversive text."
As people got up to go, I moved
into that sanctum within me where Emily
sometimes speaks a verse, and listened
for a sign of how she felt, such as,
"Thanks—Sweet—countryman—
for wanting—to Sing out—of Me—
after all that Humbug." But she was silent.

SADNESS, AN IMPROVISATION

by DONALD JUSTICE

from THE SOUTHERN REVIEW

i

Dear ghosts, dear presences, O my dear parents,
Why were you so sad on porches, whispering?
What great melancholies were loosed among our swings!
As before a storm one hears the leaves whispering
    And marks each small change in the atmosphere
    So was it then to overhear and to fear.

ii

But all things then were oracle and secret.
Remember that night when, lost, returning, we turned back
Confused, and our headlights singled out the fox?
Our thoughts went with it then, turning and turning back
    With the same terror, into the deep thicket
    Beside the highway, at home in the dark thicket.

iii

I say the wood within is the dark wood,
Or wound no torn shirt can entirely bandage,
But the sad hand returns to it in secret

Repeatedly, encouraging the bandage
    To speak of that other world we might have borne,
    The lost world buried before it could be born.

iv

Burchfield describes the pinched white souls of violets
Frothing the mouth of a derelict old mine
Just as the evil August night comes down,
All umber but for one smudge of dusky carmine.
    It is the sky of a peculiar sadness—
    The other side perhaps of some rare gladness.

v

What is it to be happy, after all? Think
Of the first small joys. Think of how our parents
Would whistle as they packed for the long summers
Or, busy about the usual tasks of parents,
    Would smile down at us suddenly for some secret reason
    Or simply smile, not needing any person.

vi

But even in the summers we remember
The forest had its eyes, the sea its voices,
And there were roads no map would ever master,
Lost roads and moonless nights and ancient voices;
    And night crept down with an awful slowness toward the
        water—
    And there were lanterns once, doubled in the water.

vii

Sadness has its own beauty, of course. Toward dusk,
Let us say, a river darkens and looks bruised,

425

And we stand looking out at it through rain.
It is as if life itself were somehow bruised
　　And tender at this hour; and a few tears commence.
　　Not that they *are* but that they *feel* immense.

ANNA LIFFEY

by EAVAN BOLAND

from AMERICAN POETRY REVIEW

Life, the story goes,
Was the daughter of Cannan,
And came to the plain of Kildare.
She loved the flat-lands and the ditches
And the unreachable horizon.
She asked that it be named for her.
The river took its name from the land.
The land took its name from a woman.

A woman in the doorway of a house.
A river in the city of her birth.

There, in the hills above my house,
The river Liffey rises, is a source.
It rises in rush and ling heather and
Black peat and bracken and strengthens
To claim the city it narrated.
Swans. Steep falls. Small towns.
The smudged air and bridges of Dublin.

Dusk is coming.
Rain is moving east from the hills.

If I could see myself
I would see
A woman in a doorway

Wearing the colors that go with red hair.
Although my hair is no longer red.

I praise
The gifts of the river.
Its shiftless and glittering
Re-telling of a city,
Its clarity as it flows,
In the company of runt flowers and herons,
Around a bend at Islandbridge
And under thirteen bridges to the sea.
Its patience at twilight—
Swans nesting by it,
Neon wincing into it.

Maker of
Places, remembrances,
Narrate such fragments for me:

One body. One spirit.
One place. One name.
The city where I was born.
The river that runs through it.
The nation which eludes me.

Fractions of a life
It has taken me a lifetime
To claim.

I came here in a cold winter.

I had no children. No country.
I did not know the name for my own life.

My country took hold of me.
My children were born.

I walked out in a summer dusk
To call them in.

One name. Then the other one.
The beautiful vowels sounding out home.

Make of a nation what you will
Make of the past
What you can—

There is now
A woman in a doorway.

It has taken me
All my strength to do this.

Becoming a figure in a poem.

Usurping a name and a theme.

A river is not a woman.
        Although the names it finds
                The history it makes
And suffers—
        The Viking blades beside it.
                The muskets of the Redcoats,
                        the flames of the Four Courts
Blazing into it
        Are a sign.
                        Any more than
A woman is a river.
        Although the course it takes.
                Through swans courting and distraught willows.
Its patience
        Which is also its powerlessness,
                From Callary to Islandbridge,
                        And from source to mouth,
Is another one.
                        And in my late forties
Past believing
        Love will heal
                What language fails to know
And needs to say—
        What the body means—
                I take this sign
And I make this mark:
        A woman in the doorway of her house.
                A river in the city of her birth.

The truth of a suffered life.
        The mouth of it.

The seabirds come in from the coast.
The city wisdom is they bring rain.
I watch them from my doorway.
I see them as arguments of origin—
Leaving a harsh force on the horizon
Only to find it
Slanting and falling elsewhere.

Which water—
The one they leave or the one they pronounce—
Remembers the other?

I am sure
The body of an aging woman
Is a memory
And to find a language for it
Is as hard
As weeping and requiring
These birds to cry out as if they could
Recognize their element
Remembered and diminished in
A single tear.

An aging woman
Finds no shelter in language.
She finds instead
Single words she once loved
Such as "summer" and "yellow"
And "sexual" and "ready"
Have suddenly become dwellings
For someone else—
Rooms and a roof under which someone else
Is welcome, not her. Tell me,
Anna Liffey,
Spirit of water,
Spirit of place,
How is it on this
Rainy Autumn night

As the Irish sea takes
The names you made, the names
You bestowed, and gives you back
only wordlessness?

Autumn rain is
Scattering and dripping
From car-ports
And clipped hedges.
The gutters are full.

When I came here
I had neither
Children nor country.
The trees were arms.
The hills were dreams.

I was free
to imagine a spirit
in the blues and greens,
the hills and fogs
of a small city.

My children were born.
My country took hold of me.
A vision in a brick house.
Is it only love
that makes a place?

I feel it change.
My children are
growing up, getting older.
My country holds on
to its own pain.

I turn off
the harsh yellow
porch light and
stand in the hall
Where is home now?

Follow the rain
out to the Dublin hills.

Let it become the river.
Let the spirit of place be
a lost soul again.

In the end
It will not matter
That I was a woman. I am sure of it.
The body is a source. Nothing more.
There is a time for it. There is a certainty
About the way it seeks its own dissolution.
Consider rivers.
They are always en route to
Their own nothingness. From the first moment
They are going home. And so
when language cannot do it for us,
cannot make us know love will not diminish us,
there are these phrases
of the ocean
to console us.
Particular and unafraid of their completion.
In the end
everything that burdened and distinguished me
will be lost in this:
I was a voice.

A HISTORY OF PAISLEY

by AGHA SHAHID ALI

from THE PARIS REVIEW

*Their footsteps formed the paisley when Parvati, angry after a quarrel, ran away
from Shiva. He eventually caught up with her. To commemorate their reunion, he
carved the Jhelum river, as it moves through the Vale of Kashmir, in the shape of
the paisley.*

You who will find the dark fossils of paisleys
one afternoon on the peaks of Zabarvan—
Trader from an ancient market of the future,
alibi of chronology, that vain
collaborator of time—won't know that these

are her footprints from the day the world began
when land rushed, from the ocean, toward Kashmir.
And above the rising Himalayas? The air
chainstitched itself till the sky hung its bluest
tapestry. But already—as she ran

away—refugee from her Lord—the ruins
of the sea froze, in glaciers, cast in amber.
And there, in the valley below, the river
beguiled its banks into petrified longing:
(O see, it is still the day the world begins:

and the city rises, holding its remains,
its wooden beams already their own fire's prophets.)
And you, now touching sky, deaf to her anklets
still echoing in the valley, deaf to men
fleeing from soldiers into dead-end lanes

(Look! Their feet bleed; they leave footprints on the street
which will give up its fabric, at dusk, a carpet)—
you have found—you'll think—the first teardrop, gem
that was enticed for a Mughal diadem
into design. For you, blind to all defeat

up there in pure sunlight, your gauze of cloud thrown
off your shoulders over the Vale, do not hear
bullets drowning out the bells of her anklets.
This is her relic, but for you the first tear,
drop that you hold as you descend past flowstone,

past dried springs, on the first day of the world.
The street is rolled up, ready for southern ports.
Your ships wait there. What other cargo is yours?
What cables have you sent to tomorrow's bazaars?
What does that past await: the future unfurled

like flags? news from the last day of the world?
You descend quickly, to a garden-café:
At a table by a bed of tzigane
roses, three men are discussing, between
sips of tea, undiscovered routes on emerald

Seas, ships with almonds, with shawls bound for Egypt.
It is dusk. The gauze is torn. A weaver kneels,
gathers falling threads. Soon he will stitch the air.
But what has made you turn? Do you hear her bells?
O alibi of chronology, in what script

in your ledger will this narrative be lost?
In that café, where they discuss the promise
of the world, her cry returns from its abyss

where it hides, by the river. They don't hear it.
The city burns; the dusk has darkened to rust

by the roses. They don't see it. O Trader,
what news will you bring to your ancient market?
I saw her. A city was razed. In its debris
her bells echoed. I turned. They didn't see me
turn to see her—on the peaks—in rapid flight forever.

for Anuradha Dingwaney

435

XXI

.

A WOOD NEAR ATHENS

by THOM GUNN

from THE PARIS REVIEW

1

The traveler struggles through a wood. He is lost.
The traveler is at home. He never left.
He seeks his way on the conflicting trails,
Scribbled with light.
          I have been this way before.

Think! the land here is wooded still all over.
An oak snatched Absalom by his bright hair.
The various trails of love had led him there,
The people's love, his father's, and self-love.

What if it does indeed come down to juices
And organs from whose friction we have framed
The obsession in which we live, obsession I call
The wood preceding us as we precede it?
We thought we lived in a garden, and looked around
To see that trees had risen on all sides.

2

It is ridiculous, ridiculous,
And it is our main meaning.

439

                    At some point
A biological necessity
Brought such a pressure on the human mind,
This concept floated from it—of a creator
Who made up matter, an imperfect world
Solely to have an object for his love.
Beautiful and ridiculous. We say:
Love makes the shoots leap from the blunted branches,
Love makes birds call, and maybe we are right.
Love then makes craning saplings crowd for light,
The weak being jostled off to shade and death.
Love makes the cuckoo heave its foster siblings
Out of the nest, to spatter on the ground.
For love has gouged a temporary hollow
Out of its baby-back, to help it kill.

But who did get it right? Ruth and Naomi,
Tearaway Romeo and Juliet,
Alyosha, Catherine Earnshaw, Jeffrey Dahmer?
They struggled through the thickets as they could.

A wedding entertainment about love
Was set one summer in a wood near Athens.
In paintings by Attila Richard Lukacs,
Cadets and skinheads, city-boys, young Spartans
Wait poised like ballet dancers in the wings
To join the balance of the corps in dances
Passion has planned. They that have power, or seem to,
They that have power to hurt, they are the constructs
Of their own longing, born on the edge of sleep,
Imperfectly understood.
                              Once a young man
Told me my panther made him think of one
His mother's boyfriend had on *his* forearm
—The first man he had sex with, at thirteen.
"Did she know about that?" I asked. He paused:
"I think so. Anyway, they were splitting up."

"Were you confused?"—"No, it was great," he said,
"The best thing that had ever happened to me."

And once, one looked above the wood and saw
A thousand angels making festival,
Each one distinct in brightness and in function,
Which was to choreograph the universe,
Meanwhile performing it. Their work was dance.
Together, wings outstretched, they sang and played
The intellect as powerhouse of love.

A DOG WAS CRYING TO-NIGHT IN WICKLOW ALSO

by SEAMUS HEANEY

from POETRY

In memory of Donatus Nwoga

When human beings found out about death
They sent the dog to Chukwu with a message:
They wanted to be let back to the house of life.
They didn't want to end up lost forever
Like burnt wood disappearing into smoke
Or ashes that get blown away to nothing.
Instead, they saw their souls in a flock at twilight
Cawing and headed back for the same old roosts
And the same bright airs and wing-stretchings each morning.
Death would be like a night spent in the wood:
At first light they'd be back in the house of life.
(The dog was meant to tell all this to Chukwu.)

But death and human beings took second place
When he trotted off the path and started barking
At another dog in broad daylight just barking
Back at him from the far bank of a river.

And that is how the toad reached Chukwu first,
The toad who'd overheard in the beginning
What the dog was meant to tell. "Human beings," he said
(And here the toad was trusted absolutely),
"Human beings want death to last forever."

Then Chukwu saw the people's souls in birds
Coming towards him like black spots off the sunset
To a place where there would be neither roosts nor trees
Nor any way back to the house of life.
And his mind reddened and darkened all at once
And nothing that the dog would tell him later
Could change that vision. Great chiefs and great loves
In obliterated light, the toad in mud,
The dog crying out all night behind the corpse house.

THE BUTTON BOX

by GRACE SCHULMAN

from WESTERN HUMANITIES REVIEW

A sea animal stalked its prey
slithering under her bed, and gorged
on buttons torn from castaways;
ever unsated, it grew large

until it became a deity
spewing out buttons in a fire
of brass for blazers, delft or ruby
for shirts—and dangerous. You'd hear

it snarl when the beds were being made.
It ate stray pins and shot out poison.
But mother, who stuffed its wooden frame,
scooped up waterfalls of suns,

enamel moons, clocks, cameos,
carved pinwheels, stars, tiny "Giottos,"
peacocks strutting out at sundown,
FDR's profile, flags of Britain,

steel helmets, each with a mission.
Mother sewed ballerinas set
in circles on your satin dress,
onyx buttons that would join

you, collar-to-hood, at graduation;
she would find in the creature's lair
"bones" of an army officer,
"pearls" of a war bride's dressing gown;

nights when the radio hissed *dive bombers*
my mother dreamed that she could right
the world again by making sure
you had your buttons, sewed on tight.

JAPAN

by BILLY COLLINS

from THE GEORGIA REVIEW

Today I pass the time reading
a favorite haiku,
saying the few words over and over.

It feels like eating
the same small, perfect grape
again and again.

I walk through the house reciting it
and leave its letters falling
through the air of every room.

I stand by the big silence of the piano and say it.
I say it in front of a painting of the sea.
I tap out its rhythm on an empty shelf.

When the dog looks up at me,
I kneel down on the floor
and whisper it into each of his long white ears.

I listen to myself saying it,
then I say it without listening,
then I hear it without saying it.

It's the one about the one-ton
temple bell
with the moth sleeping on its surface,

and every time I say it, I feel the excruciating
pressure of the moth
on the surface of the iron bell.

When I say it at the window,
the bell is the world
and I am the moth resting there.

When I say it into the mirror,
I am the heavy bell
and the moth is life with its papery wings.

And later, when I say it to you in the dark,
you are the bell,
and I am the tongue of the bell, ringing you,

and the moth has flown
from its line
and moves like a hinge in the air above our bed.

ALIENS

by KIM ADDONIZIO

from ALASKA QUARTERLY REVIEW

Now that you're finally happy
you notice how sad your friends are.
One calls you from a pay phone, crying.
Her husband has cancer; only a few months,
maybe less, before his body gives in.
She's tired all the time, can barely eat.
What can you say that will help her?
You yourself are ravenous.
You come so intensely with your new lover
you wonder if you've turned
into someone else. Maybe an alien
has taken over your body
in order to experience the good life
here on earth: dark rum and grapefruit juice,
fucking on the kitchen floor,
then showering together and going out
to eat and eat. When your friends call—
the woman drinking too much, the one who lost
her brother, the ex-lover whose right ear
went dead and then began buzzing—
the alien doesn't want to listen.
More food, it whines. *Fuck me again*,
it whispers, *and afterwards we'll go to the circus.*
The phone rings. *Don't answer it.*
You reach for a fat eclair,
bite into it while the room fills

with aliens—wandering, star-riddled creatures
who vibrate in the rapturous air,
longing to come down and join you,
looking for a place they can rest.

BELOW FOURTEENTH STREET

by GERALD STERN

from COLORADO REVIEW

Somewhere above Fourteenth he pulled up his shirt sleeves
the way he learned to do in Scotland. He found
two rubber bands and two feet of yellow string
in one of the metal baskets on Sixth. He smiled
at the color combinations but he was too stricken
to worry the way he used to. After he passed
Sam Goodys he opened his shirt. For thirty blocks
he thought of the upside-down bird; once he got
the name right he would stop in one of the restaurants
above Thirty-Fourth and write for an hour before
he went back down. Two girls wearing shorts
and yellow T-shirts made their fish faces and tried
their French on him. They wished he were dead, he ruined
their morning. Up in the sterile pear tree the bird
sang her heart out. She was a chickadee,
he was sure of that, and leaped to one perch
then to another and cleaned herself and chirped
a little more since it was the end of April
and it would never snow again. He sang
himself with his lips though there was a clicking heart
behind it and under the pear tree; across the street
from Blockbuster's there was such music, there were
so many pure complaints that when he whistled

to mark the ending, and to repeat, since who
could bear an ending, there was a quickening
and slackening in the blossoms—he even thought
he and the bird were working together, he even
waved to those girls—at least a gesture—he found
the harmony for that day, whatever you think
he was able to find his notes. He hugged
his ledger to himself—he carried a ledger—
and he adjusted his tie. When he turned left
into the forest, so to speak, those shoe stores
and ugly theatres and busy rag stores, he did
the rest of the trip in silence, that way he showed
respect for the dirt, though it was two feet down,
and for the stream that crossed there, maybe the west
side of Fifth, maybe in front of Fayvas,
and took his shoes and socks off so the muck
could bring life back into his arches and give him
back what he had lost. He put his shoes on,
he put his socks in his pocket, he tilted a stone
to see a snake, at least he thought so, and raced
past the sock store—that of all things—and past
the Moroccan cafe and up the forty-seven
steps to the right hand door beside the flutist,
she who played all day and kept her cat
in a harness, all the time looking for clover—
that's what he said—and when she opened the door
he talked about the clover, there was no life
without it, clover the rabbits needed, her cat
if there were clover would roll in her harness, clover,
in maybe a month would cover the lawns, it was
the flower closest to him, after the blooming,
after the exchange, their petals turn brown
and drop, like a skirt, it is ironic that clubs
are black when clover is white, the ace of clubs
is only a flower, he has hope and he has
three leaves in his ear, he said these things, she said
she missed the country, upstate New York, the flats
of Nebraska, but he had taken one of the leaves
and put it in his mouth and turned the bolt
twice to the right and turned the light on beside

the second refrigerator and opened the window
and found some music, Dvorak in Iowa,
a town near the Mississippi, Spillville, his cuff
like Dvorak's, already full of notes, the sound
the same, the state abounding in clover, Irma
putting her head underneath his hand, the straps
twisted around a chair but she was so tired
she had to sleep and she was so trusting she had
to purr, for this is the New World and the doors
are both open the way they should be and music
from one place is mixing with music from another,
a flute with a piano, a flute with a violin,
the cellos now taking over, the horns taking over,
hope going down the stairway, despair going up,
somewhere on that plaster the two meeting,
the man in the busy cuffs, the cat in the harness.

XXII

NO TURN ON RED

by RICHARD JACKSON

from MARLBORO REVIEW

It's enough to make the moon turn its face
the way these poets take a kind of bubble bath
in other people's pain. I mean, sure, the dumpsters
of our lives are filling with more mistakes
than we could ever measure. Whenever we reach into
the pockets of hope we pull out the lint of despair.
I mean, all I have to do is lift the eyelids
of the stars to see how distant you could become.
But that doesn't mean my idea of form is a kind of
twelve step approach to vision. I mean, I don't want
to contribute to the body count which, in our major journals,
averages 13.7 deaths/poem, counting major catastrophes and wars.
I'm not going to blame those bodies floating down some
river in Rwanda or Bosnia on Love's failures. But really,
it's not the deaths in those poems, it's the way Death arrives in a tux
and driving a Lamborghini then says a few rhymed words
over his martini. It's a question of taste, really,
which means, a question for truth. I mean, if someone
says some beastly person enters her room the way Hitler
entered Poland I'd say she'd shut her eyes like a Kurdish
tent collapsing under a gas attack, it makes about
as much sense. Truth is too often a last line of defense,
like the way every hospital in America keeps a bag
of maggots on ice to eat away infection when the usual
antibiotics fail. The maggots do a better job
but aren't as elegant. Truth is just bad taste, then?

Not really. Listen to this: "Legless Boy Somersaults
Two Miles to Save Dad," reads the headline from Italy
in *Weekly World News,* a story that includes pictures
of the heroic but bloody torso of the boy. "Twisted
like a pretzel," the story goes on. Bad taste or
world class gymnastics? Which reminds me. One afternoon
I was sitting in a bar watching the Olympics—the singles
of synchronized swimming—how can that be true?
If that's so, why not full contact javelin? Uneven
table tennis? The 1500 meter dive? Even the relay dive?
Someone's going to say I digress? Look, this is a satire
which means, if you look up the original Latin, "mixed dish,"
—you have to take a bite of everything. True, some would
argue it's the word we get Satyr from, but I don't like
to think of myself as some cloven hoofed, horny little
creature sniffing around trees. Well, it's taste, remember.
Besides my satire is set while waiting at Love's traffic
light, which makes it unique. So, I was saying you have
to follow truth's little detours—no, no, it was taste,
the heroic kid twisted like a pretzel. Pretzels are
metaphysical. Did you know a medieval Italian monk
invented them in the year 610 in the shape of crossed,
praying arms to reward his parish children?
"I like children," said W.C. Fields—"if they're properly
cooked." Taste, and its fellow inmate, truth—how do we
measure anything anymore? Everyone wants me to stick
to a few simple points, or maybe no point at all,
like the tepid broth those new formalists ladle into their
demitasse. How can we write about anything—truth,
love, hope, taste, when someone says the moment, the basis
of all lyric poetry, of all measure and meter, is just
the equivalent of 10 billion atomic vibrations of the cesium
atom when it's been excited by microwaves. Twilight chills
in the puddles left by evening's rain. The tiny spider
curled on the bulb begins to cast a huge shadow. No wonder
time is against us. In 1953, Dirty Harry, a "nuclear device,"
as the phrase goes, blossomed in Nevada's desert leaving
more than twice the fallout anyone predicted.
After thirty years no one admits the measurements.
Truth becomes a matter of "duck and cover." Even Love

456

refuses to come out of its shelter. In Sarajevo,
Dedran Smailovic plays Albinoni's *Adagio* outside
the bakery for 22 days where mortars killed 22
and the papers are counting the days till the sniper
aims. You can already see the poets lined up on
poetry's dragstrip revving up their 22 line elegies
in time for the *New Yorker* deadline, so to speak.
Vision means, I guess, how far down the road of your
career you can see. And numbers not what Pope meant
by rhythm, but $5 per line. Pythagoras (b. 570 BC)
thought the world was made entirely of numbers. Truth,
he said, is the formula, and we are just the variables.
But this is from a guy who thought Homer's soul was
reborn in his. Later, that he had the soul of a peacock.
Who could trust him? How do we measure anything?
Each time they clean the standard kilogram bar in Sevres,
France, it loses a few atoms making everything else appear
a little heavier. That's why everything is suddenly
more somber. Love is sitting alone in a rented room
with its hangman's rope waiting for an answer
that's not going to come. All right, so I exaggerate, and
in bad taste. Let's say Love has put away its balance,
tape measure and nails and is poking around in its tin
lunch pail. So how can I measure how much I love you?
Except the way the willow measures the universe.
Except the way your hair is tangled among the stars.
The way the turtle's shell reflects the night's sky.
I'm not counting on anything anymore. Even the foot—
originally defined as the shoe length of whatever king
held your life, which made the poets scramble around
to define their own poetic feet. And truth is all this?
That's why it's good to have all these details as
a kind of yardstick to rap across the fingers
of bad taste. "I always keep a supply of stimulants
handy," said Fields, "in case I see a snake;
which I also keep handy." In the end, you still need
something to measure, and maybe that's the problem
that makes living without love or truth so much pain.
I'd have to be crazy. Truth leaves its fingerprints
on everything we do. It's nearly 10 PM. Crazy.

Here comes another poet embroidering his tragic
childhood with a few loosely lined mirrors.
I'm afraid for what comes next. The birds' warning
song runs up and down the spine of the storm. Who says
any love makes sense? The only thing left is
this little satire and its faceless clock for a soul.
You can't measure anything you want. The basis of all
cleverness is paranoia. 61% of readers never finish
the poem they start. 31% of Americans are afraid to speak
while making love. 57% of Americans have dreamt
of dying in a plane crash. One out of four
Americans is crazy. Look around at your three
best friends. If they're okay, you're in trouble.

KARMA LOLLIPOP

by ALBERT SAIJO

from BAMBOO RIDGE

WHITEMAN CENTRAL BREAKDOWN—THINGS START
TO WOBBLE & FALL APART—GLASS SHATTERS METAL
CORRODES FERROCONCRETE WEATHERS &
CRUMBLES—WHITEMAN CENTRAL BECOMES POOR—
DIRT POOR—MORE POOR THAN A 3RD WORLD
COUNTRY—SO POOR IT CAN'T EVEN SUPPORT A
WEALTHY CLASS—WHITEMAN RETURNS TO HUNTER
FORAGER MODE—WHITEMAN'S LAND BECOMES TERRA
INCOGNITA—THEN ONE DAY INTO THIS NOT NECES-
SARILY UNHAPPY SITUATION IN WHICH HARDLY
ANYTHING IS HAPPENING BUT LIFE THERE COMES
NOVELTY—1ST IT'S THEIR MISSIONARIES—THEY ARE
NOT WHITE—THEY ARE ELFIN & YELLOW—THEY HAVE
HIGH CHEEKBONES SLANT EYES & BLACK HAIR—THEY
SAY THEY ARE FROM AN ADVANCED HYPERTECH
CIVILIZATION ACROSS THE GREAT WATER TO THE
WEST IN THE DIRECTION OF THE SETTING SUN & THEY
POINT IN THAT DIRECTION SO WHITEMAN UNDER-
STAND—THEY TALK LOUD—THEY SAY WHITEMAN OUR
BURDEN—THEY SAY BUDDHA LOVE WHITEMAN EVEN
IF WHITEMAN BACKWARD DIRTY & HEATHENISH—
THEY WANT WHITEMAN TO CLEAN UP & PUT ON
CLOTHES—THEIR TRIP SEEMS TO BE BUDDHA LOVES
YOU SANITATION & DON'T LET NUTHIN HANG OUT—
SO BIG DEAL IF THAT'S ALL THEY WANT—BUT THEY
BROUGHT THE KONG HONG FLU—LESS SAID ABOUT IT

THE BETTER—THEN COME THE SOCIAL SCIENTISTS—
THEY ARE FROM ANOTHER ADVANCED
TECHNOCIVILIZATION OF SMALL BROWN PEOPLE
WHERE ALTERED NEURONAL TISSUE CULTURED ON
SEWER SLUDGE GROW INTO GIANT BRAINS THAT RUN
EVERYTHING—ORGANIC BIOTECH TO THE MAX OR
NOTHING—A MARVEL OF THE NEW GOOK SCIENTIFIC
IMAGINATION—THEY SAY HEY WHITEMAN YOU DON'T
MIND IF WE SET UP OUR CAMP IN YOUR YARD DO
YOU—WE WANT TO STUDY YOU—YOU'RE VERY INTER-
ESTING TO US—HEY WHAT'S THAT TOOL YOU GOT IN
YOUR HAND—LOOK FELLAS IT'S AN ARCHAIC VICE
GRIP—WE WANT THAT—THEY GIVE WHITEMAN A MESS
OF CHEAP BEADS & A TIN MIRROR & THEY TAKE HIS
VICE GRIP—AND THEY LEAVE THE YELLOW YAW
YAWS—ALMOST 100% MORTALITY FOR WHITEMAN ON
THAT ONE—CLOSE—THE YELLOW YAW YAWS ARE LIKE
THE HEARTBREAK OF PSORIASIS ONLY MUCH MUCH
WORSE—AGAIN LESS SAID ABOUT IT THE BETTER—
THEN COME THE POWER & BUCKS PEOPLE—THEY ARE
SHORT WITH BROAD FLAT FACES & PERFECT ALMOND
EYES YOU'D DIE FOR—THEY DON'T GIVE A SHIT FOR
NUTHIN BUT POWER & BUCKS—DERE DA GUYS WHO
GOT THE VAPORIZOR GUNS—YOU GET IN THEIR WAY
THEY POINT THE VAPORIZOR AT YOU & PULL THE
TRIGGER—WHEN THE FORCE HITS IT TURNS YOU INTO
A PUFF OF INNOCUOUS VAPOR—NO GORY CORPSE—
MAYHEM MADE SANITARY—A GIANT STEP FORWARD
FOR CIVILIZATION—A MARVEL OF THE MONGOL SCI-
ENTIFIC IMAGINATION WITH ITS SURREAL
MATHEMATIC TURNS FLESH TO VAPOR—NOW BEFORE
THE VERY EYES OF WHITEMAN THESE ADVANCED
NONWHITE NATIONS ARE DIVIDING UP WHITEMAN'S
LAND INTO WHAT THEY CALL SPHERES OF INFLU-
ENCE—THEY ARE GOING TO PUT A GRID ON
WHITEMAN'S LAND & SELL IT OFF DIRT CHEAP FOR
KIWI PLANTATIONS WITH WHITEMAN DOING THE
GRUNTWORK—THEN ONCE THE PLANTATIONS ARE IN
THEY AUTOMATE PLANTATIONS—NOW WHITE MAN
ON THE DOLE & REALLY BEGINNING TO GET IN THE

460

WAY OF PROGRESS—SO THESE SUPERTECH NATIONS
ROUND UP WHITEMAN THAT IS THE REMNANT POPU-
LATIONS OF WHITEMAN STILL SCATTERED HERE &
THERE & THEY PUT THEM INTO WHAT THEY CALL
RELOCATION CENTERS THAT CAN MEAN ANYTHING
OR NOTHING LIKE RESERVATIONS—NOW THESE NON-
WHITE ADVANCED MEGATECH NATIONS BEGIN
FIGHTING AMONG THEMSELVES—INEVITABLY—ALL
POLITICS IS BULLSHIT—THEY MAKE WHITEMAN'S
LAND INTO A BATTLEGROUND FOR THEIR WARS—
THESE WARS HAVE NOTHING TO DO WITH WHITEMAN
BUT THEY ARE TRASHING HIS LAND—MEANTIME
AMIDST ALL THE CHAOS OF THIS MOTHER OF ALL
WARS ONLY THE MENEHUNES OF THE WORLD REMAIN
CLEAR CENTERED ON TIME NEUTRAL EACH A VERI-
TABLE SWITZERLAND OF THE UNIVERSAL POETIC
GENIUS

FOR THE YOUNG MEN WHO DIED OF AIDS

by JULIA VINOGRAD

from ZEITGEIST PRESS

The dead lovers are almost as beautiful
as razor-edged spaces in the air where they used to walk.
Do you remember his hand lazily playing
with the rim of a glass, making the ghost of a bell sound
for his own ghost, and the talk didn't even pause?
That glass is whole. Break it; break it now.
Break everything.
How can people go on buying toothpaste
and planning their summer vacations?
Vegetables would care more.
The potato has a thousand eyes all mourning for the lovers
who lived in their deaths like a country
foreign to everywhere for a long time before dying.
A long time watching people look away.
The potato only met them under the earth
after their deaths and still it wept. And we do not.
The ghost bell makes barely a sound forever.
The dead lovers are still in love, but no one else is.
He took his hand with him, a grave is as good
as a briefcase to keep the essentials in:
a smile, bones, a way of biting his lip
just before looking into your eyes.
Shoulder blades cutting into summer like butter.
All the commuters in a rush hour traffic jam

are cursing because the lovers are dying
faster than their cars.
The child sent to bed without dinner cries
for the lovers, also sent to bed early and without.
Unfair. Throw the dishes against the wall. Break them.
The dead lovers are almost as beautiful
as when they were alive.
You can hear the rim of a glass
tolling for the ghosts to come home.
Break the glass, break the ghosts. Pull down the sky.
Break everything.
Dance on the fragments. Scream their names.
Get splinters of ghosts under your skin
torn and bleeding because it hurts,
                    because it hurts so bad.

WHAT THE ANIMALS TEACH US

by CHARD DE NIORD

from HARVARD REVIEW

that love is dependent on memory,
that life is eternal and therefore criminal,
that thought is an invisible veil that covers our eyes,
that death is only another animal,
that beauty is formed by desperation,
that sex is solely a human problem,
that pets are wild in heaven,
that sounds and smells escape us,
that there are bones in the earth without any marker,
that language refers to too many things,
that music hints at what we heard before we sang,
that the circle is loaded,
that nothing we know by forgetting is sacred,
that humor charges the smallest things,
that the gods *are* animals without their masks,
that stones tell secrets to the wildest creatures,
that nature is an idea and not a place,
that our bodies have diminished in size and strength,
that our faces are terrible,
that our eyes are double when gazed upon,
that snakes do talk, as well as asses,
that we compose our only audience,

that we are geniuses when we wish to kill,
that we are naked despite our clothes,
that our minds are bodies in another world.

BLACKLEGS

by BRIGIT PEGEEN KELLY

from TAMAQUA

The sheep has nipples, the boy said,
And fur all around. The sheep
Has black legs, his name is Blacklegs,
And a cry like breaking glass.
The glass is broken. The glass
is broken, and the milk falls down.

The bee has a suffering softness,
The boy said, a ring of fur,
Like a ring of fire. He burns
The flowers he enters, the way
The rain burns the grass. The bee
Has six legs, six strong legs,
And when he flies the legs
Whistle like a blade of grass
Brought to the lips and blown.

The boy said, The horse runs hard
As sorrow, or a storm, or a man
With a stolen purse in his shirt.
The horse's legs are a hundred
Or more, too many to count,
And he holds a moon white as fleece
In his mouth, cups it like water
So it will not spill out.

And the boy said this. I am a boy
And a man. My legs are two
And they shine black as the arrows
That drop down on my throat
And my chest to draw out the blood
The bright animals feed on,
Those with wings, those without,
The ghosts of the heart—whose
Hunger is a dress for my song.

VOUS ÊTES PLUS BEAUX QUE VOUS NE PENSIEZ

by KENNETH KOCH

from POETRY

I

Botticelli lived
In a little house
In Florence
Italy
He went out
And painted Aphrodite
Standing on some air
Above a shell
On some waves
And he felt happy
He
Went into a café
And cried
I'll buy
Everybody a drink
And for me
A *punt e mes*
Celebrities thronged
To look at his painting
Never had anyone seen
So beautiful a painted girl
The real girl he painted
The model
For Aphrodite sits

With her chin in her hand
Her hand on her wrist
Her elbow
On a table
And she cries,
"When I was
Naked I was believed,
Will be, and am."

2

Sappho lived
In a little house
Made out of stone
On the island
In Greece of Lesbos
And she lived
To love other women
She loved girls
She went out
And was tortured by loving someone
And then was
Tortured by
Loving someone else
She wrote great
Poems
About these loves
Poems so great
That they actually seem
Like torture themselves
Torture to know
So much sweetness
Can be given
And can be taken away.

George Gordon Lord Byron lived
In a little house
In England
He came out
Full of fire
And wild
Creative spirits
He got himself in trouble all the time
He made love to his sister
He was a devil to his wife
And she to him!
Byron was making love
Part of the time
In ottava rima
And part of the time
Really
Teresa Guiccioli lived
In a big palace
In Venice
And Byron made love to her
Time after time after time.

4

Saint Francis of Assisi lived
In a little house
Full of fine
And expensive things
His father
Was a billionaire
(SIR Francis of Assisi)
And his mother was a lady
Most high and rare
Baby Francis stayed there
And then he went out
He found God
He saw God

He gave all
His clothes away
Which made
His father mad
Very mad
Saint Francis gave
To poor
People and to animals
Everything he had
Now he has a big church
Built to him in Assisi
His father has nothing
Not even
A mound of earth
With his name
SIR
FRANCIS OF ASSISI
Above it
Carved on a stone.

5

Borges lived
In a little house
In Buenos Aires
He came out
And wrote
Stories, and
When he was blind
Was director
Of the National Library
La Biblioteca Nacional
No one at the Library
Knew he was a famous man
They were amazed
At the elegant women
Who came to pick him up—
Like a book!—
At the Library's day's end.

6

Vladimir Mayakowsky lived
In a little house
In Russia
He came out
And painted pictures
And wrote poems
"To the Eiffel Tower"
"To My Passport"
"At the Top of My Lungs"
"A Cloud in Trousers."
Before he died—
Was it suicide
Or was he murdered
By the Secret Police?
Crowds of fifty thousand gathered
To hear him read his lines.

7

Maya Plisetskaya lived
In a little house
In Russia
There was snow
All around
And often
For weeks at a time
Maya Plisetskaya's feet
Didn't touch the ground
The way, afterwards
They never seemed to touch
The stage
She said The age
When you begin
To understand dance
Is the same
As that at which
You start to lose
Your "elevation."

8

Ludwig Wittgenstein lived
In a little house
In Austria
He came out
And went to live
In another house
In England
He kept coming out
And going back in
He wrote philosophy
Books that showed
We do not know how we know
What we mean
By words like Out and In
He was revered like a god
For showing this
And he acted like a god
In mid-career
He completely changed his mind.

Frank O'Hara lived
In a little house
In Grafton, Massachusetts
Sister and brother
Beside him.
He took out
Toilet articles from his house
And he took out
Candles and books
And he took out
Music and pictures and stones
And to himself he said
Now you are out
Of the house Do something
Great! He came

To New York
He wrote "Second Avenue," "Biotherm"
And "Hatred"
He played the piano
He woke up
In a construction site
At five a.m., amazed.

10

Jean Dubuffet lived
In a little house
In the south of France
He came out
And made paintings
He went back in
And made some more
Soon Jean Dubuffet had
A hundred and five score
He also did sculptures,
And paintings
That were like sculptures
And even some sculptures
That were like
Paintings Such
Is our modern world
And among the things
He did
Was a series
Of portraits
Of his artist and writer
Friends A large series
Entitled You Look
Better than You Thought You
Did *Vous Êtes*
Plus Beaux que
Vous ne Pensiez.

XXIII

THE LECTURES ON LOVE

by EDWARD HIRSCH

from THE PARIS REVIEW

1. Charles Baudelaire

These lectures afford me a great pleasure,
so thank you for coming. My subject is love
and my proposition is a simple one: erotic love,
which is, after all, a fatal form of pleasure,
closely resembles a surgical operation, or torture.
Forgive me if I sound ironic or cynical
but, I'm sure you'll agree, cynicism
is sometimes called for in discussing torture.

Act One, Scene One: The score is "Love."
The setting of a great operatic passion
At first the lovers have equal passion.
but, it turns out, one always seems to love
the other less. He, or she, is the surgeon
applying a scalpel to the patient, the victim.
I know because I have been that victim
though I have also been the torturer, the surgeon.

Can you hear those loud spasmodic sighs?
Who hasn't uttered them in hours of love?
Who hasn't drawn them from his (or her) lover?
It's sacrilegious to call such noises "ecstasy"
when they're really a species of decomposition,

surrendering to death. We can get drunk
on each other, but don't pretend being drunk
puts us in a sudden death-defying position.

Why are people so proud of that spellbound
look in the eyes, that stiffening between the legs?
Example One: She ran her hand down my legs
until I felt as if I'd been gagged and bound.
Example Two: She no longer gave me any pleasure,
nonetheless, I rested my hand on her nude body
almost casually, I leaned over and tasted her body
until her whole being trembled with pleasure.

The erotic is an intimate form of cruelty
and every pleasure can be used to prostitute
another: I love you, so I become your prostitute
but my generosity is your voluptuous cruelty.
Sex is humiliation, a terrifying game
in which one partner loses self-control.
The subject concerns ownership or control
and that makes it an irresistible game.

I once heard the question discussed:
Wherein consists love's greatest pleasure?
I pondered the topic with great pleasure
but the whole debate filled me with disgust.
Someone declared, *We love a higher power.*
Someone said, *Giving is better than receiving,*
though someone else returned, *I prefer receiving.*
No one there ever connected love to power.

Someone actually announced, *The greatest pleasure*
in love is to populate the State with children.
But must we really be no better than children
whenever we discuss the topic of pleasure?
Pain, I say, is inseparable from pleasure
and love is but an exquisite form of torture.
You need me, but I carry the torch for her . . .
Evil comes enswathed in every pleasure.

2. Heinrich Heine

Thank you, thank you ladies and gentlemen.
I have had myself carried here today
on what we may call my mattress-grave
where I have been entombed for years
(forgive me if I don't stand up this time)
to give a lecture about erotic love.

As a cripple talking about Eros,
a subject I've been giving up for years,
I know my situation (*this time he's
gone too far!*) is comical and grave.
But don't I still appear to be a man?
Hath not a Jew eyes, etc., at least today?

I am an addict of the human comedy
and I propose that every pleasure, esp. love,
is like the marriage of the French and Germans
or the eternal quarrel between Space and Time.
We are all creeping madly toward the grave
or leaping forward across the years.

(Me, I haven't been able to leap in years)
and bowing under the fiendish blows of Time.
All that can distract us—gentlemen, ladies—
is the splendid warfare between men and women.
I don't hesitate to call the struggle "love."
Look at me: my feverish body is a grave,

I've been living so long on a mattress-grave
That I scarcely even resemble a man,
but what keeps me going is the quest for love.
I may be a dog who has had his day
(admittedly a day that has lasted for years)
but I'm also a formidable intellect of our time

and I'm telling you nothing can redeem Time
or the evident oblivions of the grave
or the crippling paralysis of the years

479

except the usual enchantments of love.
That's why the night hungers for the day
and the gods—heaven help us—envy the human.

Ladies and gentlemen, the days pass into years
and the body is a grave filled with time.
We are drowning. All that rescues us is love.

3. Marquis de Sade

This is the first time I have given a lecture
on my favorite subject—the nature of love—
so thank you for courageously inviting me.
I hope you won't regret having invited me
when you hear what I think about erotic love.
These are provisional notes *towards* a lecture

since what I've prepared are some observations
which, forgive me, I will not attempt to prove
but which I offer as subjective testimony.
What I *will* claim for this evidentiary testimony
is its forthright honesty, which I cannot prove.
I offer you the candor of my observations,   ˙

and I trust I will not shock you too much
(or too little) by revealing the deep abyss
at the heart—the vertiginous core—of love.
We will always desecrate whatever we love.
Eroticism stands on the edge of an abyss:
Sex is not enough until it becomes too much.

Love is erotic because it is so dangerous.
I am an apostle of complete freedom who believes
other people exist to satisfy my appetites.
I am not ashamed to pursue those appetites
and I have the will to enact my cruel beliefs.
The greatest *liaisons* are always dangerous.

Exhibit Number One is an innocent specimen.
My niece has a face aureoled by grace,

a guileless soul, and a lily-white body.
I like to masturbate all over her body
and to enter behind while she says grace.
Her humiliation is a delicious specimen.

Exhibit Number Two takes place in church.
I sent my valet to purchase a young whore
and he dresses her as a sweet-faced num.
(Do I have any compunction about this? *None*.)
In a pew I sodomize the terrified whore
until she becomes a member of my church.

It takes courage to be faithful to desire—
not many have the nerve. I myself feed
from the bottom of a cesspool for pleasure
(and I have fed from her bottom with pleasure).
I say whosoever has the courage to feed
from the ass of his beloved will sate desire.

Please don't leave. My doctrine is *isolism*:
the lack of contact between human beings.
But strangle me and you shall touch me.
Spit in my face and you shall see me.
Suck my cock and you taste a human being.
Otherwise we are the subjects of isolism.

Forgive me if I speak with too much freedom.
I am nothing more than an old libertine
who believes in the sanctity of pleasure.
Suffering, too, is a noble form of pleasure
like the strange experience of a libertine.
I would release you to a terrible freedom.

4. Margaret Fuller

Thank you for attending this conversation on love.
I am going to argue in the Nineteenth Century
a woman can no longer be sacrificed for love.
The Middle Ages are over, ladies and gentlemen,

481

and I am going to argue in the Nineteenth Century
we are not merely wives, whores, and mothers.
The Middle Ages are over, gentleman. And ladies,
we can be sea captains, if you will.

We are not merely wives, whores, and mothers.
We can be lawyers, doctors, journalists,
we can now be sea captains, if you will.
What matters to us is our own fulfillment.

We can be lawyers, doctors, journalists
who write ourselves into the official scripts.
What matters to us is our own fulfillment.
It is time for Eurydice to call for Orpheus

and to sing herself into the official scripts.
She is no longer a stranger to her inheritance.
It is time for Eurydice to call for Orpheus
and to move the earth with her triumphant song.

She is no longer a stranger to her inheritance.
She, too, leaves her footprints in the sand
and moves the earth with her triumphant song.
God created us for the purpose of happiness.

She, too, leaves her footprints in the sand.
She, too, feels divinity within her body.
God created us for the purpose of happiness.
She is not the betrothed, the bride, the spouse.

She, too, feels divinity within her body.
Man and Woman are two halves of one thought.
She is not the betrothed, the bride, the spouse.
The sexes should prophesy to one another.

Man and Woman are two halves of one thought.
They are both on equal terms before the law.
The sexes should prophesy to one another.
My love is a love that cannot be crucified.

We are both on equal terms before the law.
Our holiest work is to transform the earth.
(My love is a love that cannot be crucified.)
The earth itself becomes a parcel of heaven.

Our holiest work is to transform the earth.
Thank you for attending this conversation on love.
The earth itself becomes a parcel of heaven.
A woman can no longer be sacrificed for love.

5. Giacomo Leopardi

Thank you for listening to this new poem
which Leopardi has composed for the occasion:
he regrets he cannot read it here himself
(he is, he suggests, but a remnant of himself),
especially on such an auspicious occasion.
He has asked me to present you with this poem:

Poetry Would Be a Way of Praising God if God Existed

Deep in the heart of night
I stood on a hill in wintertime
and stared up at the baleful moon.
I was terrified of finding myself
in the midst of nothing, myself
nothingness clarified, like the moon.
I was suffocating inside time,
contemplating the empty night

when a bell rang in the distance
three times, like a heart beating
in the farthest reaches of the sky.
The music was saturated with stillness.
I stood listening to that stillness
until it seemed to fill the sky.
The moon was like a heart beating
somewhere far off in the distance.

But there is no heart in a universe
of dying planets, infinite starry spaces.
Death alone is the true mother of Eros
and only love can revivify the earth.
Look at the sky canopied over earth:
it is a black sea pulsing without Eros,
a world of infinitely dead, starry spaces.
Love alone can redeem our universe.

6. Ralph Waldo Emerson

Thank you for coming to this lecture on love.
I have been told that in public discourse
my true reverence for intellectual discourse
has made me indifferent to the subject of love,
but I almost shrink at such disparaging words
since I believe love created the world.
What else, after all, perpetuates the world
except enacted love? I savor the words.

The study of love is a question of facts
and a matter of dreams, a dream that matters.
Lovers are scientist studying heavenly matters
while their bodies connect the sweetest facts.
Please don't blush when I speak of love
as the reunion of two independent souls
who have drifted since birth as lost souls
but now come together in eternal love.

There can be no love without natural sympathy.
Let's say you're a hunter who excels at business
(I'm aware this may be none of my business)
but for me it doesn't arouse much sympathy.
Let's say, however, you drink tea in the morning
and like to eat apple pie for breakfast;
we both walk through the country very fast
watching the darkness turn into early morning

and this creates a mutual bond between us
that leads to a soulful sharing of sabbaths.

The heart has its jubilees and sabbaths
when a fiery lightning strikes between us.
I do not shy away from the subject of sex
which is, after all, a principle of the universe
(it is also, alas, a principle of my verse)
since we are bound to each other through sex.

Look how the girls flirt with the boys
while the boys slowly encircle the girls.
The village shops are crowded with girls
lingering over nothing to talk with boys.
Romance is the beginning of celestial ecstasy,
an immortal hilarity, a condition of joy:
civilization itself depends on the joy
of standing beside ourselves with ecstasy.

Love is a bright foreigner, a foreign self
that must recognize me for what I truly am;
only my lover can understand me as I am
when I am struggling to create myself.
So, too, I must love you as you truly are—
but what is that? Under your cool visage
and coy exterior, your advancing age,
I sense the young passion of who you are.

The lover comes with something to declare—
such declarations affirm the nature of love.
Here is what the lover says to his love
in the heat of passion, this I declare:
My love for you is a voluptuous world
where the seasons appear as a bright feast.
We can sit together at this delicious feast.
Come lie down with me and devour the world.

7. Colette

My young friends, this is the final lecture,
though not the last word, on the subject of love,
so thank you for listening. It is my pleasure
to address a passion I know something about

485

(which is something, forgive me, I can't say about
all the previous lecturers)—not just pleasure,
but the unruly depths we describe as love.
Let's call our tête-à-tête, "A Modern Lecture."

My mother used to say, "Sit down, dear,
and don't cry. The worst thing for a woman
is her first man—the one who kills you.
After that, marriage becomes a long career."
Poor Sido! She never had another career
and she knew firsthand how love ruins you.
The seducer doesn't care about his woman,
even as he whispers endearments in her ear.

Never let anyone destroy your inner spirit.
Among all the forms of truly absurd courage
the recklessness of young girls is outstanding.
Otherwise there would be far fewer marriages
and even fewer affairs that overwhelm marriages.
Look at me: it's amazing I'm still standing
after what I went through with ridiculous courage.
I was made to suffer, but no one broke my spirit.

Every woman wants her adventure to be a feast
of ripening cherries and peaches, Marseilles figs,
hothouse grapes, champagne shuddering in crystal.
Happiness, we believe, is on sumptuous display.
But unhappiness writes a different kind of play.
The gypsy gazes down into a clear blue crystal
and sees rotten cherries and withered figs.
Trust me: loneliness, too, can be a feast.

Ardor is delicious, but keep your own room.
One of my husbands said: is it impossible
for you to write a book that isn't about love,
adultery, semi-incestuous relations, separation?
(Of course, this was before our own separation.)
He never understood the natural law of love,
the arc from the possible to the impossible . . .
I have extolled the tragedy of the bedroom.

We need exact descriptions of the first passion,
so pay attention to whatever happens to you.
Observe everything: love is greedy and forgetful.
By all means fling yourself wildly into life
(though sometimes you will be flung back by life)
but don't let experience make you forgetful
and be surprised by everything that happens to you.
We are creative creatures fueled by passion.

Consider this an epilogue to the lectures on love,
a few final thoughts about the nature of love.
Freedom should be the first condition of love
and work is liberating (*a novel about love
cannot be written while you are making love*).
Never underestimate the mysteries of love,
the eminent dignity of not talking about love.
Passionate attention is prayer, prayer is love.

Savor the world. Consume the feast with love.

THE BOOK OF THE DEAD MAN #87

by MARVIN BELL

from POETRY

1. Accounts of the Dead Man

The dead man likes it when the soup simmers and the kettle hisses.
He wants to live as much as possible at the ends of his fingertips.
To make sense, to make nonsense, to make total sense, lasting sense,
    ephemeral sense, giddy sense, perfect sense, holy sense.
The dead man wants it, he requires it, he trusts it.
Therefore, the dead man takes up with words as if they had nowhere
    in mind.
The dead man's words are peacock feathers, bandages, all the
    everyday exotica ground under by utility.
The dead man's book foresees a flickering awareness, an ember at
    the end of the Void, a glitter, a glow beneath the ash.
The dead man's book is the radical document of time, nodding to
    calamity and distress, happy in harm's way.
To the dead man, the mere whistling of a pedestrian may signal an
    onslaught of intention.
The dead man calls his spillover a journal because it sounds helpless
    and private, while a diary suggests the writings of someone
    awaiting rescue.
The dead man doesn't keep a diary.
The dead man sweeps under the bed for scraps, pieces, chips, tips,
    fringework, lace, filings and the rivets that rattled and broke.

His is a flurry of nothing-more-to-give, the echo of a prolonged note
    struck at the edge of an inverted bowl.
Now he must scrub his brain before a jury of his peers.

2. More Accounts of the Dead Man

The dead man has caused a consternation, but he didn't mean to.
He was just clocking his pulse, tracking his heart, feeling his way.
He was just dispersing the anomalous and otherwise scouting the
    self-evident and inalienable.
It was just that sometimes he couldn't stand it because he was happy.
It was the effect that he effected that affected him.
Some say it was his fervor for goose bumps took his breath away.
Some say it was the dead man's antsiness that put him in the dirt.
Some say he was too much the live wire, the living will, the holy
    spirit, the damn fool.
His was a great inhalation, wanton, a sudden swivel in the midst of
    struggle, a death dance with demons and other dagnabbits.
The dead man was well into physical geezerhood when he came to a
    conclusion and declared his independence.
At once he was chockablock with memories, the progeny of design
    and of blooper, boner and glitch.
He had his whole life to live.
When there is no more beseeching or gratitude, no seats remaining
    on the metaphysical seesaw, no zero-sum activity, no acquisition
    that is not also a loss, no finitude, then of course the dead man
    smiles as he blows a kiss through the wispy curtain of closure.
Some say the dead man was miserable to be so happy.

HISTORIES OF BODIES

by MARIKO NAGAI

from NEW LETTERS

for J.R.
Be ahead of all partings.
—Rainer Maria Rilke

I.

That's how we can distinguish a man from a woman, or from
    ourselves: only in
a moment of embrace. Judgment on bodies has already passed,
    they say we are
like any other, cock is a breast, balls another pair that
    swings like hands
of a clock. Our stories have no listener, our stories are like
    any other.
We misunderstood each other, our bodies the only proof of intimacy,
    a repetition
of bodies coming together as we move on top or under each other,
we fill each other with ourselves in the moment of embrace, an imago
stretching its wings out, two bodies connected by embrace.

II.

"Hush," you say, "I love your body," "I get hard only for you," "I am
    yours only."

490

You say that sex is another word for how we leave the body, or, how, like the Whirling
Dervishes, we seek the eternal in the embrace, in the moment of unveiling
the white so much like a butterfly, or our selves. You hold your cock, your release
comes like a magician releasing the doves. They land on my stomach, they stay there until they dry like scabs over wounds.

I love you: "Love is another way to say how unoriginal we are," or, "You and I are separated
by a word, a mere word." Love is a division, it is a barrier that makes us what we are,
another word for how repetition becomes the way we part from each other, over
and over again, Love is another way of saying, *Your face in this light is how I want to remember*
you, a face only a few steps away from death; this is when I like you best.

III.

You call it *shoah,* the unrepeatable. Here's a picture: soldiers burning books.
Another picture: soldiers dragging an old man who held the Torah as if it were
his child, or God. Let us move thirty years ahead: here's a picture of students burning
books, another of students pushing an old man clutching the Classics.
The faces of these boys are so many years before any partings they can understand,
their bodies taut with how little years they have. Pictures are repeatable, so are events.
God loves innocence and children, but two are not the same.
I say that the holocaust is an image of bodies ahead of all partings.
The souls have already forgotten the rib cages, the backbones that protrude like a broken
violin. A picture: bodies after bodies thrown into a ditch. The only thing

491

separating a man from a woman is by how their sacks are carelessly
   placed:
here is a man, his balls have shriveled to the size of a large pea;
   there, a woman,
where her breasts once were, two broken pendulums that no longer
   tell time hang. *I want*
to say, the shaved heads tell all: holocaust is the debasement of
   bodies,
where bodies turn into grotesque universality. In this picture, a
   woman lies
on top of two men, their mouths open as if almost a kiss, an embrace.

IV.

The proof is the body, not in words: you lie on your stomach, slowly
   rocking yourself
to sleep as if the bed is another body you can ease yourself into. I lie
next to you, my thighs slightly open like a window, or a door,
   anyone can look
in, even you. But we have stopped our movements already. In this
   early morning, words are bodies
heaped up high, each body imprinted with past, they are
   remembrance. But we have already turned
our eyes inward, we do not hear. Each come-cry hides in the cave
   of the mouth,
stays inside of us like doves in a magician's pockets, waiting for the
   signal they've been trained to recognize.

LIKE GOD

by LYNN EMANUEL

from BOSTON REVIEW

You hover above the page staring
down on a small town. By its roads
some scenery loafs in a hammock of
sleepy prose and here is a mongrel
loping and here is a train pulling into
a station in three long sentences and
here are the people in galoshes waiting.
But you know this story and it is not
about those travelers and their galoshes,
but about your life, so, like a diver
climbing over the side of a boat and
down into the ocean, you climb, sentence
by sentence, into this story on this page.

You have been expecting yourself
as the woman who purrs by in a dress
by Patou, and a porter manacled to
the luggage, and a matron bulky as
the *Britannia,* and there, haunting
her ankles like a piece of ectoplasm
that barks is, once again, that small
white dog from chapter twenty.
These are your fellow travelers and
you become part of their logjam of
images of hats and umbrellas and
Vuitton luggage, you are a face

behind or inside these faces, a
heartbeat in the volley of these
heartbeats, as you choose, out of all
the passengers, the journey of a man
with a mustache scented faintly with
Prince Albert. "He must be a secret
sensualist," you think and your awareness
drifts to his trench coat, worn, softened,
and flabby, a coat with a lobotomy, just
as the train arrives at a destination.

No, you would prefer another stop
in a later chapter where the climate is
affable and sleek. But most of
the passengers are disembarking, and
you did not choose to be in the story
of the white dress. You did not choose
the story of the matron whose bosom
is like the prow of a ship and who is
launched toward lunch at The Hotel Pierre,
or even the story of the dog-on-a-leash,
even though this is now your story:
the story of the man-who-had-to-
take-the-train and walk the dark road
described hurriedly by someone
sitting at the cafe so you could discover it,
although you knew all along it
would be there, you, who have been hovering
above this page, holding the book in
your hands, like God, reading.

ONCE A SHOOT
OF HEAVEN

by BECKIAN FRITZ GOLDBERG

from FIELD

Even when you see through the lies, the lies they
fed you as a child, you
believe some of it, still, when you drift
from thinking. When the air's true and simple
like a sheet you've laundered for as long

as you can remember, and your mother before you. There was an
    end,
and a beginning, and love, wrong and right and
someone who loved the world and someone who did not
and someone who made the moon and the moon that just was.
Always.

Now there's a white disappearing brow at the edge of September,
    usual stars.
        A siren sets off a dog.
        A car radio flies down the road.
        In between the acacias tick, tick in a lightness not yet wind.

The early bird is asleep,
        The world still isn't safe for democracy.

There was a mother and a father and a child and an hour
and exactly so many minutes, and left and right,

and people who ascended like doves and people
who slept in the earth, and apples that could make you strong
and sugar that could make you weak, and people who burned.

And tonight you still talk to someone who is not there, not
    yourself—crazy promises, little pleas, momentary

thanksgivings. This no one who has never been there is like the cat
    who only went away they said

to live and raise a family in the Christenson's barn. So there was the
    one who went on living forever and the one you realized could not
    live forever.

Here there's the sound of a neighbor dragging his trash cans down
    the driveway to the curb. No one on this street sleeps.
        The crickets are poor not lucky.
        The ear might as well be gold.

THE CUP

by KATRINA ROBERTS

from HOW LATE DESIRE LOOKS (Gibbs-Smith) and BOSTON BOOK REVIEW

PLEASED TO CONSIDER THE CUP. On a high-up shelf it stands, waiting to be fingered. Finders keepers. It's its simplicity, to envy. This configuration of complicity with air, and arms enact handles to tilt it. Roundelay for a sip and care beneath it, cantankerous baby. Upholds the light in holes, holding in liquid minutia as though a sister. Or twinned slippers hushing carpet stairs; four hands with glasses, crown glass with milk and a nipple knob in it.

*

Cucurbit for the spilly pieces. Pleased to consider the cup. Precisely why it matters most emphatically. Usufruct of quantities of unknown property. By which method of doing. If saucers—a dado below in difference. Or blue, for example. Teethed with crenels like castle turrets, yes.

*

What I want is to hand around it, insideways often. It hurts less to know its absence is natural. Pleased to consider. The cup lobs lookingly like honey.

So, abandon hope. Of course, it's most natural to want it intact; the crack from lip to base faces south and south. Smooth lazy susan whirls and twirls so. But, if it basks in perfection, call it cul-de-sac. Call it caved-in-cup, spinning—unpleased to consider the consequences of indabbing fingers, which lose their gloves—minus the digit-mask, like some anemone from the sea.

Enemy is the pace. In which manner of thinking. Space to curl into it. So pleased! Drink up. To consider most lovingly intonations of refusal, drains your energy. Gully dint is coming. Bees don't squeeze from honeycomb fumes. Out back the hat-hive-house stands, pleased to squat in sun—most roundly. Only to have itself to consider.

*

Enclosed spaces with borders not to be crossed—jimpson fences. So that's why the bell stings. Orchestrated petals reek havoc in the shade of night. Sweet and sour pork. Pleased to be sure to lock all doors, to hit the light. Casuistry says this is the way the gentlemen ride—hippety, then, but, oh—from toe to heel the campanile shifts, suffering contrecoup. An elegant silence darkened by sidelighting.

In the cup she puts five things. Today the tides, some crumbs, a lunar key. The wolf of Gubbio leaves five teeth, a bloody kiss by her negligee. Put them in, and then. . . . So what of laughter bouncing within? Intaglioed complaints brim her blown-glass goblet. What he cups in his hands is neither, nor water.

*

Slip on his hands, the cup grows. Soft underneath, it will harden. *Cunning,* She says, *touch.* She says: *Massage and mass . . . sage . . . message . . . mess and age . . .* and the cup grows most pleasingly. *Don't touch,* she says—*much, to consider.*

—*for Robert Antoni*

XXIV

MITCH

by ROBERT CREELEY

from SOLO 2

Mitch was a classmate
later married extraordinary poet
and so our families were friends
when we were all young
and lived in New York, New Hampshire, France.

He had eyes with whites
above eyeballs looked out
over lids in droll surmise—
"gone under earth's lid" was Pound's phrase,
cancered stomach?

A whispered information over phone,
two friends the past week . . . ,
the one, she says, an eccentric dear woman,
conflicted with son?
Convicted with ground

tossed in, one supposes,
more dead than alive.
Life's done all it could
for all of them.
Time to be gone?

Not since 1944–45
have I felt so dumbly, utterly,

in the wrong place at
entirely the wrong time,
caught then in that merciless war,

now trapped here, old, on a blossoming earth,
nose filled with burgeoning odors,
wind a caress, sound blurred reassurance,
echo of others, the lovely compacting
human warmths, the eye closing upon you,

seeing eye, sight's companion, dark or light,
makes out of its lonely distortions
it's you again, coming closer, feel
weight in the bed beside me,
close to my bones.

They told me it would be
like this but who could
believe it, not to leave, not to
go away? "I'll hate to
leave this earthly paradise . . ."

There's no time like the present,
no time in the present. Now it floats, goes out like a boat
upon the sea. Can't we see,
can't we now be company
to that one of us

has to go? *Hold my hand, dear.*
I should have hugged him,
taken him up, held him,
in my arms. I should
have let him know I was here.

Is it my turn now,
who's to say or wants to?
You're not sick, there are
certainly those older.
Your time will come.

In God's hands it's cold.
In the universe it's an empty, echoing silence.
Only us to make sounds,
but I made none.
I sat there like a stone.

GRAVITAS

by ELIZABETH ALEXANDER

from THE AMERICAN VOICE

Emergency! A bright yellow schoolbus
is speeding me to hospital. My pregnant belly bulges
beneath my pleated skirt, the face
of my dear niece Amal a locket inside my stomach.

Soon she will be born healthy,
and after, her sister, Bana.
Labor will be tidy and effortless.
In fact, I will hardly remember it!

All of this is taking place in Kenya, where they live.
This is my first dream of pregnancy
since I have been actually pregnant,
therefore I dream in reality, not metaphor.

I am gravid, eight weeks along.
My baby, I have read, has a tail
and a spine made of pearls,
and every day I speak to her in tongues.

ALSO LOVE YOU

by REGINALD SHEPHERD

from THE GETTYSBURG REVIEW

for Chris

I think of you when I am dead, the way rocks
think of earthworms and oak roots, tendrils
that break them down to loam and nutrients,
something growing out of every
disappearance. I will be simpler then, sheer
molecule, much easier to understand:
steam rising from sidewalk vents, rain
accumulating on ailanthus leaves
after the rain has ended, the lingering smell
of rain and rotting leaves. (*Look for me,
I'll be around,* that's every song: I'll be that
too.) I will you kites unraveled from their tangled lines
(so far up you can't tell what they want to imitate),
weather balloons and evening stars, easily
mistaken objects of luminosity; observation
satellites to record you just out of sight
and tell you what you've missed. I will be
the lichen bubbling from a crack in the
Belmont Rocks, where you don't go,
between the brilliant men loitering
in their temporary beauty. You will. I will
you every artificial slab that makes a beach

if you think hard enough, anchored
fronds of blue-green algae bobbing
in the surface motion just like kelp
weaving in waves on Long Island Sound,
like, come to think of it, sirens' hair combed out
to tourmaline and emerald. I could be this fallen
branch across your path in Lincoln Park, marker: grasp it
and push it aside. I will you people bicycling
just past sunset and joggers straying from
their path, whole evenings of various exercise,
and this first of a whole series of lampposts
burned out, blocks of them. I will be the wind
that messes up your hair, you've just
gotten it cut, pollen, pawn of light and
light winds, air sultry and somehow
sexual, those men still sunning themselves,
giving themselves up to light and passing
eyes, your eyes perhaps. I'll be the things
left behind for you, I'll be much kinder
then. I'll kiss the drowsing atmosphere
all of a summer's afternoon, and that's not all.

THE SKY-BLUE DRESS

by CATHY SONG

from THE KENYON REVIEW

The light says *hurry* and the woman
gathers the perishables to the table, the fish
thawed to a chilled translucency, the roses
lifted out of a sink of rainwater, the clean hunger
on the faces of her husband and children faithful
as the biscuits they crumble into their mouths.
Hunger is the wedge that keeps them intact,
a star spilling from the fruit
she slices in a dizzying multiplication of hands
wiping a child's mouth of butter, hands
wiping a dishrag across a clean plate.
She stands at the door waving the dishrag—
ready, set, go!—calling the children in, shooing
the children out, caught in a perpetual
dismantling, a restlessness she strikes the rag at
as if she could hush the air invented by flies.

The light says *hurry* and the family
gathers at the table, the tablecloth washed through countless
fumblings of grace, its garland hem of fruits clouds
into blue pools, faded as a bruise or a reckless tattoo or the roses
the woman hurried that morning into the house,
rushing to revive the steaming petals out of wet
bundles of newspaper the roses traveled in
up the mountain from the market by the sea,
flowers more precious than fish

she left spoiling in the backseat of the car.
Petals and flesh are perishable as the starfruit
a friend of the family climbed the tree to save,
tossing to earth what the sun, the birds, the insects
were days, hours, minutes from rotting.
The roses, stems cut at a slant under rainwater,
breathe cool nights into the air thick with biscuits.
On the table beside the roses a dish of butter disappears
as each knife swipes
its portion, its brightness, its wedge of cadmium lemon.

The light says *hurry* and the man
begins to paint roses while his wife tosses in her sleep
and dreams of a dress she wore long before
she was married, a dress that flowed to her feet
when her hair swirled at her knees, swirled
even when she was simply standing under a tree.
The man who was just a boy then remembers
the first time he saw her, she was standing in a river of hair,
remembers this as he begins to paint roses.
She dreams of the sky-blue dress,
how she once filled it with nothing but skin.
Flesh does not fill it.
Neither does wind.
The girl who wore it left it
pinned like a hole in the sky
the woman passes through, sleep
pouring out of her into water,
all the broken water that leaves
the dress empty, simply hanging from a tree.
She throws off the covers and the moon
washes her in a light that is disturbing,
lifts her into a restlessness
that coincides with the appearance of flies
earlier in the week dragging a net of buzzing,
blue and claustrophobic,
forcing her to examine the roses.

The light says *hurry* and the boy
who came to the man and the woman late in marriage

slips his tooth under his parents' pillow.
In this way he knows they will remember to wake up.
He fills the night with his sweet breath,
breath unimpeded, flowing out of the space
once blocked by the tooth.
Behind the rock there is a cave.
Behind the moon there is simply dark space.
His mother will find the tooth when she makes the bed.
She will save it with all the other teeth hidden under pillows—
broken and intact, smooth and milky—
petals and buttons,
slices of the star-shaped fruit,
shells found nesting in the crevice of pools.

SAND, FLIES & FISH

by MÔNG-LAN

from QUARTERLY WEST

1

I take a glass of the expiring sun, sipping it.
Cambodia's terse mountains to my right. the Gulf
of Thailand in front of me. the border police in their
rumpled uniforms are still as backdrop characters.
the hot sun mats their hair down in neat sweat lines.
a white gull pecks at the black sand. the sand is so
black you think you're close to hell. I wait for the
sun to come down on the sea. the nausea for it. in
the evenings the national Vietnamese news blares
from the loudspeakers. the world's slow motions.
fires' haze. sky's blood draining over the boneless
ocean.

2

even if I described detail by detail to you, the whole
would escape you. how can you see
the southern edge of the continent— what would
that matter? or the black sand grading into the
blueness of the sea, or the vigilant Cambodian

mountains. what would it matter if I told you ships
dock in front of my window. that when not in my
room, I wander through villages eating dirt, whatever
I can beg. it happens to a woman. these things
happen. these accidents. I watch my stomach
bloat with the seed of a man who was a shadow. I
pick at the salt crop gleaming in evening light, and
steal whatever I can to sell in the markets. the
land's lungs are strong. it fills my baby's ears
with its tenor.

3

this edge of the world is a knife. the motorcycle taxi
drivers wait humped, clocks on the dock, that dulled
look for a customer. everything an illusion of
another.

4

salt fields glisten from ocean light. there is so much
light here you could die from it. bamboo houses
stilted on black sand. houses so close they share
the same reflection on the water. pepper fields like
black eggs dry in the sun. here I became pregnant
and had my first child. his fingers learned to
quicken at the touch of sand. he let fish swim in
and out of his lungs and bloodstream. the ocean and
sky, one medium to him, he walked in both. one
day I let him go too far, and the black waves came
down and took him.

5

fishermen, wrapt in another world. their harvest
dries on large metal nets laid aslant—dust settles on
the squid's splayed arms. squatting, smoking,
noticing every ripple on the road. their skins
sinewy, pasty as clay. lying on their hammocks,
crowns of mosquitoes and flies over their heads.
they know your real name without asking.

6

her rat's nest hair. she peels it from her face. the
children pound her with fists. she sweeps her cane,
left and right, screaming something. the children
laugh. hysteria in her eyes. bobbing up and down,
she slaps down money at a cafe stand to buy food.
they laugh. in a tremor she throws the food at the
crowd. they laugh again. her clothes are ragged,
shirt torn at the seams, her skirt dusty, feet thick
and calloused. more fists at her. jab of her cane. a
man scoops the children away from her. clasping
the seams of the crowd, she exhales something
orange and white. eyes pierce her back. in her
drunken momentum she crosses the floating bridge
without paying toll. frothing fire down her chin, her
rat's nest hair blazes to the skies.

7

they watch the land, watch the air. the dust
gathering. strips of white ghost-cloth tied across
their foreheads. the grey-haired, heads down, talking.

the young with round eyes full of fruit, rice, cradles
of incense, yellowing black & white photos of
grandparents, great-grandparents. they dress him up,
the resemblance of him. powdered, rouged, his hair
combed back. what he was in life, more so in death.
my baby died a quiet death. except for the birds,
there was no one to witness.

8

the ocean curves around the land like a fish caught
on a hook, murmuring something to itself. bodies
crooning. stark bamboo houses. the women beat
shrimp into dust, after they're laid out in perfect
pink squares to dry. bowels unload, unweave into
the Gulf of Thailand.

9

pigs arrive at the dock each morning squealing for
their lives. rows of squid drying on nets like
ghosts. the whole village is well preserved smelling
of dried fish and squid. Vietnamese boys watch
Cambodian TV. the black sand wet under my feet
speaks too in another language, teeth chafing against
teeth sound against sound, tongue buckling north
and south into the land. what country is this. it
used to be my home. it was where my child was
born, where he died. it was probably best that he
didn't see anything else but this sun.

ALL THE APHRODISIACS

by CATHY HONG

from MUDFISH

blowfish arranged on a saucer. Russian roulette. angelic slivers.
ginseng. cut antlers allotted in bags. dogs on a spit, a Dutch girl

winking, holding a bowl of shellfish.

white cloth, drunkenness. a different language leaks out—
the idea of throat, an orifice, a cord—

you say it turns you on when I speak Korean.

the gold paste of afterbirth, no red—

Household phrases	-pae-go-p'a	(I am hungry)
	-ch'i-wa	(Clean up)
	-kae sekki	(Son of a dog)

I breathe those words in your ear which makes you climax,
afterwards you ask me for their translations. I tell you it's a secret.

gijek niin tigit rriil—the recitation of the alphabet, guttural
    diphthong, gorgeous.

what are the objects that turn me on, words—

han-gul, the language first used by female entertainers, poets,
    prostitutes—

the sight of shoes around telephone wires,
    pulleyed by their laces, the blunt word cock

little pink tutus in F.A.O. Schwarz,
they used to dress me as a boy when I was four.

white noise, white washed. The whir of ventilation in the library.

Even quarantined amongst books, I tried to kiss you once. Tried to
    touch your cock.

strips of white cotton, the color of the commoner, the color of virtue,
the color that can be sullied—

my hand pressed against your diaphragm, corralling your pitch—

a pinch of rain caught between mouths,

analgesic tea. poachers drawing blood—

strips of white cotton I use to bind your wrist to post, tight
enough to drawl vein, allow sweat—

sweat to sully the white of your sibilant body,

the shrug of my tongue, the shrug of command, ssshhht.

XXV

MY DEAD DAD

by DAVID KIRBY

from THE SOUTHERN REVIEW

Our rue Albert apartment has this pre-Napoleonic water heater
    that lurches to life with a horripilating bang
when, for example, Barbara is taking a bath, as she is now,
    and every time she turns the handle for
more hot water, the heater hesitates a second, then ka-pow!

as though there's a little service technician sitting inside
    working a crossword, his elbows on his knees,
and suddenly he gets the more-hot-water signal and jumps up
    off his little dollhouse chair and runs down
the walkway and throws a shovelful of coal in the furnace

and then walks back, wiping his brow, only to have Barbara
    crank that faucet again, and thwack! he's off
and running while I'm sitting in our French living room
    reading *Journey to the End of Night* by Céline,
whose prose is sweaty and overheated in the first place,

and boom! there he goes once more, sprinting toward
    the furnace, and in the other room
Barbara is giving these little cries of either pleasure
    or surprise or both, as she often does
when bathing, and ba-boom! there he goes again.

I imagine him in neatly pressed khakis and a hat
        with a patent-leather brim,
like the gas-station attendants of my youth,
        and I wonder if he is not a relative of the equally little man
in the refrigerator whose job it was, according to my dad,

to turn the light on whenever anyone opened the
        door and off when they closed it
and who, in my child's mind, bore a striking resemblance
        to my dad not only in appearance
but also patience and love of word games and other nonsense.

And if there is such a little man in my French refrigerator
        and water heater and one
in my refrigerator and water heater back home,
        and if there are five billion of
us big people in the world, there must be twenty billion of them!

I think, like us, they'd have entertainments, such as
        circuses, barbecues, and *thés dansants*,
but also wars and horrible acts of cruelty!
        Though when peace returned, entire towns of
little people would finish the evening meal and then go on

the *passeggiata* the way the Italians do, the young flirting,
        the old sighing as they admire and envy the young,
the children and dogs getting mixed up in everybody's legs
        as they stroll and chat and ready themselves for
sleep as the clock in the little clock tower strikes eleven,

twelve, one, and the moon comes up—the moon! Which also
        has its little men, according to my dad,
though these are green and, to our eyes, largely invisible,
        since they live on the dark half,
though every once in a while they, too, become curious,

and a few will sneak over into the glary, sunlit side,
        so that when the moon is full, he said,
we should stare at it with every optical instrument at our

disposal, because if we do, we just might see
one of those little fellows nibbling the piece of cheese

he holds in one hand as he shields his eyes with the other
        and squints down at us. And I haven't even got
to the good little people who live inside each bad one
        of us, according to pop psychologists,
though I don't think my dead dad would have bought that one;

yet since the few people left who knew us both often say
        how much I remind them of him, then I think
if my dead dad lives anywhere at all, he lives inside me.
        Well, and my brother, too, if not
our mother, though there's nothing unusual about that,

because the older I get, the more widows I know, and
        none of them ever says anything about
her dead husband, suggesting perhaps these champions
        weren't so fabulous after all, at least
to them. Sad thought, isn't it, that these men should live

only in the minds of their children. Or maybe my dead dad's
        on the moon, since the alternate point
of view to my smug phenomenological one is that people
        go to heaven when they die,
and heaven's in the sky, and so's the moon,

so who's to say that's not my dead dad up there, his mouth
        full of Limburger or provolone,
shielding his eyes as he tries to find the house
        where we used to live, but he can't,
because it's been torn down, though he'd have no way

of knowing that, so he looks for my mother, and she's there,
        but she lives in a retirement community now,
and he can't believe how old she is, and he's shocked
        that she's as beautiful as he always knew
her to be, only she can't walk now, can't hear, can't see.

And he looks for my brother in Ohio, and he's there,
　　　and me in Florida, where he left me,
but I'm not in Florida anymore. Hey, Dad! Over here! It's France!
　　　No, France! Great country! Great cheese.
I wish I could take you in my pocket with me everywhere I go.

BIBLICAL ALSO-RANS

by CHARLES HARPER WEBB

from LIVER (University of Wisconsin Press)

Hanoch, Pallu, Hezron, Carmi,
Jemuel, Ohad, Zohar, Shuni:
one Genesis mention's all you got.

Ziphion, Muppim, Arodi: lost
in a list even the most devout skip over
like small towns on the road to L.A.

How tall were you, Shillim?
What was your favorite color, Ard?
Did you love your wife, Iob?

Not even her name survives.
Adam, Eve, Abel, Cain—
these are the stars crowds surge to see.

Each hour thousands of Josephs,
Jacobs, Benjamins are born.
How many Oholibamahs? How many

Mizzahs draw first breath today?
Gatam, Kenaz, Reuel? Sidemen
in the band. Waiters who bring

the Pèrignon and disappear.
Yet they loved dawn's garnet light
as much as Moses did. They drank

wine with as much delight.
I thought my life would line me up
with Samuel, Isaac, Joshua.

Instead I stand with Basemath, Hoglah,
Ammihud. Theirs are the names
I honor; theirs, the deaths I feel,

their children's tears loud as any
on the corpse of Abraham, their smiles
as missed, the earth as desolate

without them: Pebbles on a hill.
Crumbs carried off by ants.
Jeush. Dishan. Nahath. Shammah.

THE WORKFORCE

by JAMES TATE

from HARVARD REVIEW

Do you have adequate oxen for the job?
No, my oxen are inadequate.
Well, how many oxen would it take to do an adequate job?
I would need ten more oxen to do the job adequately.
I'll see if I can get them for you.
I'd be obliged if you could do that for me.
Certainly. And do you have sufficient fishcakes for the men?
We have fifty fishcakes, which is less than sufficient.
Would fifty more fishcakes be sufficient?
Fifty more fishcakes would be precisely sufficient.
I'll have them delivered on the morrow.
Do you need maps of the mountains and the underworld?
We have maps of the mountains but we lack maps of the underworld.
Of course you lack maps of the underworld,
there are no maps of the underworld.
And, besides, you don't want to go there, it's stuffy.
I had no intention of going there, or anywhere for that matter.
It's just that you asked me if I needed maps. . . .
Yes, yes, it's my fault, I got carried away.
What do you need then, you tell me?
We need seeds, we need plows, we need scythes, chickens,
pigs, cows, buckets and women.
Women?
We have no women.
You're a sorry lot then.
We are a sorry lot, sir.

Well I can't get you women.
I assumed as much, sir.
What are you going to do without women, then?
We will suffer, sir. And then we'll die out one by one.
Can any of you sing?
Yes, sir, we have many fine singers among us.
Order them to begin singing immediately.
Either women will find you this way or you will die
comforted. Meanwhile busy yourselves
with the meaningful tasks you have set for yourselves.
Sir, we will not rest until the babes arrive.

PENUMBRA

by BETTY ADCOCK

from SHENANDOAH

The child in the cracked photograph sits still
in the rope swing hung from a live oak.
Her velvet dress brims with a lace frill.

Her pet bantam is quiet in her lap.
It is the autumn day of a funeral
and someone has thought to take a snap-

shot of the child who won't be allowed
to go to the burying—the coffin in the house
for days, strange people going in and out.

She's dressed as if she'd go, in the blue church-
dress from last Christmas, almost too short.
The rooster loves her. She guards his perch

on her lap, his colors feathering the mild air.
She concentrates on this, now that her father
is unknowable, crying in the rocking chair.

Her mouth knife-thin, her small hands knotted hard
on the ropes she grips as if to be rescued,
she is growing a will that won't be shed.

And something as cold as winter's breath
tightens in her, as later the asthma's vise
will tighten—hands on the throat, the truth.

Black and white, she is hiding
in every one of my bright beginnings.
Gold and deep blue and dark-shining

red the cockerel's feathers, gold the sun
in that skyblue southern fall, blue
over the four-o'clocks and the drone

of weeping draining like a shadow from the house
where someone is gone, is gone, is gone—
where the child will stay to darken like a bruise.

I am six years old, buried
in the colorless album.
My mother is dead.
I forgive no one.

TO GRASP THE NETTLE

by EAMON GRENNAN

from THE KENYON REVIEW

Empty your hands. Shake off even the sweat
of memory, the way they burned

to find the cool indented shell of flesh
at the base of her spine, how they cupped themselves

to hold her head, feeling the weight and bones of it,
every angle of her face and the curve of each earlobe

finding its place in your palm or at your fingertips,
flesh whispering to flesh in its own dialect; or the way

one of them would creep through the breathlessness
of sleep—the sheer unlikely fact of being there, and there

when the light came back—to come to rest on a breast
or claim a hand or settle a warm spot on her belly

or between stilled thighs. Shake it all off:
for as long as they bear the faintest trace

of such hard evidence against you, your hands
will not be steady and the thing will sting you.

JASPER, TEXAS, 1998

by LUCILLE CLIFTON

from KESTREL and PLOUGHSHARES

i am a man's head hunched in the road.
i was chosen to speak by the members
of my body, the arm as it pulled away
pointed toward me, the hand opened once
and was gone.

why and why and why
should I call a white man brother?
who is the human in this place,
the thing that is dragged or the dragger?
what does my daughter say?

the sun is a blister overhead.
if i were alive i could not bear it.
the townsfolk sing we shall overcome
while hope drains slowly from my mouth
into the dirt which covers us all.
i am done with this dust, i am done.

XXVI

MEMORY

by ANTHONY HECHT

from SOUTHWEST REVIEW

Sepia oval portraits of the family,
Black-framed, adorned the small brown-papered hall,
But the parlor was kept unused, never disturbed.
Under a glass bell, the dried hydrangeas
Had bleached to the hue of ancient newspaper,
Though once, someone affirmed, they had been pink.
Pink still were the shiny curling orifices
Of matching seashells stationed on the mantle
With mated, spiked, wrought-iron candlesticks.
The room contained a tufted ottoman,
A large elephant-foot umbrella stand
With two malacca canes, and two peacock
Tail-feathers sprouting from a small-necked vase.
On a teak side-table lay, side by side,
A Bible and a magnifying glass.
Green velvet drapes kept the room dark and airless
Until on sunny days toward midsummer
The brass andirons caught a shaft of light
For twenty minutes in late afternoon
In a radiance dimly akin to happiness—
The dusty gleam of temporary wealth.

A SHORT HISTORY OF THE SHADOW

by CHARLES WRIGHT

from YALE REVIEW

Thanksgiving, dark of the moon.
Nothing down here in the underworld but vague shapes and black
 holes,
Heaven resplendent but virtual
Above me,
             trees stripped and triple-wired like Irish harps.
Lights on Pantops and Free Bridge mirror the eastern sky.
Under the bridge is the river,
                     the red Rivanna.
Under the river's redemption, it says in the book,
It says in the book,
Through water and fire the whole place becomes purified,
The visible by the visible, the hidden by what is hidden.

Each word, as someone once wrote, contains the universe.
The visible carries all the invisible on its back.
Tonight, in the unconditional, what moves in the long-limbed
 grasses, what touches me
As though I didn't exist?
What is it that keeps on moving,
                     a tiny pillar of smoke
Erect on its hind legs,
            loose in the hollow grasses?

A word I don't know yet, a little word, containing infinity,
Noiseless and unrepentent, in sift through the dry grass.
Under the tongue is the utterance.
Under the utterance is the fire, and then the only end of fire.

Only Dante, in Purgatory, casts a shadow,
L'ombra della carne, the shadow of flesh—

                    everyone else *is* one.
The darkness that flows from the world's body, gloomy spot,
Pre-dogs our footsteps, and follow us,

                diaphanous bodies
Watching the nouns circle, and watching the verbs circle,
Till one of them enters the left ear and becomes a shadow
Itself, sweet word in the unwaxed ear.
This is a short history of the shadow, one part of us that's real.
This is the way the world looks
In late November,

        no leaves on the trees, no ledge to foil the lightfall.

No ledge in early December either, and no ice,
La Niña unhosing the heat pump

                up from the Gulf,
Orange Crush sunset over the Blue Ridge,
No shadow from anything as evening gathers its objects
And eases into earshot.
Under the influx the outtake,

           Leonbattista Alberti says,
Some lights are from stars, some from the sun
And moon, and other lights are from fires.
The light from the stars makes the shadow equal to the body.
Light from fire makes it greater,

      there, under the tongue, there, under the utterance.

INHERITANCE

by KWAME DAWES

from THE CARIBBEAN WRITER

for Derek Walcott

I

In the shade of the sea grape trees the air is tart
with the sweet sour of stewed fruit rotting
about his sandalled feet. His skin,
still Boston pale and preserved with Brahmanical
devotion by the hawkish woman
who smells cancer in each tropical wind,
is caged in shadows. I know those worn eyes
their feline gleam, mischief riddled;
his upper lip lined with a thin stripe
of tangerine, the curled up nervousness
of a freshly shaved mustache. He is old
and cared for. He accepts mashed food
though he still has teeth—she insists and love
is about atoning for the guilt
of those goatish years in New England.
A prophet's kind of old. Old like casket-
aged genius. Above, a gull surveys
the island, stitches loops through the sea and sky—
an even horizon, the bias on which

teeters a landscape, this dark loam of tradition
in which seeds split into tender leaves.

II

I can see the smudge of light colors
spreading and drying quickly in the sun.
The pulpy paper takes the water color,
and the cliché of sea and a fresh beach
seems too easy for a poem. He has written
them all, imagined the glitter and clatter
of silver cuirasses, accents of crude
Genoese sailors poisoning the air,
the sand feeling for the first the shadow
of flag and plumed helmet—this old story
of arrival that stirred him as a boy,
looking out over the field of green,
as he peopled the simple island
with the intrigue of blood and heroes,
his gray eyes searching out an ancestry
beyond the broad laughter and breadfruit-
common grunts of the fishermen, pickled
with rum and the *picong* of *kaiso*,
their histories as shallow as the trace
of soil at the beach's edge where crippled
corn bushes have sprouted. That was years ago;
he has exhausted the language of a broken civilization.
These days he just chips at his epitaph,
a conceit of twilight turning into
a bare and bleak night. He paints, whistling
Sparrow songs while blistering in the sun.

III

The note pad, though, is not blank. The words start,
thirteen syllables across the page, then seven
before the idea hesitates—these days
he does not need to count, there is in his head
a counter dinging an alarm like the bell
of his old Smith Corona—his line breaks

are tidy dramas of his entrances
and exits, he will howl before the darkness.
This ellipsis is the tease of a thought,
the flirtatious lift of a yellow skirt
showing a brown taut thigh—a song he knows
how to sing but can't line-up the lyrics again—
an airy metaphor of one taken up
by a flippant sea breeze going some place
inland, carrying the image, snagged
by the olive dull entanglement
of a bramble patch. At eight he lays
the contents of his canvas book bag
on the sand, organizing the still life
in honed stanzas. He scoops the orange pulp
of papaya relishing the taste of fruit, this bounty
harvested from the ant-infested fragile
tree behind the cottage, a tree that bleeds
each time its fruit is plucked away. The flesh
is sunny. He knows the fishermen warn
that it will cut a man's nature; dry up
his sap, that women feed their men pureed
papaya in tall glasses of rum-punch
to tie them down, beached, benign pirogues
heading nowhere. He dares the toxins
to shrivel him, to punish him
for the chronic genius of crafting poems
from the music of a woman's laugh
while he chews slowly. A poem comes to him
as they sometimes do in the chorus
of a song. It dances about in his head.
He does not move to write it down—it will wait
if it must, and if not, it is probably
an old sliver of long discarded verse.

IV

The old men in the rum shop are comforted
as they watch him limp along the gravel
road, wincing at the sharp prod of stones
in his tender feet, the knees grinding

538

at each sudden jar—just another ancient
recluse with his easel folded under
his arm, a straw hat, the gull-like eyes
seeing the sea before he clears the hill.
They know him, proud of the boy—bright as hell
and from good people. There is no shared language
between them, just the babel of rum talk
and cricket sometimes. Under his waters
he talks of Paris, Florence, barquentines,
Baudelaire, rolling the words around
like a cube of ice—they like to hear
the music he makes with tongue; the way
he tears embracing this green island,
this damned treasure, this shit hole of a treasure.
Sometimes when you don't mind sharp, you would think
he white too, except for the way he hold
the rum, carry his body into the sun
with the cool, cool calm of a drinker.
He say *home* like it in a book;
hard to recognize when he say *home*.
Yes, they like it anyway, the way
they like to hear "Waltzing Matilda" sung
with that broad Baptist harmony to a *cuatro*
plucked, to hear it fill an old time night.

V

If he is my father (there is something
of that fraying dignity, and the way
genius is worn casual and urbane—aging
with grace) he has lost much over the years.
The cigarette still stings his eyes and the scent
of Old Spice distilled in Gordon's Dry Gin
is familiar here by the sea where a jaunty
shanty, the cry of gulls and the squeak
of the rigging of boats are a right backdrop—
but I have abandoned the thought, the search
for my father in this picture. He's not here,
though I still come to the ritual death watch
like a vulture around a crippled beast,

the flies already bold around its liquid
eyes, too resigned to blink. I have come
for the books, the cured language, the names
of this earth that he has invented,
the stories of a city, and the way
he finds women's slippery parts in the smell
and shape of this island, the making
and unmaking of a city through
the epic cataclysm of fire,
eating the brittle old wood, myths dancing
in the thick smoke like the gray ashen debris
of sacrifice. It is all here with him—
this specimen living out his twilight days,
prodigious as John's horror—the green
uncertain in the half light. When we meet
he is distant, he knows I want to draw
him out, peer in for clues—he will not be drawn
out, he is too weary now. He points
to the rum shop, to an old man, Afolabe,
sitting on the edge of a canoe, black
as consuming night. I can tell
that he carries a new legend in his terrible
soul each morning, a high tower over the sea.

VI

I could claim him easily, make of him
a tale of nurture and benign neglect;
he is alive, still speaks, his brain clicks
with the routine of revelations
that can spawn in me the progeny
of his monumental craft. These colonial
old men, fed on cricket and the tortured
indulgences of white school masters
patrolling the mimic island streets
like gods growing gray and sage-like in the heat
and stench of the Third World; they return
to the reactionary nostalgia
during their last days—it is the manner
of aging, they say, but so sad, so sad.

I could adopt him, dream of blood and assume
the legacy of a divided self.
But it would ring false quickly; after all
my father saw the Niger eating out
a continent's beginnings; its rapid
descent to the Atlantic; he tasted
the sweet *kelewele* of an Akan
welcome, and cried at the uncompromising
flame of *akpetechi*. The blood of his sons
was spilled like libation into the soil,
and in nineteen twenty six, an old midwife
buried his bloodied navel string, the afterbirth
of his arrival at the foot of an ancient
cotton tree there on the delta islands
of Nigeria. My blood defines the character
of my verse. Still, I pilfer (a much better word),
rummage through the poet's things to find the useful,
how he makes a parrot flame a line
or a cicada scream in wind; the names
he gives the bright berries of an island
in the vernacular of Adam and the tribe.

VII

I carry the weight of your shadow always,
while I pick through your things for the concordance
of your invented icons for this archipelago.
Any announcement of your passing
is premature. So to find my own strength,
I seek out your splendid weaknesses.
Your last poems are free of the bombast
of gaudy garments, I can see the knobs
of your knees scarred by the surgeon's incisions
to siphon water and blood from bone;
I stare at your naked torso—the teats
hairy, the hint of a barreled beauty
beneath the folding skin. I turn away
as from a mirror. I am sipping your blood,
tapping the aged sap of your days while you grow
pale. You are painting on the beach, this is how

the poem began—I am watching you watching
the painting take shape. I have stared long enough
that I can predict your next stroke—your dip
into the palette, your grunts, your contemplative
moments, a poised crane waiting for the right
instance to plunge and make crimson ribbons
on a slow moving river. These islands
give delight, sweet water with berries,
the impossible theologies
of reggae, its metaphysics so right
for the inconstant seasons of sun and muscular
storm—you can hear the shape of a landscape
in the groan of the wind against the breadfruit
fronds. I was jealous when at twenty, I found
a slim volume of poems you had written
before you reached sixteen. It has stitched in me
a strange sense of a lie, as if all this
will be revealed to be dust—as if I learned
to pretend one day, and have yet to be found out.

LIMEN

by NATASHA TRETHEWEY

from DOMESTIC WORK (Graywolf Press)

All day I've listened to the industry
of a single woodpecker, worrying the catalpa tree
just outside my window. Hard at his task,

his body is a hinge, a door knocker
to the cluttered house of memory in which
I can almost see my mother's face.

She is there, again, beyond the tree,
its slender pods and heart-shaped leaves,
hanging wet sheets on the line—each one

a thin white screen between us. So insistent
is this woodpecker, I'm sure he must be
looking for something else—not simply

the beetles and grubs inside, but some other gift
the tree might hold. All day he's been at work,
tireless, making the green hearts flutter.

BEETLES

by STEVE KOWIT

from *The Dumbbell Nebula* (Heyday Books)

*The famous British biologist J.B.S. Haldane, when asked by a churchman . . . to
state his conception of God, said: "He is inordinately fond of beetles."*
Primo Levi

Spotted blister beetles. Sacred scarabs.
Water beetles whirling on the surface of still ponds.
Little polkadotted ladybugs
favored by the Virgin Mary & beloved of children.
Those angelic fireflies sparkling in the summer evenings.
Carrion beetles sniffing out the dead.
June bugs banging into screens.
Click beetles. Tumblebugs. Opossum beetles. Whirligigs
& long-horned rhino beetles,
Cowpea weevils snuggling into beans.
The diving beetle wintering in mud.
Macrodactylus subspinosus: the rose chafer
feasting upon rose petals, dear to the poet Guido Gozzano.
The reddish-brown *Calathus gregarius*.
Iridescent golden brown-haired beetles.
Beetles living in sea wrack, dry wood, loose gravel.
Clown beetles. Pill beetles.
Infinitesimal beetles nesting in the spore tubes of fungi.
There is no climate in which the beetle does not exist,
no ecological niche the beetle does not inhabit,

no organic matter, living, dead, or decomposed
that has not its enthusiast among the beetles,
of whom, it has been estimated, one and one-half
million species currently exist,
which is to say one mortal creature
out of five's a beetle—little armored tank
who has been rolling through the fields her ball of dung
these past three hundred million years: clumsy
but industrious, powerful yet meek,
the lowly, dutiful, & unassuming beetle—
she of whom, among all earth-born creatures, God is fondest.

INVENTORY

by EAMON GRENNAN

from HAYDEN'S FERRY REVIEW

To lay claim to something, even
this old half-barrel with its
rusty hoops and painted staves,
weather-bleached, as it starts
to look back, be a true thing
in the world, offering crumbs
to small birds, two streaks of
birdshit brightening its side.
Or bodies stretched to a limit
in that incessant present
they'd stumbled into, living
the truth of hand to mouth.
But there they go now, falling
forward with small cries of pain,
calling back the long vowels
and that short clamouring
from her mouth riding the
air, eager for it, swimming into
his open mouth. Evening,
he can hear the wind
off the Atlantic—oceanic uproar
among the high branches
and see the sycamores which
sky the garden, swaying shipwise,
and two gulls down the valley
backlit by brightness. A swallow

reams the garden's air and
ragged bushes show at once
their bones and bright flowers,
their leafy summer-swollen
plenitude taking the wind in
to sigh its big life among them,
waves and waves of it
gathering, greeting, going on,
where he sits singing the
praises of shelter, trying to
fathom what it is that glints
through hedge-windows or at the edge
of clouds, or what the wind
insists to high branches or among
the agitated leaves. Clouds now
changing shapes and changing
as they marshall and disperse: their
weight unimaginable, almost
on fire with themselves, coasting
towards change and change about
in such bodies, maybe, as angels
might borrow, spreading themselves
in light and through it, or turning
all to tears while the mountains
like immense gentle animals
lie down under the hand of light
itself and are settled by it.

XXVII

COCK ROBIN

by MIRANDA FIELD

from POST ROAD

Not eat the thing you took. Not pluck its feathers, peel its skin.
Not kiss your own face on the mouth, imagining
the tasting. Nor bury the thing you bring down from the sky.

Not interpret the meaning of its cry. Not clothe the cooling thing
in woollens. Not reel it in. Not wind it while it writhes.
Not breathe hard while you work, not speak of it, not burrow in.

But barely look upon the garden where the weight fell, sudden.
Where the falling broke it open, the plummet stopped.
Where rain falls down in dying angles and damage blooms.

Not touch the entry wound. Not stitch it up. Nor enter.
Not with a finger. Not the Viking eye. Not wonder.
But leave be what you took. But let what spills congeal.

And wager everything you own the grass grows over it in time.
It will not rise again. The sky assists this with its rain.
And the garden, and the mind.

THE CHURCH OF OMNIVOROUS LIGHT

by ROBERT WRIGLEY

from MĀNOA

On a long walk over the mountain you'd hear
them first, the pang and chorus
of their jubilations, as though you'd strayed
out of Hawthorne into Cotton Mather—
such joyous remorse, such cranky raptures.

And you'd love their fundamental squawking,
little Pentecostal magpies, diminutive
raven priests. You'd walk into their circle
like a drag queen into a Texas truck stop—
silence first, then the caterwauls, the righteous gacks.

Someone's gutted out a deer is all.
In the late autumn snow you'd see the deacons'
tracks—ursine, feline, canine—sweet eucharist of luck
and opportunity for them all. Take and eat,
clank the birds, but not too much. It might be a while.

You'd wonder, yes you would,
and maybe nudge with the toe of your boot
the seeming rigidity of the severed esophagus.
It's gently belled, like a deaf man's antique horn.
Breathless, the lungs subside to carnate blood.

You'd want to go, but you'd want to stay;
you'd want a way to say your part in the service
going on: through high windows
the nothing light, the fourteen stations
of the clouds, the offertory of the snow.

Imagine the brethren returned, comical,
hopping in surplice and cassock, muttering,
made dyspeptic by your presence there, but hopeful too,
that something might yet come and open
your coarse, inexplicable soul to their sight.

RED BERRIES

by JANE HIRSHFIELD

from THE YALE REVIEW

Again the pyrocanthus berries redden in rain,
as if return were return.

It is not.

The familiar is not the thing it reminds of.
Today's *yes* is different from yesterday's *yes*.
Even *no*'s adamance alters.

From painting to painting,
century to century,
the tipped-over copper pot spills out different light;
the cut-open beeves,
their caged and muscled display,
are on one canvas radiant, pure; obscene on another.

In the end it is simple enough—

The woman of this morning's mirror
was a stranger
to the woman of last night's;
the passionate dreams of the one who slept
flit empty and thin
from the one who awakens.

One woman washes her face.
another picks up the boar-bristle hairbrush,
a third steps out of her slippers.
That each will die in the same bed means nothing to them.

Our one breath follows another like spotted horses, no two alike

Black manes and white manes, they gallop.
Piebald and skewbald, eyes flashing sorrow, they too will pass.

SONNET

by KAREN VOLKMAN

from NEW ENGLAND REVIEW

Lease of my leaving, heartfelt lack, what does
your plunge propose, its too-loose turning?
A deepfall trill, always-again returning
when Leaving, stepchild of Staying, is and was

always already going, condition, cause
of future's rapture—the baby always burning—
and present never present, always yearning
for plummet's pivot—articulate pause.

Lack lurks, blue and black. What acrid, airy sea
will give the whither anchor, heed the calling
for harbor, shore, to stall the listing lee

of always-motion, infant and appalling?
My infinite late, dark nascence: Tell me,
will there be an end to all this falling?

THE PART OF THE BEE'S BODY EMBEDDED IN THE FLESH

by CAROL FROST

from LYRIC

The bee-boy, *merops apiater*, on sultry thundery days
filled his bosom between his coarse shirt and his skin
with bees—his every meal wild honey.
He had no apprehension of their stings or didn't mind
and gave himself—his palate, the soft tissues of his throat—
what Rubens gave to the sun's illumination
stealing like fingers across a woman's thigh
and Van Gogh's brushwork heightened.
Whatever it means, why not say it hurts—
the mind's raw, gold coiling whirled against
air currents, want, and beauty? I *will* say beauty.

AUTOCHTHONIC SONG

by REBECCA SEIFERLE

from BITTERS (Copper Canyon Press)

We knew the buffalo were dangerous, but, most of the time
as we drifted among them, longing to touch

the bright curls of one of the spring calves,
their coats the color of new pennies, they lowered

their heads to the wild grasses, and shied away
only when we drew too near. For months

we moved among them, circling
the sweet expressions of the calves,

as they kept circling that hill that seemed a ziggurat,
pointed at the summit, like that odd vision

of Columbus—off the coast of South America
"the earth was round and something rising

in the distance like a breast"—who thought
he had reached the beginning

of all creation, the nipple
of time and space. The hill glittered

with mica—flakes, the size and breadth
of a human hand—scattered

over its flanks. We tried many times to bevel by hand
the stones into a clear plane, an eyeglass

through which we could view the world,
but the crystals only split along the cleavage,

until, running among that shaggy tribe,
we forgot our mothers, our fathers, as if, running among

that remnant, we could save some part of ourselves
from extinction. Crazy with liberty,

I veered toward a calf, drew so close
that I could never remember

if I had touched it or not. But the mother,
her malevolence, one movement with her desire

to protect, wheeled in alarm,
and as she did so the herd wheeled with her, as a flock of sparrows

will turn in the sky to enfold a red-tailed hawk. A current
of rippling fear or anger, the buffalo

turned to charge us. We ran, the breath scattering
out of our child-lungs, barely able to keep ahead

of that rhythm that had always seemed like that of a choppy
rocking horse but which now seemed as fluid

as a flash flood churning down an arroyo.
We ran toward the hill, hoping the slope would save us

by wearing them down, the climb exhaust their fury,
and it did, but so slowly that by the time the buffalo stopped,

milling about halfway up, we were ourselves stampeding,
seized by a panic, so ancient, it kept our ribs

splintering in our chests all the way up the hill
until we crammed ourselves into the tiny cave

at its summit, clinging to ourselves
among the black widow spiders, the sloppy cobwebs

of fear, and it was only then that I understood—
the earth is not our mother but a wild music beyond the self.

XXVIII

PRIMER OF WORDS

by DAVID BAKER

from THE GEORGIA REVIEW

I.

Hard to picture him here in the lake grass,
taking notes, up to his knees in mud, bugs,
but here he is, August 1880,
in Canada, tracing the flights of birds.

Like a bird he takes whatever he finds
to make words, the backs of letters, homemade
notebooks, and writes sometimes without looking,
they are so plentiful, the shy *Shore-lark*

and all the Sparrows, Oriole (hanging
bird—golden robin), Scarlet Tanager;
Swallows, the (very common) cedar-bird.
Lists, lists, enlivening his mind, like his

better father said they would do, for "bare
lists of words are found suggestive to an
imaginative and excited mind."
Yet he is half-paralyzed from the strokes

and must hang on Wm. Saunders' firm arm
to continue. Lists in manuscript are
his poems now, his greatest Leaves fallen
years past, consigned to infamy or fame.

Lists draw their power straight from nature, as
from his expressions. *Words of ~~all~~ the Laws*
of the Earth—he closes his eyes to feel
the sun bathe his face, softly now he breathes—

Words of the Sun and Moon,
Words of Geology, ~~Chemistry Gegro~~ History, Geography,
Words of ~~Me~~ the Medieval Races,
Words of the Progress of ~~Law~~, Religion, Law, Art, Government,

Words of the ~~Topography~~ surface of the Earth, grass, rocks, trees,
   flowers, grains, and the like,
Words of the Air and Heavens,
Words of the Birds ~~of the~~, and of insects,
Words of ~~the~~ Men and Women—the hundreds of different na-
   tions, tribes, colors, and other distinctions . . .

2.

He's sixty-one, famous if half infirm.
He's doted on by Addington Symonds, Bucke,
hounded for his views on Lincoln and Life,
yet now, in Ontario, by the lakes,

he is simply Walt, noting here when one
little black-and-yellow bird [the goldfinch]
lights from his billowy flight on a low
pine bough not ten feet off. In one gesture

he considers the significant trait
of civilization Benevolence—
and thinks it *doubtful whether ~~it~~ this is*
anywhere illustrated to fuller

degrees than in Ontario, *with its*
countless institutions for the Blind, one
for the Deaf and Dumb, one for Foundlings,
a Reformatory for Girls, one for

Women, and no end of homes for the old
and infirm, for waifs, and for the Sick—and
then adjusts the list . . . (all ~~vario~~ sorts)
otter, coon, mink, martin, ~~and buffalo~~

musk-rat, & c. Equality
is nature's law and must be government's.
The rich, abundant, wild various hues
of the birds, the hunting hawks, the ruby-

throated whirring hummingbirds, the brave gold-
finch full of song—so many genera—
should not confuse the mind. In his rough-hand
Primer of Words he traces the native

people's phrases, found in the north prairies,
their *wardance, powwow, Sachem, Mohekan,*
then notes as in a new poem the fate
of the Africans, the poignant irony . . .

3.

> barracoon—collection of slaves
> in Africa, or anywhere
> ("I see the slave barracoon")

how hybrid songs of "nigger dialect"
have furnished *hundreds of outre ~~names~~
words,* many of them adopted into
the common speech of the mass of people.

In another notebook, in years past, he
fretted with this problem so, writing *I
know there are strong and solid arguments
against slavery—arguments addressed*

*to the great American thought Will it pay?
We will go ~~directly~~ stand face to face*

with the / chief of the supreme bench. We will
speak with the soul. [new page] *For ~~free~~ as great*
   as any worldly wealth to a man,—or

~~her~~ womanhood to a woman,—greater
than these, I think, is the right of liberty,
to any and to all men and women.—
Lists. Lists. Bare words. Nature's compositions

stretch before the receptive eye. He has
found a cool, moss-covered slab of limestone
to light on, looking south, over the lake.
Tomorrow, he thinks, he'll speak yet with Bucke

about the poems, and a lecture tour.
There is so much to say about the world.
These grasses, for instance, growing so tall
in the wild—*what are they?* Timothy, joe-

pye weed, rip-gut, perhaps? Of what nature,
what kind are they? There's another question
here, a hope—he needs to frame this better . . .
how they blow in the wind . . . how they go on . . .

or, *how they may seed.* Yes. How continue.

THE DRAGON

by BRIGIT PEGEEN KELLY

from NEW ENGLAND REVIEW

The bees came out of the junipers, two small swarms
The size of melons; and golden, too, like melons,
They hung next to each other, at the height of a deer's breast
Above the wet black compost. And because
The light was very bright it was hard to see them,
And harder still to see what hung between them.
A snake hung between them. The bees held up a snake,
Lifting each side of his narrow neck, just below
The pointed head, and in this way, very slowly
They carried the snake through the garden,
The snake's long body hanging down, its tail dragging
The ground, as if the creature were a criminal
Being escorted to execution or a child king
To the throne. I kept thinking the snake
Might be a hose, held by two ghostly hands,
But the snake was a snake, his body green as the grass
His tail divided, his skin oiled, the way the male member
Is oiled by the female's juices, the greenness overbright,
The bees gold, the winged serpent moving silently
Through the air. There was something deadly in it,
Or already dead. Something beyond the report
Of beauty. I laid my face against my arm, and there
It stayed for the length of time it takes two swarms
Of bees to carry a snake through a wide garden,
Past a sleeping swan, past the dead roses nailed
To the wall, past the small pond. And when

I looked up the bees and the snake were gone,
But the garden smelled of broken fruit, and across
The grass a shadow lay for which there was no source,
A narrow plinth dividing the garden, and the air
Was like the air after a fire, or before a storm,
Ungodly still, but full of dark shapes turning.

COMMERCE

by MICHAEL WATERS

from THE GETTYSBURG REVIEW

Niagara Falls, 18—

Some half-wit Barnum, amateur Noah,
fashioned an ark—a salvaged, broken barge—
to populate with creatures trapped or bought:
black bear, wolverine, a fox like a flame,

peacocks, possum, hogs, raccoon, wailing tribe
of forsaken dogs, weasel, skunk, even—
according to eyewitness reports—six
silver monkeys shipped by rail from New York,

God's mange-thumbed menagerie chained to planks
that would have floated three runaway slaves
had not abolitionists threatened court.
Then Noah bid his bestiary good-bye,

the raft of lamentation set adrift,
its creatures more confused than crazed, almost
calm as the ark spiraled toward the maelstrom,
the waters' vast uproar drowning weak cries,

white mists like shrouds enveloping the crew
while spectators whooped and scrambled both banks

and newsboys shilled beer a nickel a glass
till it perched midair on the precipice. . . .

Folklore swears the bear survived, pummeled ashore
where men beat her with clubs and muzzled her,
then dragged that rough beast saloon to saloon
where drafts of whiskey were chugged down her throat.

By morning she lay a rank heap on State—
schoolchildren leapfrogged the raggedy corpse.
Then one cat was found, eyeless, legs broken,
so for the next decade tramps tortured strays

to sell them to tourists, farm boys, and Poles
as The Cat Swept Over Niagara Falls,
singular souvenir, His living hand,
New World miracle—only one dollar.

IS

by BRUCE BEASLEY

from THE SOUTHERN REVIEW

> *[B]eing is twofold. . . . Being conveys the truth of a proposition which unites together subject and attribute by a copula, notified by this word "is"; and in this sense being is what answers to the question, "Does it exist?"*
> —Thomas Aquinas

> *When Eve was still in Adam, death did not exist. When she was separated from him, death came into being. If he enters again and attains his former self, death will be no more.*
> —The Gospel of Philip

Male and female He created them,
ʾîš   and ʾiššâ
bone/flesh   *of my*   *bone/flesh*

—Stripped
in the woods   *Naked came I*
crouched in the charred   lightning-gutted pine tree,
twelve, hard, and scared of it,

feeling what it felt to touch myself
till the blood rushed, and the shiver
rose, and the change

came on, I could just barely hold back . . .
                    Woman, what have I to do with thee?

                    ❖   ❖   ❖

Like a little dick inside,   my sister said, not showing me

Girls have a little spot that's like a dick:

Like a long splinter   (I imagined it)
stabbed inside, blue,   half-visible,
gone soft and snaking up   through their bellies,
a Thing   like mine
It's a penis, my father said,   drunk, his only
version of the Facts of Life,   *don't call it your Thing anymore,*
        it's called a penis . . .

penalis: punishment   vulva: from *volvere,* to turn
        penetrate: to pierce, to grasp the inner meaning of

Learning the turned-
inward, the con-
volute   Tampon-string

the undivulged

    I/upreared   S/encoiled
        the vertical, the rigid   lips inside lips

        Differ: to dis-ferry, to carry

apart

                ❀   ❀   ❀

And the copula (*the link*) carries together—dissolves difference—
        X *is* Y
                One in Being
        —as in metaphor, that rut of words, that
        lust across the copula . . .

As out of the burning,
unconsumed bush
to Moses It said:

I am who am
Thus shalt thou say, I AM hath sent me unto you

—pure Being, or pure
metaphor, or
tautology (say the same say the same)   *Is* is *is*
Then pure
profusion   (fruitful: multiply)
in whatever form It *Is*—

So, in the storm cellar, yeast smell
of my bread-mold lab, fuzzed
piecework of black and GI Joe green,
stale bread-crusts in rows of wooden bowls

How strangely the patterns   *differed*, side by side:
pinkish peach-fur on one,   black whiskers, pubic
                                    thatch on the next

Mold spores called out of the air, the rank
fecundity made visible, in three days—

I couldn't stop
laying out the molds on my slides,
under microscope,   threads, runners, webs,
couldn't stop breeding
my apricot and golden hamsters,
at eleven, waiting   night after night for estrus,
the sniff, the telltale   lifting of the tail
(Latin *oestrus*,   frenzy)

In the medicine cabinet, my mother's
little silver, punched-out packet of pills
She takes them so she fuck   *with Daddy*

The female's hissing,   her bared incisors,   a grinding of the
                                                        teeth

It is   so that it might be   *Is*

573

My grandfather's *Playboys*, in their stash by his whiskey
        cabinet,
behind his pirate's sword
with the blood spot, in the long
crawlspace:
my parents caught
me looking, and made me stay down there and look

so I'd know they were upstairs knowing
I was turning the glossed pages
(*and I was ashamed   and hid myself*)
string of pearls around the nipples and the flicking tongue . . .

"After mounting,   the male
becomes tired   and uninterested"

        The hamsters frenzied again on their separate wheels

                    ✿ ✿ ✿

In "our" image, male and female   Split, and teeming
                        out of that one "Am"

*So she can fuck with Daddy you know that's what they're
        doing when they say they're "taking a nap"*

Inwardly penetrated and inflamed
by divine love, the soul
passes utterly into that other glory—

that *Is*, penetrant and burning

God's unspeakable name
made out of the *imperfect*
of *to be*,

vowel-less merge:
Y   H   W   H
I am whoever I will come to be

ʾîš / male   ʾîššâ/fe-male
                    is, the fastener

To *grasp*   the inner meaning
                of that "other glory":
We have our own little spot
                        That's why it feels good to us too

                    ✿   ✿   ✿

Under the dripping waterspout,
behind the bars, the day-old litter
bled: torn-
off foot in the mother's mouth, and the naked,
pink, uneyed babies
squirming, still, toward her teats—
The runt
stuffed kicking in the mother's cheek-pouch as she
gnawed—

It's just how Nature
works, my mother kept saying,
whiskey on her breath, lifting
the mangled body out with a napkin,
It's just how Nature works,
her face
contorted above me.

                    ✿   ✿   ✿

When Eve was still   in Adam,
when death had not   "come into being,"
breasts and vulva buried there inside his sealed-in rib

                    —Calling
out of the body of the bread (sopped
crusts, in their trapped-air Mason jars) the invisible
teeming,

and out of the Fungus Book, the language I loved:

Rhizopus
nigricans,

mycelia, sporangia, hyphae—

Spora, seed   *Sporas*, scattered

—The much-warned-
against   "nocturnal emission": being told
by *Moving into Manhood*   our bodies
were seeded now,   and seeding
White eyelash-threads   over thistledown mats
of spread black   split
spore-cases, on the wet   Wonder Bread

All the girls   single file
leaving the auditorium   pushing open
the red velvet drapes   their hushed,
barking laughs   the nurse
leading   What were they told
          Don't call it a "Thing"

E-
missions

—Pearls   on the nipples,
pearls   on the tongue . . .

                    ✿ ✿ ✿

Nature's works: the littering, the
waste, flashlight
on my new, barely visible, pubic hair,
in Boy Scout camp, in the tent:

Don't be shy, guy,
the sixteen-year-old said,
I may have more of what you've got
and you may have less of what I have,
but we've all got the same

stuff . . .
      (A little spot,
a little dick inside . . .)

Who I am, I am,
copula: reach
hither thy finger.

               ❁   ❁   ❁

How deep does the *is*   in the sentence
penetrate,   with what *quick*ness does it
burn,
            the copula, the subject and predicate's
                    fuse?
(as the mold and bread are made one:
root-cases   digging through the grain,

as I imagined for a while my
    sister,   hermaphroditic,
with her   Thing
          all coiled inside)—

My mother's face
as she turned away, bloodied
napkin in her hand

Then all night the hamster's
wheel-screak, her gnawed
wood bar, smell of afterbirth
she never even licked off the litter.

—Then metaphor's
quick copulation
(hiss, sniff, lifted
tail), its resistless   thrusting-into-one—

      (bread mold, bred hamsters, Yahweh
        breeding out from His *Is*)

Crumble of mold-dust   as the taken bread
disintegrates   What's left of the host
body?, when the change

comes

I am Am

Sporangia everywhere,   bursting

CAIN'S LEGACY

by RICHARD JACKSON

from CRAZYHORSE

You can't stop the boxcars of despair.
You can't stop my voice from hiding out
like a virus inside your words, their knives
clamped between your teeth. You can't stop
the dogs gnawing on the bones from mass graves.
Thus your mirrors holding other faces. Thus your lungs
filled with someone else's words.
The eyelids of the heart closing. The sky drunk
on vapor trails. Otherwise, a few packages of conscience
to the refugees. You can't stop the sounds
of exploding stars as they approach you.
The anxious triggers. The land mines of idealism.
You can't stop Dismay from stumbling
out of the trenches of your dreams.
You can't stop these ghosts sitting around your table
gnawing on the past. Their candles burn down
to shimmering wounds in their cups.
Everyone holding their favorite flags like napkins.
The sound of bugles spilling from the room like laughter.
I know, you kill what you love just to hate yourself
all the more. You put on the cloak of distance.
A wind that blows away the weeks. The lovers' wilted embrace
that was your only, your last hope.
Everyone his own Judas. After a while
even the moon is just an excuse not to look too closely.

You can't stop the past boiling up in the heart like lava.
Otherwise, a history written by shadows.
For example, someone says the universe is expanding,
more anxious optimism, but where would it expand into?
There's only the vacuum that's always inside us.
There's Stephen Hawking saying the past is pear shaped
but that doesn't feed anyone. You can't stop the brain
of the starving child turning into a peach pit,
not his body terrorizing itself for food,
not his face wrinkling like the orange you leave on your table,
his liver collapsing, the last few muscles snug
over his bones like the tight leather gloves of your debutante.
Otherwise your old lies yawning to wake in the corner.
You can't stop the pieces of the suicide bomber
from splattering all over the café walls.
You can't stop the walls the tanks crush from rising again.
Otherwise a few tired rivers, a few fugitive stars.
The seasons that ignore us. The cicadas giving up on us.
Hope's broken antennas. Love trying to slip out of the noose.
The betrayed lives we were meant to live.
You can't stop that town from turning its soul on a spit,
not the light chiseling away desire, the morning
wandering dazed through the underbrush of deception.
You can't stop these sails of tomorrow hanging limp
from their masts. All you have are these backwaters of touch,
this voice spinning like a broken compass,
this muzzle made from your own laws.
But you can't stop the bodies piling up.
You can't stop the deafening roar of the sky.
You can't stop the bullet you've aimed at your own head.

ADEPT

by DANA LEVIN

from AMERICAN POETRY REVIEW

Stomach with a skin of light.

Without a knife he opened himself up.

Without a knife.

Chinese letters marched around him in formation,
  a military equestrian parade—

He was an adept, in my book on the golden flower.

On a bed of peacock tails.

And he was opening his abdomen with both his hands,
  parting it like curtains.

And I thought if I looked at him long enough, I might go through
 there.

Through the flame-shaped opening.

Where there sat another lotus-sitting figure.

And the caption said, Origin of a new being in the place of
 power.

And I thought, was that the flower.
—

What was the body but a scalpel and a light what was it—

Rubbing an oil into scars like a river for the first time I touched
     them—

I was an adept in the book of vivid pain, I used my finger like a
     knife—

Not
     to hurt myself, but to somehow get back *in*—

like the little man opening his belly right up.
     and the little man resting inside there.

But how could I. When I would not enter the flame-shaped opening.

When I hovered
                    above.

But never leaving it, always nearing it, a fly on the verge of some-
     thing sweet—

Was that what the body was, a sweetness?

Hive ringed by fire.
—

And the adept says, That's you on the bed: Empty Chamber.

And your stomach
                    is open like a coat—

It's black in there, deep.
It's red in there, thick
                    with the human loam—

And all along your ghost head and your shoulders
          you can feel the wet

as you slide back in,
      your tissues cupping you like hands.

The body: worm round an ember of light.

You're in it now.

Flower.

XXIX

WONDER: RED BEANS AND RICELY

by SYDNEY LEA

from THE SOUTHERN REVIEW

He blew the famous opening figure of "West End Blues"
and then—a long pause. A long long pin-drop pause.
This sounded like nothing the four of us had been hearing out here
at the Famous Sunnybrook Ballroom in East Jesus, PA,
which was in fact a moth-eaten tent to which in summer
the big postwar bands, then fading into the '50s—
the likes of the Elgars or Les Brown and His Band of Renown—
would arrive to coax the newly middle-aged and their elders
into nostalgia and dance. My second cousin, our steadies,
and I were younger, cocksure, full of contraband beer,
but the moment I speak of knocked even us in the know-it-all chops.

I suddenly dreamed I could see through the vast canvas top
clear to stars as they stopped their fool blinking and planets
    standing
stock-still over cows and great-eyed deer in the moonlight
and ducks ablaze on their ponds because everything in God's world
knew this was nothing like anything they'd known before.
It's still a fantasy, that sorry tent a lantern,
transparent as glass, through which I beheld the landscape around it
as though it showed in some Low Country more-than-masterpiece
while no one danced. The crassest fat-necked burgher in the crowd

sat rapt, as did his missus, the moment being that strong.
It lingered strong, beginning to end, through the "Blues" that
   followed.

Then Velma Middleton got up to jive and bellow.
She broke the charm, her scintillant dress like a tent itself,
and people resumed the lindy and fox-trot as she and he
traded the always-good-for-laughs double meanings
of "Big Butter and Egg Man," "That's My Desire,"
and so on. And so we four, or rather we two boys,
resumed our drinking and boasting until the band took its break.
Full enough by now of the Bud and some of the rum
that the cousin had brought, which would take him in time, too
   sadly short
a time, to another shore forever, I stood and pledged:
I'll get his autograph. It made no sense at all.

I staggered to and through the canvas's backstage hole,
the mocking jibes of cousin and sweethearts dying behind me,
and beheld four semi-tractor trucks—his equipage.
There were doors as to a house in each, and a little set
of metal steps underneath. Without a hitch, I climbed
one stair of the bunch. It made no sense except it did.
I *knew.* . . . Something had burned into my fogged brain
when that opening solo started, he would have to be
just there where he was when I knocked on one of the several doors
inside the truck, and the growl was Fate: it didn't surprise me:
Come in, he said. How could he? How could he not? I came.

It had had to be, and yet I stammered with puzzlement, shame.
I'd had a vision, yes, and yet to have the vision
there before me. . . . Wonder! Great Armstrong at his desk
in an undershirt, suspenders flapping, his face near blinding,
sweat beads charged by the gimcrack string of fluorescent lights
so that he seemed to wear an aura—it was all
one supple motion, the way he reached into a drawer,
drew out a jug of Johnny Walker, sucked it down
to the label, squared before him a sheet of paper (where
did *that* come from?), flourished a fountain pen, and wrote:
Red Beans and Ricely Yours at Sunny Brook Ballroom. Pops.

Back at the table they judged it was real enough by the looks.
"I just walked in and got it," I bragged, as if a miracle
hadn't transpired, surely as great as any I'd know.
I bragged as if my part in it all were important somehow,
and God hadn't just looked down and said, "Well OK—him."
And what remains from then? Not the paper, long since lost,
nor the lovely, silken girls, Sally and Margot,
nor the cousin, as I've said, who became the Guy with the Liver.
Nor that old, that old brash blessèd younger I. . . .
Just the heaven-struck beasts and the trees and the moon and the
   sky

below that spray of opening notes which are there forever.

LANDSCAPE WITH HUNGRY GULLS

by LANCE LARSEN

from GRAND STREET

If I said burial, if I said a lovely morning
    to prepare the body, who would I startle?
Not this pair of teenage girls in matching swimsuits
    making a mound of their brother.
And not the boy himself, laid out like a cadaver
    on rye, who volunteered for interment.

In the language of skin, he knows that sand rhymes
    with patience, and that patience worketh
a blue sky dotted with gulls, if only he remains
    still enough. And he does, his face a cameo
dusted with sparkling grains. Meanwhile, my son
    brings me offerings he has dug up—

a jawbone, a pair of vertebrae, ribs like planks, three teeth.
    At my feet, an ancient horse assembles.
A lesson in calcification? A beginner's oracle kit?
    If the seagulls canvassing the beach
are questions, then the pelican riding the dihedral breeze
    above the buoys is an admonition, but to what?

The sisters are at work again, making a giant
    Shasta daisy of their brother's face,

six pieces of popcorn per petal, his eyes blinking.
    Now they scatter leftover kernels across the mound
like sextons scattering lime. To my left,
    ankle-deep in shallows, my son catches minnows.

No, not minnows, damselfly larvae,
    which swim like minnows but have six legs.
He places them in a moat, so they can swim freely.
    Soon enough they will climb this castle wall.
Soon enough they will shed their syntax and leave
    one language for another, like a good translation.

The sisters have moved farther down the beach
    in hopes that the seagulls will gently
nibble their brother. So many motives. Theirs: to dress
    a body in the sands of is as though tomorrow isn't.
His: to taste the world, mouth to beak.
    The gulls draw closer, to peck at his heart.

I am trying to pretend the body is only an idea.
    I watch the pelican. I have to keep reminding myself.
A pelican is not a pterodactyl with feathers.
    A pelican is not doing moral reconnaissance.
A pelican does not know my name.
    I close my eyes long enough to drift up and up.

Poor man, napping there, far below, who looks
    and smells like me, but is stuck in a beach chair.
Quick, someone teach him to bank and hover.
    And this horse my son is decorating the moat with,
broken into pieces so small and various and eloquent—
    why do I worry whether it has enough to eat?

HORSEFLIES

by ROBERT WRIGLEY

from THE IDAHO REVIEW

After the horse went down
    the heat came up,
and later that week
    the smell of its fester yawed,
an open mouth of had-been air
    our local world was licked
inside of, and I,

the boy who'd volunteered at twilight—
    shunts of chawed cardboard
wadded up my nostrils
    and a dampened bandana
over my nose and mouth—
    I strode then

into the ever-purpler sink
    of rankness and smut,
a sloshful five-gallon bucket of kerosene
    in my right hand,
a smoking railroad fusee
    in my left,
and it came over me like water then,

into my head-gaps and gum
    rinds, into the tear ducts

and taste buds and even
　　　into the last dark tendrils
of my howling, agonized hair
　　　that through the windless half-light
hoped to fly from my very head,

and would have, I have no doubt, had not
　　　the first splash of kerosene
launched a seething skin
　　　of flies into the air
and onto me, the cloud of them
　　　so dense and dark my mother in the distance
saw smoke and believed as she had feared

I would, that I had set my own
　　　fool and staggering self aflame,
and therefore she fainted and did not see
　　　how the fire kicked
the other billion flies airborne
　　　exactly in the shape
of the horse itself,

which rose for a brief quivering
　　　instant under me, and which for a pulse thump
at least, I rode—in a livery of iridescence,
　　　in a mail of exoskeletal facets,
wielding a lance of swimming lace—
　　　just as night rode the light, and the bones,
and a sweet, cleansing smoke to ground.

MY BROTHER, ANTONIO, THE BAKER

by PHILIP LEVINE

from FIVE POINTS

Did the wind blow that night? When did it not?
I'd ask you if you hadn't gone underground
lugging the answer with you.
Twenty-eight years old, on our way home
after a twelve-hour shift baking Wonder Bread
for the sleeping prisoners in the drunk tank
at the Canfield Station dreaming of a breakfast
of horse cock and mattress stuffing.
(Oh, the luxuries of 1955! How fully we lived—
the working-classes and the law abiding dregs—
on buttered toast and grilled-cheese sandwiches
as the nation braced itself for pate and pasta.)
To myself I smelled like a new mother minus
the aura of talcum and the airborne, acrid aromas
of cotton diapers. Today I'd be labeled
nurturing and bountiful instead
of vegetal and weird. A blurred moon was out,
we both saw it; I know because leaning back,
eyes closed on a ruined sky, you did your thing,
welcoming the "bright orb" waning in the west,
"Moon that rained down its silver coins
on the darkened Duero and the sleeping fields
of Soria." Did I look like you, my face
anonymous and pure, bleached with flour,
my eyes glistening with the power of neon light

594

or self-love? Two grown men, side by side,
one babbling joyfully to the universe
that couldn't care less, while the other,
practiced for middle age. A single crow settled
on the boiler above the Chinese restaurant,
his feathers riffling, and I took it for a sign.
A second sign was the couple exiting
the all-night pharmacy; the man came first
through the glass door, a small white sack in hand,
and let the door swing shut. Then she appeared,
one hand covering her eyes to keep
the moonlight at bay. They stood not talking
while he looked first left, then right, then left
again as flakes of darkness sifted upward
toward the streetlight. The place began to rumble
as though this were the end. You spoke again,
only this time you described someone humble
walking alone in darkness. I could see
the streetcar turning off Joy Road,
swaying down the tracks toward us,
its windows on fire. There must have been a wind,
a west wind. What else could have blown
the aura of forsythia through the town
and materialized one cross-town streetcar
never before on time? A spring wind
freighted with hope. I remember
thinking that at last you might shut up.
An old woman stood to give you
her seat as though you were angelic
or pregnant. When her eyes spilled over
with happiness, I saw she took your words
to heart as I never could. Maybe she recalled
the Duero, the fields asleep in moonlight,
maybe the words were music to her,
original and whole, words that took her home
to Soria or Krakow or wherever,
maybe she was not an old woman at all
but an oracle in drag who saw you as you were
and saw, too, you couldn't last the night.

CAN'T YOU HEAR THE WIND HOWL?

by FRANK X. GASPAR

from THE GEORGIA REVIEW

I'm shivering here with Coleman Hawkins and cup of gin
and no idea what hour of the night it is—feeling ashamed
of how time passes when everyone knows I should be the
responsible party and put a stop to all this waste: What good
is a night if there's a dawn always lurking somewhere in the future?
How can I ever be completely certain of the stars if they fade
so easily before such cheap theatrics? When will I learn, as all
my betters have, to live in the moment? Out in the alley there's
a possum looking for a home. Out in the city lights there's an
alley looking for a street. You can hear the wind blowing
all along the window screens. It's singing to the voices in my head,
it's saying, *Quiet!* It's saying, *Shooo!* Coleman Hawkins isn't
saying a word. He's occupied with some friends. He's living
in the moment among certain characters with names like Dizzy
and Django and Pee Wee and Cozy. He ain't going nowhere,
he is all past *and* future, if you know what I mean. I don't have
the nerve to say my heart is aching—not with *that* crowd all
around me, not with that bass line shaking the books and their
cracked spines and rocking the pens and pencils. Am I wrong?
Am I wrong to let Cicero rest awhile and to let Sappho, in her
tatters, sleep under the seven sisters, and to breathe in deeply
and to breathe out deeply? And to let the ice in my blue cup bark
in its quiet cataclysms and let the brown air blow down a hundred
   miles

from the deserts because I have no choice in these matters? Now
let me tap my foot in a certain way. In a certain way because there
was a machine once that could cull every kind of music from a room
and save it for a while, unharmed. Can't you hear the wind howl?
Here, all around my feeble senses. Here, in the iron lung of the
    night.
Here it comes again, all teeth in the palm leaves, looking for a
    home.

BEETLE ORGY

by BENJAMIN SCOTT GROSSBERG

from WESTERN HUMANITIES REVIEW

Bloom up from the earth, blooming and curling
like ribbon, and at semi-regular intervals
sprouting leaves: almost the border art
of a Celtic manuscript, the vines up along the fence
of this old tennis court. Amid the wreck

of the net, the cracks of the surface, the rust
along the poles still standing, the vines
are a saving delicacy. Not jarring at all,
though incongruous—except as a reminder
that the school yard will gladly take this place

back in a few untended years, that between
the vines and grass, the tennis court
will be ground into meal and digested.
I stop at one of the vine edgings caught
by even finer detail: the leaves themselves

are digested; they have been eaten to
irregular lace, and the perpetrators are still here—
five of them across one particular leaf, lined up
straight and even, like cars in a parking lot.
Beetles: their backs a lustrous green and copper,

taken hot from the kiln, thrown on a bed of saw dust
that burst into flame, then lidded over

so the vacuum could draw the metal oxides
to the surface. At first it looks like there are five,
but now I see that there are seven, no eight—

and that in three of the spaces, beetles
are doubled up, one mounting, back legs
twitching, as if running and getting no where;
and one mounted, also moving, slightly rocking
in back, close to the point of intersection—

or penetration—in any case, where the bodies
touch. And here I come to it—amid the advancing
vines and decrepit court: they're on other leaves, too,
all around—coupling in company, hundreds of them,
the rows melding to make a single metallic band.

Back in Houston, a friend had parties—
lawn bags in the living room numbered with tape
to store guest clothing; plastic drop cloths
spread out in the spare bedroom (cleared of furniture
for the occasion), a tray of lubricants, different

brands in tubes or bottles, labels black, red, and silver
—a high tea sensibility. The artifacts remained
uncollected in his apartment for days, even weeks
after, when I would drop by to find his talk
transformed, suddenly transcendental—

the communality, he told me, the freedom: not
just from the condom code (HIV negative I
was never invited) but freed of individuation—
nothing less than rapture, men more than brothers,
a generosity of giving and taking, to both give

and take greedily, that he had experienced
no where else. Could I understand that?
The room pulsing as if inhabited by
a single animal, caught up in a single sensibility.
Could I understand? I could read transformation

in his face, could see his eyes, feel him trying
to tell me something: to offer this reliable revelation—
what he always knew would come, but what always
in coming disarmed him. As he talked I looked around
the spare bedroom, attempting to see it

in terms other than lust—a couple of dozen men,
how they would have lined up, become a single
working unit on clear plastic, how their bodies
might have formed a neat chain. I looked around
and tried; couldn't I understand that?

So each beetle a tiny scarab, a dime-size jewel
that glints in the sun. I lean over and touch
their backs with the tip of my finger: running
up and down the bright, smooth surface
like piano keys, hard enough to feel resistance

but not to interject foreign music. Together they form
a band of light, a band of glaze, the gold leafing
that shadows the vines in Celtic manuscripts, a living art.
Maybe that's how it was at my friend's parties—
God leaning over the house on a casual tour

of the wreck of the world, noticing ornamentation
where it wasn't expected. Moved to add
his touch, he reaches a hand through the clouds, runs
his finger over the hard arch of their backs, covering
the length of each spine with the tip;

each man brightens at the touch, comes to know
something expected, unexpected, and tenuous—
and God, also, comes to some knowledge
as if for the first time, is distracted and pleased
by the collective brightness of human skin. . . .

Then I think of God fitting the roof back on
my friend's house, and exhaling, satisfied—
just like me as I walk away
from the tennis court, just like the men inside.

ROSE OF SHARON

by BRIGIT PEGEEN KELLY

from THE ORCHARD (BOA Editions)

I loved the rose of Sharon. I would have loved it
For its name alone. I loved its fleshy blossoms.
How fat they were. How fast they fell. How the doves,
Mean as spit, fought the finches and the sparrows
For the golden seed I spilled beneath the bush.
How I threw seed just to watch the birds fight.
And the blossoms fallen were like watered silk
Loosely bound. And the blossoms budding
Were like the dog's bright penis first emerging
From its hairy sheath. And the blossoms opened wide
Were like the warm air above the pool of Siloam.
Tree of breath. Pink flowers floating on water.
The flushed blossoms themselves like water.
Rising. Falling. The wind kicking up skeins
Of scented foam. High-kicking waves. Or laughing
Dancers. O silly thoughts. But a great sweetness. . . .
And then it was over. An ice storm felled the tree.
With a clean cut, as if with a hatchet. One year
A whole flock of birds. One year a crop of fruit
That melted on the tongue, a kind of manna, light
As honey, just enough to sustain one. And then nothing.
The breasts gone dry. The window opening onto
Bare grass. The small birds on the wire waiting
For the seed I do not throw. *Pride of my heart*,
Rose of Sharon. *Pool of scented breath*. Rose

Of Sharon. How inflated my sorrow. But the tree
Itself was inflated. A perpetual feast. A perpetual
Snowfall of warm confetti. . . . And now I worry.
Did the bush fear the ice? Did it know of the ice's
Black designs? Did its featherweight nature darken
Just before it was felled? Was it capable of darkening?

BEST AND ONLY

by ANDREW FELD

from MICHIGAN QUARTERLY REVIEW

I: THE SHIP OF STATE

The way a carp's speckled brown and white head
flashes just below the surface of the Potomac
night waters, Richard Nixon's penis almost enters

the national consciousness, as a thin gold thread
of urine stitches him to an August night in 1973,
on the stern of the *Sequoia*. Standing beside him

is the Cuban financier Bebe Rebozo, who is also
pissing into the river. The image is a small shame
in the middle of many greater ones: the damp dots

on his pants as he shakes off with an awkward
drunk step back and zips up: the president pissing
on the Republic, over which he stands. Exposed

briefly before being pulled back below decks,
the two men are easy targets for anyone's
anger or condescension. Jowly, soft with

the executive spread of men in the era before
exercise was invented, their bodies bulge oddly,
pumpkin-like growths swelling the crotches

and stomachs of their pin-stripped suits, as if
their own flesh had risen up against them. But for
the marksman stationed near, their appearance

at his post is an allegation he'd die to deny. Eyes
trained to see elsewhere, he holds his cool
weapon and a bead drops from the little jungle

of his armpit as twin diesel engines push the boat
past the riverbank where the hippie who jumps up
to grab a Day-Glo Frisbee out of the air hears

their voices and mistakes the drunken laughter
of two old men in a boat for the drunken laughter
of two old men in a boat, unaware that History

is passing so close he's breathing its exhaust,
its strain of scorched fuels distinct for a few
seconds and then folded back into the ordinary

summer night smells of mass transportation
and river water. We now know on this particular
August night they're shifting funds, arranging pay-offs

for the plumbers and harassing Henry the Jew,
denying they've *even heard* of Cambodia, as they sail
several martinis outside anyone's jurisdiction.

For these and other crimes, may they be lodged
in the sulphurous cavern of Satan's anus forever.
But what of the genuine warmth all the biographers

agree burnt between these two men, the actual,
human love they felt for each other: is it only
the gaseous fire of butane tentacles wrapping around

a bushel of asbestos logs in the below-deck bar's
mahogany dark, or is it the quicksilver spirits
in the funneled glasses they lift to each other,

a whisper of vermouth tasting like amnesia
in the gin's frostbitten false fire, the warmth
in each sip drawing them closer together?

II: FROM THE APOCRYPHA OF BEBE REBOZO

3.
Protesters under the cherry trees: notice
how each fallen petal rots from the inside
with a small brown dot on its delicate center-seam,
like a piece of used toilet paper:
so corruption is essential in us. It's in our guts.

7.
The young no longer dance.
Instead they *twitch*, as if
their electric guitars were electrodes
taped to their genitals. If only.

But their children will rediscover
the steps they abandon
and follow them back to us.

12.
Richard, I dreamed we walked the fine silver sands
shoring the Bay of Pigs, and there, beside your wing-
tip's tip, we found a gull poking its bill into the gills
of a still-living fish. Out in the surf, girls' voices called

for your attention as Tricia and Julie came riding shoreward
on the crests of waves; and this length of scaled muscle
was eaten alive at our feet, drowning in our oxygen.

III: 19—: AN ELEGY

Apollo. Bebe Rebozo. Beatniks.
The Car. Counting backwards.
Cold Warriors. The century

I was born in. Disney. The Great
Depression and Anti-Depressants.
Everest. The Evil Empire. Electric
light and atomic energy. Frost
at Kennedy's Inaugural. Fucking.
Free love. Gridlock. Harley-Davidson
and Hell's Angels. *Ho Ho Ho Chi Minh*.
The Ivory-billed woodpecker. The Iron
Curtain. Joke: how many right-wing
neo-conservative, conspiracy theory,
survivalist, NRA, MIA, VFW,
free-market, anti-establishment
radio talk show host-loving loners
does it take to screw in a light bulb?
The Killing fields. Love-Beads.
Love-Ins. Love Canal. The Mall
of America. Medical waste. Richard
Nixon. No one's home. The century
when oral sex came into its own.
The overdose. *People*. Peaceniks.
Plutonium. Post-. Pop-. Plastic-wrapped
bundles of cocaine washing up
on Florida beaches. Queer theory.
Race. A small car like a stereo
on wheels, the Soul-Singer's voice
tearing through paper speaker cones
the way the spirit is formed and deformed
by the flesh. The century of the Teenager.
Televangelists. Uncut. Unadulterated.
Vietnam. Watergate. World Wars. The X-ray.
Yeah Yeah Yeah. Zen Koan. Ground Zero.

MEDITERRANEAN

by ROSANNA WARREN

from POETRY

—when she disappeared on the path ahead of me
I leaned against a twisted oak, all I saw was evening light
                              where she had been:

gold dust light, where a moment before
and thirty-eight years before that

my substantial mother strode before me in straw hat, bathing
                              suit, and loose flapping shirt,
every summer afternoon, her knapsack light across her back,

her step, in sandals, firm on the stony path
as we returned from the beach

and I mulled small rebellions and observed the dwarfish cork trees
with their pocky bark, the wind-wrestled oaks with elbows
                              akimbo,

while shafts of sea-light stabbed down between the trunks.
There was something I wanted to say, at the age of twelve,

some question she hadn't answered,
and yesterday, so clearly seeing her pace before me

it rose again to the tip of my tongue, and the mystery was
not that she walked there, ten years after her death,

but that she vanished, and let twilight take her place—

BRIGHT WORLD

by CARL PHILLIPS

from FIELD

—A<small>ND IT CAME TO PASS</small>, that meaning faltered; came detached
unexpectedly from the place I'd made for it, years ago,
fixing it there, thinking it safe to turn away, therefore,
to forget—hadn't that made sense? And now everything
did, but differently: the wanting literally for nothing
for no good reason; the inability to feel remorse at having
cast (now over some; now others), aegis-like, though it
rescued no one, the body I'd all but grown used to waking
inside of and recognizing, instantly, correctly, as mine,
my body, given forth, withheld, shameless, merciless—
for crying shame. Like miniature versions of a lesser
gospel deemed, over time, apocryphal, or redundant—both,
maybe—until at last let go, the magnolia flowers went on
spilling themselves, each breaking open around, and then
apart from, its stem along a branch of stems and, not of
course in response, but as if so, the starlings lifting, unlifting,
the black flash of them in the light reminding me of what I'd
been told about the glamour of evil, in the light they were
like that, in the shadow they became the other part, about
resisting evil, as if resistance itself all this time had been
but shadow, could be found that easily . . . *What will you do?*
Is this how you're going to live now? sang the voice in my
head: singing, then silent—not as in desertion, but as
when the victim suddenly knows his torturer's face from

before, somewhere, and in the knowing is for a moment
distracted, has stopped struggling—And the heart gives in.

ELEVENS

by STANLEY PLUMLY

from THE KENYON REVIEW

1.

The sun flatlining the horizon, the wind
off the Atlantic hard enough to swallow—
arctic, manic and first thing—
the morning beach walk north lasting less
than half an hour, while you've stood
in the middle of the room that long
trying to get your breath back to normal.
It seems to take all the time there is,
as if a flake of ash burning off the sun
had entered at the mouth, turned ice,
and had, in slow-borne seconds, grown

2.

glacial, granite, dark. The summer
in the mountains there was snow, new snow,
you could walk in fifteen minutes down
the narrow gravel road and there'd be
ghostweed, spiraea, and stunted laurel trees
blossoming their own snow-on-the-mountain.
Ten, eleven thousand feet, and the water,
with a spirit of its own, moving over rock

without once touching, flying toward the world.
The thin fresh air too spiritual as well.
Down below, with lights, Durango, Colorado.

3.

City snow, especially, transforms backwards—
antique, baroque, medieval, hand-to-mouth.
Karel Čapek, in a book called *Intimate
Things*, says Prague can go back one, two
hundred years just overnight in a three-
or four-inch snowfall, as in the stillness
of a postcard of the Charles, looking from
the square in Mala Strana toward the sad-faced
saints along the high sides of the bridge,
snow-capped, blessed and even fouled with
the Old World and other-worldly, since Prague

4.

is a winter city, night city, streetlights
blurred in mist, the centuries-looming
buildings basic gothic under the glow.
Čapek adds "that you are startled at the
darkness deep within you" standing in
the history and cold beauty of the place.
Kundera, too, clarifies the quality of light,
as if among the weight of intimate things
you were lifted, and the face in the water
looking up from the river were not yours,
and those weren't your footprints in the snow.

5.

Water filling a void created by a glacier—
hundreds of these lakes healing over wounds.
And when you choose you must be silent.

So we'd row out slowly, barely lifting up
our oars, in order to fool the fish, who'd
rise to see what foolish fish we were, then
go back down. Fresh water, black water deep.
You had the sense, at dusk, of dreaming,
of floating in a light now almost gone—
the anchor tied to a ladder, oars like wings,
but nowhere to go but drifting until morning.

6.

At a height above Punto Spartivento,
the point at which the northern wind divides,
Como and Lecco assume their separate waters,
deep enough they've drained the deepest sky.
The lift from the lakes' sun surfaces is
swallows, terns, and Mediterranean gulls,
green hills and granite mountains, white
tourist boats and seaplanes circling in, then
steps beyond the timed arrivals and departures,
terraces and gardens of terra cotta towns
that look like, from here, no one lives there.

7.

Eliot says that home is where you start from,
memory and body so confused they are the same.
In London, in Holland Park, in late October
on a Sunday, in an after-rain late afternoon,
I stood under the great horse chestnut
I'd stood under in the spring when it lit
its candelabra into flame. The chestnuts,
like the eyes of deer, were gone—buckeyes
if you'd grown up in Ohio, conkers if you
played them or fed them to the horses.
And half the leaves were gone. Yet through

8.

the intricate yellow lattice of what was left
the changing sky took on a shape less random.
Eliot, in "East Coker," also says that as we
grow older the world becomes stranger, the sky,
the painter's sky, transformative as earth—
Constable's wool-gathering, towering clouds,
Turner's visceral, annihilating sunsets.
I went to this tree every season for a year.
In winter it was purity, in summer full green
fire. The sky's huge island canopy felt focused
through its branching, the ground more certain.

9.

The way a child might hide. I remember walking
into the sharp high grass of a hayfield, lying
down, closing my eyes. If you were patient
with the insects and the papercuts of blades
you could, after awhile, hear the Moloch
under the earth, and in your mind, if you tried,
ascend into the afterlife of air hovering
just above you. It had to be that falling
time of day the sun is level with the dead last
word. Levitation was the first word you thought
of down on a knee in the hospital, kissed . . .

10.

When I saw my heart lit up on the screen,
the arteries, veins and ventricles
all functioning, pictured, as if removed,
in picture-space, I knew that this is
what is meant by distance, the way, flying
once at forty thousand feet, the needle nose
of the needle flashing in the sun, traveling
alone, and nothing but clarity under us,

I felt like a visitor inside my own body.
I could see myself invisible on the ground
following the threadbare vapor trail. We

.

11.

claim the body as a temple or cathedral,
meaning the house in which I am that I am,
breath and bone, water, mortar, earth.
Brunelleschi, bricking up the eggshell
of his dome, understood the soul must live
in space constructed out of nature.
He could see within his double-vaulted,
self-supporting ceiling a sky "higher
than the sky itself." When I was there,
in the Duomo, looking up, the terror of
a bird took all the heart out of the air.

ON THE REALITY OF THE SYMBOL

by GEOFFREY HILL

from LITERARY IMAGINATION

1

That he feared death—Karl Rahner—unrevealing.
Fine theologian with or against
the world, in senses that are not the world's,
his symbolism, both
a throwback and way forward, claims its own
cussedness, yet goes with the mystery.
Parturition of psalm like pissing blood
I múst say, the formal evidence
so much an issue. Though not painful
pain's in the offing, somewhere signifies
its needled presence. Plus, the prostate's
a nasty beast even at the best of times.
But for translation the old linguaduct
works not too badly. This is a translation.

2

So? Say it again: ephemeralities
ever recurring. There are numerous
things you can't speak or think. Must confess I
sometimes rape her ghost? The olive trees
oblige with well-reft branches. Scapegoats are not

hunted but driven out. There yet remain
impassioned and strange readings: a remote
cry of the blood sugars.
Try *melos* for desired numbness of breath.
And you a poet in all justice. Too
many signs: call scourings from fouled pipes
purification. There! the white dove plumps
her spectral finery. Building my ark begins
late in the terminal welter of the flood.

3

Pity love could not act us. No scarcity
of drama schools where I live. In some of them
refusal's not much worse than other failings
I won't elaborate. We refused each other:
loss is what we are left with. Re-audition.
They'd take us back, instruct us to be old.
Here's bargain-gelt to move things on a stage.
More than a sexy trial a *Trauerspiel*
needs make-believe to launch the sordid fact.
Does this miscast us as a tragic chorus?
Can't answer that, I'm working on my rôle.
Shyster's from a Yiddish word for shit.
It's not, you know.
This is late scaffold-humour, turn me off.

4

On vision as a mode of neural tort:
and I could find myself becoming
overseer for rehabilitation,
imprinting with due licence the late-cancelled
stanzas that hymn roulette. Everything mortal
has to give from life. When we're exhausted
by ill-willing, the fictions of our joys,
violin, pleach-toned harp, and grand piano
melodize; the contessa's niece
glitters her gift three lengths of the salon.
Symbol burns off reality: take *The Red Shoes*—

618

since I'm to show beholden—how for instance
those awkward, svelte, death-struck, life enhancers
labour their immortality proclaimed.

5

Gold, silver, to gel-blaze the dark places.
Black has its own gleam. Pascal's
name is a blank to many people (blank
being blanc); so too are yours and mine.
There must be unnamed stars but all are numbered
de profundis. Check these on the web
spun by their own light. And does such knowledge
firm up allegiance to the stoic heavens?
And is the question real or rhetorical
when finally the all-or-nothing man
presses his wager? Such extravagance
here to expand on, to elect chaos
where there's a vacancy and peradventure
if chaos is the word.

6

The work of mourning—the *Trauerarbeit*—
bugles dead achievements. Regardless
and in spite of, what a memory
topped out by glittering breakage. Bitter stabs
at the long jump (juniors) from a greased run up,
off a rain-swathed board. Five seconds' freedom
I nominate to be the normal freedom
of the mob-ruled. Subsequent fables,
men of stale will nursing their secret wounds,
the token of the scarecrow as sufferer,
seem done for. Death fancies us but finally
leaves us alone. Metaphysics remain
in common language something of a joke.
Mourning my meaning is what I meant to say.

PRESSES FEATURED IN THE PUSHCART PRIZE EDITIONS SINCE 1976

Acts
Agni
Ahsahta Press
Ailanthus Press
Alaska Quarterly Review
Alcheringa/Ethnopoetics
Alice James Books
Ambergris
Amelia
American Letters and Commentary
American Literature
American PEN
American Poetry Review
American Scholar
American Short Fiction
The American Voice
Amicus Journal
Amnesty International
Anaesthesia Review
Another Chicago Magazine
Antaeus
Antietam Review
Antioch Review
Apalachee Quarterly
Aphra
Aralia Press
The Ark

Art and Understanding
Arts and Letters
Artword Quarterly
Ascensius Press
Ascent
Aspen Leaves
Aspen Poetry Anthology
Assembling
Atlanta Review
Autonomedia
Avocet Press
The Baffler
Bakunin
Bamboo Ridge
Barlenmir House
Barnwood Press
Barrow Street
Bellevue Literary Review
The Bellingham Review
Bellowing Ark
Beloit Poetry Journal
Bennington Review
Bilingual Review
Black American Literature Forum
Blackbird
Black Rooster
Black Scholar

Black Sparrow
Black Warrior Review
Blackwells Press
Bloom
Bloomsbury Review
Blue Cloud Quarterly
Blue Unicorn
Blue Wind Press
Bluefish
BOA Editions
Bomb
Bookslinger Editions
Boston Review
Boulevard
Boxspring
Bridge
Bridges
Brown Journal of Arts
Burning Deck Press
Caliban
California Quarterly
Callaloo
Calliope
Calliopea Press
Calyx
Canto
Capra Press
Caribbean Writer
Carolina Quarterly
Cedar Rock
Center
Chariton Review
Charnel House
Chattahoochee Review
Chautauqua Literary Journal
Chelsea
Chicago Review
Chouteau Review
Chowder Review
Cimarron Review
Cincinnati Poetry Review
City Lights Books
Cleveland State Univ. Poetry Ctr.

Clown War
CoEvolution Quarterly
Cold Mountain Press
Colorado Review
Columbia: A Magazine of Poetry and
    Prose
Confluence Press
Confrontation
Conjunctions
Connecticut Review
Copper Canyon Press
Cosmic Information Agency
Countermeasures
Counterpoint
Crawl Out Your Window
Crazyhorse
Crescent Review
Cross Cultural Communications
Cross Currents
Crosstown Books
Cumberland Poetry Review
Curbstone Press
Cutbank
Dacotah Territory
Daedalus
Dalkey Archive Press
Decatur House
December
Denver Quarterly
Desperation Press
Dogwood
Domestic Crude
Doubletake
Dragon Gate Inc.
Dreamworks
Dryad Press
Duck Down Press
Durak
East River Anthology
Eastern Washington University Press
Ellis Press
Empty Bowl
Epoch

Ergo!
Evansville Review
Exquisite Corpse
Faultline
Fence
Fiction
Fiction Collective
Fiction International
Field
Fine Madness
Firebrand Books
Firelands Art Review
First Intensity
Five Fingers Review
Five Points Press
Five Trees Press
The Formalist
Fourth Genre
Frontiers: A Journal of Women Studies
Fugue
Gallimaufry
Genre
The Georgia Review
Gettysburg Review
Ghost Dance
Gibbs-Smith
Glimmer Train
Goddard Journal
David Godine, Publisher
Graham House Press
Grand Street
Granta
Graywolf Press
Great River Review
Green Mountains Review
Greenfield Review
Greensboro Review
Guardian Press
Gulf Coast
Hanging Loose
Hard Pressed
Harvard Review
Hayden's Ferry Review

Hermitage Press
Heyday
Hills
Holmgangers Press
Holy Cow!
Home Planet News
Hudson Review
Hungry Mind Review
Icarus
Icon
Idaho Review
Iguana Press
Image
Indiana Review
Indiana Writes
Intermedia
Intro
Invisible City
Inwood Press
Iowa Review
Ironwood
Jam To-day
The Journal
Jubilat
The Kanchenjuga Press
Kansas Quarterly
Kayak
Kelsey Street Press
Kenyon Review
Kestrel
Latitudes Press
Laughing Waters Press
Laurel Review
L'Epervier Press
Liberation
Linquis
Literal Latté
Literary Imagination
The Literary Review
The Little Magazine
Living Hand Press
Living Poets Press
Logbridge-Rhodes

Louisville Review
Lowlands Review
Lucille
Lynx House Press
Lyric
The MacGuffin
Magic Circle Press
Malahat Review
Mānoa
Manroot
Many Mountains Moving
Marlboro Review
Massachusetts Review
McSweeney's
Meridian
Mho & Mho Works
Micah Publications
Michigan Quarterly
Mid-American Review
Milkweed Editions
Milkweed Quarterly
The Minnesota Review
Mississippi Review
Mississippi Valley Review
Missouri Review
Montana Gothic
Montana Review
Montemora
Moon Pony Press
Mount Voices
Mr. Cogito Press
MSS
Mudfish
Mulch Press
Nada Press
National Poetry Review
Nebraska Review
New America
New American Review
New American Writing
The New Criterion
New Delta Review
New Directions

New England Review
New England Review and Bread Loaf
    Quarterly
New Letters
New Orleans Review
New Virginia Review
New York Quarterly
New York University Press
News from The Republic of Letters
Nimrod
9 × 9 Industries
Noon
North American Review
North Atlantic Books
North Dakota Quarterly
North Point Press
Northeastern University Press
Northern Lights
Northwest Review
Notre Dame Review
O. ARS
O. Blēk
Obsidian
Obsidian II
Oconee Review
October
Ohio Review
Old Crow Review
Ontario Review
Open City
Open Places
Orca Press
Orchises Press
Orion
Other Voices
Oxford American
Oxford Press
Oyez Press
Oyster Boy Review
Painted Bride Quarterly
Painted Hills Review
Palo Alto Review
Paris Press

Paris Review
Parkett
Parnassus: Poetry in Review
Partisan Review
Passages North
Penca Books
Pentagram
Penumbra Press
Pequod
Persea: An International Review
Perugià Press
Pipedream Press
Pitcairn Press
Pitt Magazine
Pleiades
Ploughshares
Poet and Critic
Poet Lore
Poetry
Poetry East
Poetry Ireland Review
Poetry Northwest
Poetry Now
Post Road
Prairie Schooner
Prescott Street Press
Press
Promise of Learnings
Provincetown Arts
Puerto Del Sol
Quaderni Di Yip
Quarry West
The Quarterly
Quarterly West
Raccoon
Rainbow Press
Raritan: A Quarterly Review
Red Cedar Review
Red Clay Books
Red Dust Press
Red Earth Press
Red Hen Press
Release Press

Review of Contemporary Fiction
Revista Chicano-Riquena
Rhetoric Review
Rivendell
River Styx
River Teeth
Rowan Tree Press
Russian *Samizdat*
Salmagundi
San Marcos Press
Sarabande Books
Sea Pen Press and Paper Mill
Seal Press
Seamark Press
Seattle Review
Second Coming Press
Semiotext(e)
Seneca Review
Seven Days
The Seventies Press
Sewanee Review
Shankpainter
Shantih
Shearsman
Sheep Meadow Press
Shenandoah
A Shout In the Street
Sibyl-Child Press
Side Show
Small Moon
The Smith
Solo
Solo 2
Some
The Sonora Review
Southern Poetry Review
Southern Review
Southwest Review
Speakeasy
Spectrum
Spillway
The Spirit That Moves Us
St. Andrews Press

Story
Story Quarterly
Streetfare Journal
Stuart Wright, Publisher
Sulfur
The Sun
Sun & Moon Press
Sun Press
Sunstone
Sycamore Review
Tamagwa
Tar River Poetry
Teal Press
Telephone Books
Telescope
Temblor
The Temple
Tendril
Texas Slough
Third Coast
13th Moon
THIS
Thorp Springs Press
Three Rivers Press
Threepenny Review
Thunder City Press
Thunder's Mouth Press
Tia Chucha Press
Tikkun
Tin House
Tombouctou Books
Toothpaste Press
Transatlantic Review
Triplopia
TriQuarterly
Truck Press
Turnrow
Undine
Unicorn Press

University of Georgia Press
University of Illinois Press
University of Iowa Press
University of Massachusetts Press
University of North Texas Press
University of Pittsburgh Press
University of Wisconsin Press
University Press of New England
Unmuzzled Ox
Unspeakable Visions of the Individual
Vagabond
Verse
Vignette
Virginia Quarterly
Volt
Wampeter Press
Washington Writers Workshop
Water-Stone
Water Table
Western Humanities Review
Westigan Review
White Pine Press
Wickwire Press
Willow Springs
Wilmore City
Witness
Word Beat Press
Word-Smith
Wormwood Review
Writers Forum
Xanadu
Yale Review
Yardbird Reader
Yarrow
Y'Bird
Zeitgeist Press
Zoetrope: All-Story
ZYZZYVA

MORE OUTSTANDING POEMS

Volume XVI

Volume XVII

Volume XVIII

Volume XIX

Volume XX

Volume XXI

Volume XXII

Volume XXIII

Volume XXIV

Volume XXV

Volume XXVI

Volume XXVII

Volume XXVIII

Volume XXIX

Volume XXX

Printed in the United States
70761LV00001B/49-498